Maenam.

The Thai word for "river."

Literally translates to "mother water." In Buddhism, water is the strongest of

all the elements, representing an ever-replenishing flow.

maenam

maenam

A FRESH APPROACH TO THAI COOKING

ANGUS AN

Forewords by DAVID THOMPSON and NORMAND LAPRISE

appetite

Appetite by Random House® and colophon are
registered trademarks of Penguin Random House LLC.

Library and Archives Canada Cataloguing in Publication is available upon request.

ISBN: 9780147530943

eBook ISBN: 9780147530950

Written with Joie Alvaro Kent

Cover and book design by Terri Nimmo

Photographs by Darren Chuang, except those on pages 4, 5, 63, 243, 265, 266

Photos on pages 4–5, 265, 266 by Chris Mason Sterns

Photo on page 63 by Ellen Ho

Photo on page 243 by Hamid Attie

Printed and bound in China

Published in Canada by Appetite by Random House®,
a division of Penguin Random House LLC.

www.penguinrandomhouse.ca

10 9 8 7 6 5 4 3 2

To my late grandparents with love,
for their belief and support.

Contents

Foreword

A photographer, a degree in fine arts, a love of architecture; these points intrigued me as I read Angus' letter asking to stage in the kitchen at Nahm in London. Good chefs have many surprising skills but most are based solidly in kitchen practice. It is not so common to come across a cook with such a polished education in the arts. Of course it was no guarantee of quality of Angus' cooking but at least I could expect some decent conversation.

I was not disappointed. Angus could certainly chat. He was thoughtful and interesting, colouring everything with a wonderfully dry sense of humour. I smile as I write this.

He could cook too.

It was very evident that Angus had had some rigour and discipline in his culinary background, but just as noticeable were his talent and palpable love of cooking.

Sooner than most, Angus was put in charge of a section, the soup section. Each and every soup was made and finished individually. Perhaps the most testing dish for a cook to cook is a *dtom yam*, the classic hot and sour soup on every Thai menu, worth its fame when done well but the very devil of a dish to get right. It should be simple as there are only a few seasoning components. It isn't. To achieve a good one is an exercise in elegance, balancing the lemongrass with the coriander, and the chillies with the lime and fish sauce. It demands an adroit hand at seasoning and a knowing tongue. It can confound the best of cooks.

When Angus was thrown into the mess, I knew he'd need some guidance. Before his soup was served, I tasted it. It wasn't bad, but it wasn't quite right. A final adjustment is essential to every dish. Proper balance and honed seasoning can transform the taste. It is what makes Thai food so remarkable, so addictive, and so damned difficult.

So I stirred the pot and tinkered a little. It became acceptable to serve. However, what was more interesting was watching Angus's face as he tasted, almost chewing the soup as if to extract as much knowledge as possible in each sip. And as he savoured the last of the taste, his eyes brightened and he smiled. I knew Angus would be staying for quite some time.

Angus stayed at Nahm for a few years, tasting, growing in experience, chuckling at his own jokes and meeting his wife, Kate, He moved back to Vancouver where he has flourished due to his talent and dedication to his craft and industry. This book recounts the development of his own style as a cook and restaurateur. And what an excellent book it is.

David Thompson

Avant-propos

Après avoir complété avec succès sa formation au sein de l'Institut culinaire français de New York (aujourd'hui le Centre culinaire international), Angus a débuté sa carrière culinaire professionnelle au sein de la brigade du Toqué! Pendant ces années montréalaises, Angus a été assigné à tous les postes de travail en cuisine : du « froid au chaud », de la « production à la création ». C'était un cuisinier dévoué et un bon joueur d'équipe. Sa rigueur, son attitude positive et sa gourmandise (!), ont fait de lui un membre respecté et apprécié de ses collègues.

Probablement motivé par sa curiosité et encouragé d'aller diversifier ses expériences, Angus s'est dirigé vers un parcours d'enrichissement professionnel exigeant : il a choisi des milieux de travail différents de ceux qu'il avait connus, en plus de déménager en Europe ! C'était risqué, sauf qu'Angus a une ouverture d'esprit qui lui permet de se concentrer sur son apprentissage et de franchir les préjugés.

Aujourd'hui, je suis convaincu que cet amalgame de toutes ces années d'apprentissage et de découvertes de nouvelles expériences sont au cœur de son succès remarquable (et selon moi, bien mérité).

En effet, à son retour au pays, Angus a réussi, non sans effort, à développer sa signature avec son restaurant Maenam : il y sert des des produits locaux canadiens, auxquels il intègre des techniques contemporaines afin de revisiter certaines recettes traditionnelles thaï sans toutefois en dénaturer l'origine.

C'est ainsi qu'avec les années, Angus a su construire et partager son monde culinaire avec ses 6 restaurants qu'il a ouverts à Vancouver au cours des dernières années, en toute complicité avec son épouse et partenaire d'affaires.

D'ailleurs, c'est en famille qu'ils réussissent annuellement, à travers leurs voyages, à faire un retour aux sources ou découvrir de nouvelles tendances: Les voyages sont généralement des sources d'inspiration qui peuvent générer de nouvelles créations si on sait se donner l'espace et le temps pour les interpréter à notre façon.

Ce livre retrace, de façon juste et authentique, le cheminement d'un chef, de ses débuts jusqu'à sa réussite, à Vancouver évidemment, mais également à travers le Canada et finalement, sur la scène de la gastronomie internationale. En plus, vous y trouverez d'excellentes recettes que vous pourrez réussir et partager en toutes circonstances.

Angus a souvent dit que j'ai été son premier mentor. Permettez-moi d'ajouter qu'avec les années, je suis devenu son ami et un amateur de sa cuisine : c'est donc un immense plaisir pour moi que de participer à la préface de son livre, un livre que je qualifierai de sincère, réfléchi et généreux : Un livre à son image.

Normand Laprise, C.M.,C.Q.
Chef copropriétaire Restaurant Toqué!

Foreword

After having successfully completed his training at the French Culinary Institute in New York (now known as the International Culinary Center), Angus began his professional culinary career as part of the Toqué! brigade. During those years in Montreal, he was assigned to all of the kitchen's workstations, from cold to hot food, from production to creation. He was a dedicated cook and a valued team player. His precision, positive attitude, and immense love for good food (!), made him a respected and appreciated member among his colleagues.

Likely motivated by his curiosity and by the encouragement of others to diversify his culinary experiences, Angus headed to pursue a demanding professional enrichment course: he chose working environments different from those he already knew, on top of moving to Europe! It was a risky move, except Angus has an open mind that allows him to focus on his apprenticeship and overcome any preconceptions.

Today, I am convinced that the combination of his years of learning and discovering new experiences is at the heart of his remarkable (and, in my opinion, well-deserved) success. Indeed, upon his return to Canada, Angus succeeded, not without effort, to develop his signature style at his restaurant Maenam:

he serves locally sourced Canadian foods, integrating contemporary techniques to revisit traditional Thai recipes without compromising their origins.

Thus, over the years, Angus has been able to build and share his culinary world at the six restaurants that he has opened in Vancouver in full collaboration with his business partner: his wife.

Furthermore, it's as a family that, through their annual travels, they succeed in returning to the roots [of Thai cooking] or discovering new trends. Trips are, generally, sources of inspiration for new creations if one knows to give the space and time for interpreting them in their own way.

This book, in a fair and authentic way, traces the path of a chef from his beginnings to his success in Vancouver, but also across Canada and, finally, on the international gastronomic scene. In addition, you will find excellent recipes that you can create and share for any occasion.

Angus has often said that I'm his first mentor. Let me also add that, over the years, I have become his friend and a fan of his cooking. As such, it's been an immense pleasure for me to write a foreword for his book, a book I would describe as sincere, thoughtful, and generous. A book in his image.

Normand Laprise, C.M., C.O.
Co-Owner and Executive Chef Toqué!

Introduction

Maenam. The Thai word for "river." Literally translates to "mother water." In Buddhism, water is the strongest of all of the elements, representing an ever-replenishing flow.

Thai food. Why Thai food? It's a question I'm often asked. Thai food came to me serendipitously, and it might have been the happiest accident I've ever had. This book is about Thai cooking—more specifically, a modern interpretation of classical Thai cuisine.

My wife and business partner, Kate, chose Maenam as the name of our restaurant, and it immediately felt right. Water is the strongest of all the elements in Buddhist culture, the predominant religion in Thailand, and Maenam represents its constant, ever-replenishing flow. Just as a river continues its course around boulders and obstacles, the name mirrors our willingness to persist in the face of adversity and change, and my ongoing evolution as a chef.

Maenam was born at a trying time. My first French-inflected fine-dining restaurant, Gastropod, fell victim to the global economic recession in 2009, and we had to do an immediate about-face to curtail our growing losses. My confidence and desire to cook definitely took a bit of a hit. Kate and I had always planned a Thai concept as our second restaurant; our shift in fortunes dramatically stepped up this goal. Within three short weeks, we closed Gastropod and reopened as Maenam, a more casual neighborhood spot featuring family-style Thai sharing plates at an approachable price.

There was an immediate uptick in business, yet, admittedly, I struggled for the first couple of years. Emotionally, I was bitter about the restructuring, seeing it as a defensive survival move, and humbled by Gastropod's failure. And I saw myself as an inadequate Thai cook, having worked for only a year and a half with chef David Thompson at Nahm a couple of years prior. But using the lessons I learned at Nahm as a springboard, I immersed myself in establishing my own subtle refinement of Thai cuisine's sharp, clear flavors.

Since then, I've been a passionate student of Thai food, with Kate as my knowledgeable guide to the food of her home country. As with most households in Thailand, food is a focal point for Kate's family, the centerpiece that brings people together for celebrations and everyday meals. Together with our son, Aidan, we've traveled extensively through Thailand to eat, research, and learn. And that learning process never ends. With this cookbook, I hope to bring you along on my ongoing journey of discovering Thai cuisine and give you some insight on blending traditional Thai flavors and cooking techniques with my local, seasonal inspirations from Canada's west coast and your own regionally sourced ingredients.

•••

I grew up in Taiwan, where my father and mother were my culinary role models. They were both very keen cooks—not because we couldn't afford to eat out, but because they knew they could prepare food better at home. Five-year-old me would stand in our kitchen, fascinated by the process of watching Mom cook. From time to time, I'd ask if I could help her with the sauces, and eventually she taught me to fry an egg in a traditional wok. Long before I was tall enough to see over the sides of the wok, Mom stood me on a stool and let me try. I quickly graduated from fried eggs to scrambled eggs to fried rice, and suddenly a whole new cooking world opened its doors to me.

Mom would also take me shopping at the wet market in Taiwan, immersing me in all the sights and sounds of the hawkers butchering fish and meat, and teaching me how to choose the freshest produce. It's where I first learned that the process of making a meal starts with a connection to the ingredients.

My grandmother was another figure who played a big role in shaping my culinary perspective. She was an extremely good cook, very meticulous in her methods. She moved to the United States when I was young, and it was always exciting when she came to visit. We spent countless hours together in the kitchen, and she'd teach me how to bake Western treats like carrot cake and lemon loaf—exotic tastes for a young boy in Taiwan. When our family eventually moved to Canada, we'd visit her in California, where the Meyer lemon tree in her backyard was especially significant to me. Its lemons were the size of my fist, and I'd help her pick them when they were perfectly ripe, then zest and juice them to make lemon cake. This is one of my strongest food memories, and I'm transported straight back to childhood every time I smell Meyer lemons. Grandma helped to instill my visceral appreciation for food, teaching me to involve all my senses in discerning tastes and building flavors.

When we moved to a two-acre hobby farm in Maple Ridge, BC, my dad proudly raised ducks, geese, and rabbits, and he grew all sorts of vegetables, from tomatoes to garlic and various Chinese greens. There was no shortage of eggs from our chickens, and Dad butchered all our poultry before the words "free range" entered my lexicon. Our family literally ate from the land, buying very little from the sterile supermarkets that seemed so alien to me. It wasn't very special to me as a teenager, but I definitely learned to understand and appreciate the taste of vine-ripened heirloom tomatoes still warm from the sun, and the difference between chickens from our farm and hormone-filled battery-raised chickens. Collectively, these experiences established the roots of my desire to become a chef.

I continued cooking through high school and university, where I studied fine arts in pursuit of

architecture. Yet every odd job I had, whether as a delivery driver or busboy or burgeoning line cook, was linked to food; I had a strong desire to maintain a connection to the culinary world. Stuck eating dorm food, my friends became willing guinea pigs for my gastronomic explorations. I made a deal with them: they'd buy groceries, and I had free rein to cook whatever I wanted to for dinner—a perfect win-win situation. By the time I hit second year, my passion for cooking had fully crystallized; despite my desire to drop out, I promised my parents I would finish my degree. And finish I did, graduating with a bachelor's degree in fine arts, specializing in photography and installation art.

That's when I made the formal leap into pursuing cooking as a career, and applied to New York's prestigious French Culinary Institute (now known as the International Culinary Center). There, I completed an externship at Jean-Georges Vongerichten's restaurant JoJo, and ultimately graduated top of my class. I moved to Montreal for my first "real" restaurant job, at Toqué! Chef Normand Laprise was my first mentor, and the three years I spent in his world-class kitchen were some of the best in my career. He had a respect for produce and a deep-seated connection with farmers and foragers long before it was trendy. The array of impeccable locally sourced ingredients we worked with was virtually limitless—a luxury I only truly realized in hindsight, after staging in various European restaurants that didn't prioritize freshness and seasonality in nearly the same way. Normand was a zen master in the kitchen. Quiet and thoughtful, he gave me the room and freedom to be imaginative and encouraged me to discover my own path. As I worked my way up through Normand's brigade, I thrived under his kitchen philosophy. I'm still inspired by the creative process in Toqué's kitchen to this day, and wholeheartedly appreciate the elegance of always starting with the best possible ingredients and letting nature speak through my dishes.

In 2004, my culinary travels led me to the United Kingdom and to a number of stages at Michelin-starred restaurants. I ended up working with Chef David Thompson at Nahm on a whim. Truth be told, I had zero intention of learning how to cook Thai food; coming from a classical French background, I thought that Thai cooking was too casual. Little did I know how arrogant my preconceptions were.

I'd been on the line for only a few days when I was tasked with making the hot sour soup for lunch service. Although I followed David's instructions to the letter, my soup was over-the-top spicy, and I was sweating bullets because I didn't know how to fix it. It was so bad, in fact, that I was loath to bring it to Chef for tasting.

It took only two spoonfuls of soup for David to discern my shortcomings. What followed was a five-minute master class in Thai cuisine as he began adding ingredients to the pot, showing me an approach to balance, seasoning, and intensity that I'd never seen before. Palm sugar was first, followed by tamarind, fish sauce, fried garlic, and shallots. He tasted it again before adding fresh herbs, then handed me a spoon. I was absolutely blown away by the transformation. Chef had turned my train wreck into a completely different creation, an incredibly balanced and rounded soup with phenomenal depth of flavor.

That moment at Nahm was a turning point for me—the moment I really decided to take Thai food seriously. It showed me how narrow the scope of my classical French-based knowledge really was and how much I still needed to learn. Cooking with David was a humbling experience. Over the next 18 months, he taught me about the intricacies of Thai cooking and the nuances of seasoning food by layering intense flavors, aromas, and textures. The time I spent at Nahm changed my world; it led me to my beautiful family (I met my wife, Kate, during my first shift at Nahm—we started our training on the same day!), and it eventually saved my career.

• • •

I am still a passionate student of Thai food. Ten years after opening, Maenam's menu is more assertive and more confident than it's ever been. Funny enough, I feel that my earlier studies in fine arts really help hone my skills as a chef, developing my appreciation for aesthetics and the unique beauty of things, which dovetails directly with the process of conceptualizing, refining, and executing a new dish. Whether taking a picture, planning a new building, or composing a new menu item, I think that creating all forms of art comes down to the design process.

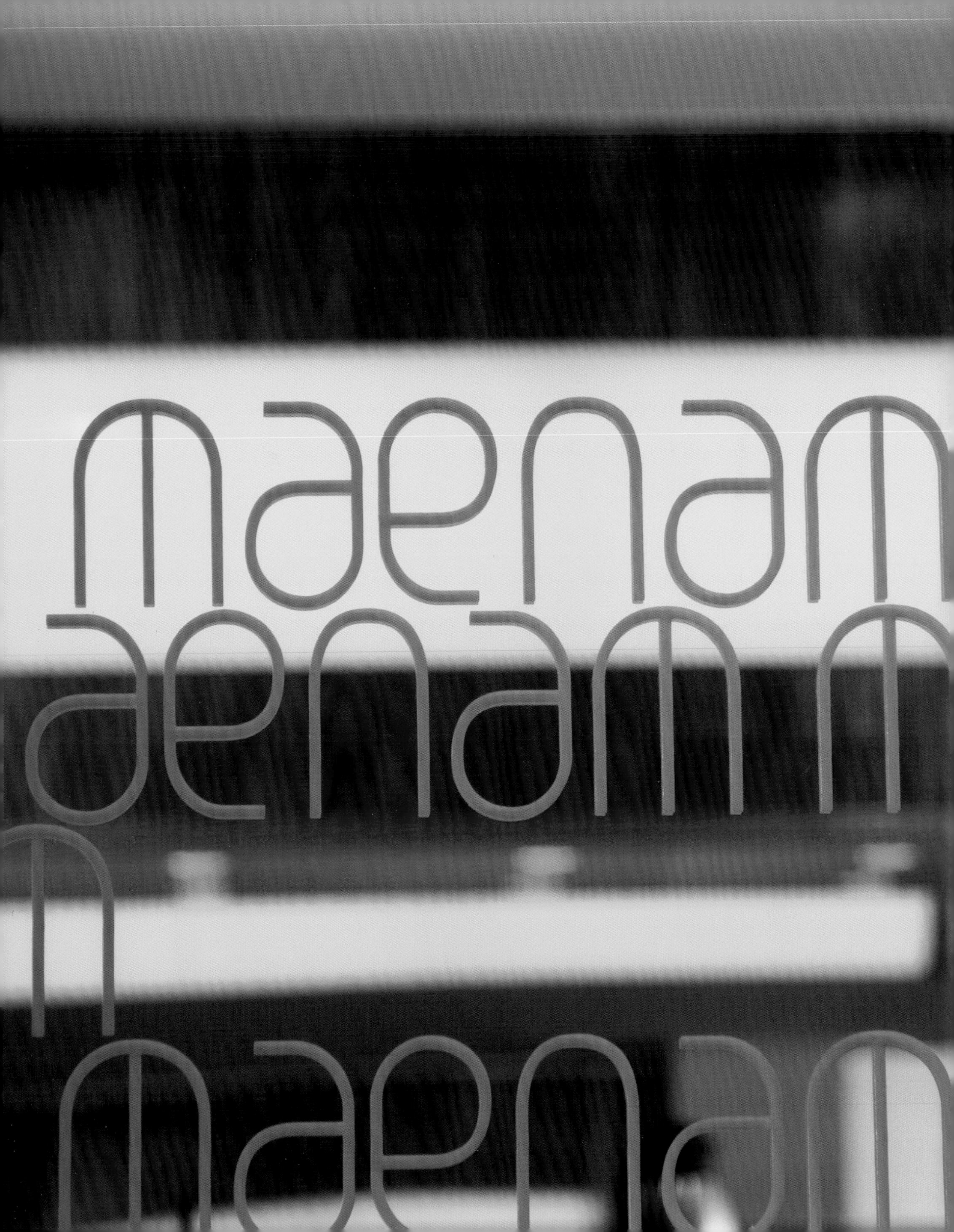
maenam

The words of iconic architect Frank Gehry have been a mantra of sorts for me: he cites 15 percent as the magic figure that's left over for unfettered creativity in his design process after adhering to the boundaries of building codes, city bylaws, and client requirements. It may not seem like much, but that 15 percent is what he credits for shaping his uniquely spectacular pieces of work. The same holds true for chefs—we're up against boundaries in the kitchen every day. Some young chefs fall into the trap of thinking that the plate is a blank canvas free of boundaries, and they overcomplicate their dishes with too many ingredients. Conversely, I struggled with too many boundaries at the outset of my Maenam journey, putting myself under pressure to create dishes that were authentic in both voice and tradition, as well as being fresh and modern, and taking into consideration what neighborhood diners would want to eat. As a result, my creativity was stifled. Over the years, though, we've worked hard to earn the trust of our guests, and the window for creativity has expanded because people are enthusiastically willing to leave their dining experience in our hands.

I've opened four more restaurants in the last 10 years, and the success of each one encourages me to be bolder still with Maenam. I've stopped being restricted by expectations of authenticity. Using advances in culinary techniques and technology to cook a dish differently how it was prepared 100 years ago doesn't make it less authentic—it just makes it more modern. I've made my peace with that realization, and now build Maenam's menu on a foundation of traditional Thai flavors and classic recipes, elevating them with finesse and the very best west coast ingredients we can find to strongly reflect our current sense of place.

Now in our 10th year, I feel the name Maenam— beyond the strict meaning of the word—represents a moment of change. It will forever connect me to the serendipitous hot sour soup moment at Nahm that shifted my perspective on cooking Thai food. Each of the five Thai-related restaurants we now own is a result of the life-changing day I walked into Nahm, a celebration of just how far we've come.

Notes on Thai Cooking

Food is a huge part of Thai culture and is the centerpiece of most, if not all, celebrations and gatherings. Thai cuisine incorporates historic recipes and influences from neighboring countries, including India, China, Burma, and Vietnam, along with Muslim influences—these instances are highlighted throughout. There are countless regional variants of dishes between provinces and villages, with subtle differences in the tastes and flavors of the same recipe, even between families.

When passing down recipes from one generation to another, Asian grandmas teach their kids and grandkids how to cook intuitively, a prominent trait of Thai cooking. Specific quantities of ingredients and cooking times are rarely used; instead, you taste as you go, adding a little bit of this and some of that to achieve the desired tastes and textures.

Understanding the flavors of a particular dish is an important step in Thai cuisine; its complexity is the primary element that differentiates Thai cooking from Western cooking. Western dishes tend to focus on a central ingredient with a couple of supplemental flavors to enhance it. Thai cuisine, on the other hand, spotlights the flavors of a dish first. A well-seasoned Thai dish incorporates robust, intense flavor to achieve harmony, balancing the interrelationship of hot, sour, sweet, and salty, with bitter flavors thrown in on occasion for good measure. It should have fresh, bold characteristics, yet still be subtle and sophisticated with carefully crafted layers of seasoning. For example, you can have a dish with a lot of chilies if the flavors are well balanced; in fact, the flavors will sing to one another beautifully (and you won't be overwhelmed by the heat).

Thai food is also flexible. Some people prefer their papaya salad to be on the sweeter side, while others prefer it sharp, intense, and hot! All of this should be taken into consideration when you're seasoning not only dishes from this book but your cooking overall. Often, you'll need to adjust the seasoning of a dish at the end, and knowing how to do this is a good skill. If something is too spicy or sour, add a little more sweetness or salt to balance the taste. Likewise, adding more acid and salt is a good way to correct a dish that's too sweet. If you prefer things on the salty side, you can adjust a recipe accordingly—just make sure to adjust your flavor balance too so that the dish doesn't just taste of salt.

As I've noted, Thai food is all about balance—this means textural balance too. To achieve this textural balance, the recipes featured in this book often incorporate the same ingredient in different forms and at different stages of the recipe to create a unifying flavor thread that contributes to the dish's overall balance in complexity. For example, I often pound garlic into curry paste as a flavor accent, braise the meat with garlic as an aromatic to add depth and character, and finish the dish off with fried garlic for textural contrast.

Keep this in mind when cooking from this book, and use all your senses to discern flavor and doneness. Is your batter thick enough to coat the back of a spoon? Have you fried your curry paste long enough to make it fragrant? Above all, trust your instincts and your palate. As you familiarize yourself with the spectrum of Thai ingredients and tastes, you'll become more adept at making fine balance adjustments to suit your personal tastes.

To introduce you to the joys of Thai cooking, I have included some general tips as well as techniques and equipment that will collectively make each dish unique.

Preparation

Mise en Place

Mise en place is a culinary term that means having "everything in its place," yet it encompasses much more than just physically laying out your prepared ingredients within arm's reach so that you don't have to turn off the heat and walk away to grab something. On top of all the physical preparations, I think it also signifies the mental organization and timing of steps so that you know which things you can get ahead on and which must be done *à la minute* to maintain freshness and sharpness of flavor. For example, rushing to get a five-hour braise done right before your guests arrive isn't realistic. Yet you can cook and cool down your braise properly the night before and then simply reheat and garnish before serving. Similarly, you may not want to make your hot sour soup the night before, but have your aromatics ready to go so that all it takes is 10 minutes in the pot before dishing it out. And a beautiful fresh salad dressing will lose its luster if made the night before. There's a line you draw in every recipe, and I've taken great care in this book to highlight steps you can do in advance versus critical preparations that must be done just before bringing a dish to the table.

Cook Times

Thai street food, especially soups and noodles, is prepared quickly à la minute. As such, you'll notice prep times (as in everything you can make ahead of time) may be longer, but cook times and assemble times (the final steps to finish the dish) are incredibly quick—hence the importance of your mise en place. You'll also notice that I haven't built in steps you can do in advance to the total time, such as overnight marinades, freezing sorbet, or dehydrating pork skin, but have indicated these instances in the recipes. There may be many recipe steps to achieve the utmost in flavor, but if you plan your mise en place strategically, the total recipe time won't seem as daunting.

Ingredients

The ingredients featured in this book are a mix of Thai produce available at your Asian grocer and local ingredients that are in season. Where possible, I've included substitutes and other tips in the glossary (page 251). Undoubtedly, there'll be foreign ingredients that are unfamiliar. Take the time to go through the glossary and do some research online before starting a recipe. In most cases, if you find the right store, you should be able to source specialty ingredients from one location instead of driving around town to find them.

Rice

Rice is the most important part of any Thai meal. In fact, the equivalent of "Let's eat" in Thailand is "Eat rice!" All the other food on the table is thought of as a side dish that encourages you to indulge in more rice. Thai jasmine rice is the best type of rice to accompany the recipes in this book. As each rice producer is different, make sure to wash the rice thoroughly—stirring your fingers through it and allowing the grains to scrub against each other, then pouring out the water, adding fresh water, and repeating this process until the water runs clear. This washes away excess starch and gives the rice a wonderfully bouncy texture when cooked. The second most important step is to follow the instructions on the bag. Rice may differ from harvest to harvest due to its age; the starch in a younger crop of rice hasn't fully matured, so it won't need as much water as a later-harvest variety. Strain the rice right after washing to drain off all excess water, and measure the appropriate amount of water for cooking.

Spices

In Thai cuisine, it's always better to cook with whole spices. Not only do they last longer, but you're also able to toast them to bring out more flavor. Ground or powdered spices purchased from the store don't keep that well—their flavors are almost always flat and you can't toast them without burning. When toasting spices, it's important to do it over medium or medium-low heat. Slowly toast them until they release their flavors and smell sweet and nutty. If you toast them in a pan that's too hot, you'll end up burning the spices before their fragrance releases.

Stock and Master Stock

I love master stocks. It's sacrilegious to throw away stock, and master stocks are flavor bases you can add to any braise or stock to get it going. Keep any leftover liquid from that recipe for the next batch—it's the gift that keeps on giving. Chicken is the obvious one to have and the easiest to incorporate into any dish; at home, we always have chicken stock in our fridge because we go through it quickly enough without worrying that it may spoil. You can also freeze stock in ice-cube trays and add it to your stocks and braises as needed (page 62). If you cook often, you may need to have a dark stock and a light stock. A dark stock tends to incorporate soy sauce for braising pork or beef, which is perfect for those types of proteins but not chicken or fish because it may overpower their flavors. A light stock, like chicken or pork, is easy for kick-starting a simple soup.

Batter vs. Slurry

What is batter, what is slurry, and when do you use them?

Batter is used when an ingredient needs to be cooked quickly with a thick coating to prevent it from being overcooked. For me, this thicker mixture is made with flour, water, eggs, and sometimes baking soda. Tempura is a classic use of batter, as are my Crispy Fried Oysters (page 32).

Personally, I prefer cooking with slurry, a thinner solution made with either cornstarch or rice flour stirred into water. It creates a thin coating from which the water evaporates as it's frying, forming a delicate but crispy shell. Slurry is typically used with ingredients that require more time to fry, such as the Fried Chicken Wings with Nahm Jim Jiao (page 30). Note that the cornstarch sinks if you aren't cooking with the slurry right away, so you'll need to stir it again before using.

Techniques & Tools

Mortar and Pestle

In my opinion, a mortar and pestle is the most essential tool to own if you want to use this book. I highly recommend buying a stone mortar and pestle instead of a marble one, and it should be a minimum of 6 inches in diameter, but preferably 7 to 8 inches if available. Make sure to soak your new stone mortar and pestle in water overnight before

using it. The stone is quite porous, and soaking it allows moisture to penetrate; skipping this step means the stone is more likely to crack as you're pounding. Use only a light amount of soap to clean your mortar and pestle, and be sure to rinse it well.

The proper way to use your mortar and pestle depends on what you're making. When grinding dry spices, for example, a grinding motion is all you need. But when making curry pastes (pages 202–04) or dressings (pages 132–33), a combination of pounding and grinding is the right technique. In most cases, a pinch of coarse sea salt will act as an abrasive to help break down the aromatics in curry pastes and dressings. Correct technique doesn't involve a lot of arm movement. Instead, use your wrist to strike the pestle down on the front side of the bowl, then grind it through and come up on the backside of the bowl—this way you're pounding and grinding simultaneously. You may also need to use your opposite hand to cover the mortar to prevent splashing, and to scrape the bowl down from time to time with a spoon or spatula to ensure even consistency of the ingredients. It's also wise to put a thick dish towel underneath the mortar to reduce noise and prevent slippage.

Another trick to efficiently processing ingredients is to not overcrowd your mortar. Do things in batches and mix them together afterward.

Boiling

Boiling simply refers to blanching ingredients in a large pot. When cooking anything in boiling water, make sure to select the appropriately sized vessel for the job. Don't overcrowd the pot, as this causes the water temperature to drop too quickly, and the ingredients will end up stewing rather than boiling. Always have your spider—a long-handled shallow mesh strainer—or slotted spoon immediately handy so you're able to quickly pick up the items that you're boiling.

Braising

Braising should always be done nice and slow. After bringing the stock to an initial boil, turn the heat down to a very low simmer with little to no movement left in the liquid; this ensures slower cooking time and more tender proteins. Another trick to braising is the cool-down process: always cool down your cooked protein in the stock to prevent it from drying out. Thai people typically use non-reactive brass woks to reduce sauces or cook desserts because they heat evenly and because of the prevalence of highly reactive coconut milk and cream in Thai cuisine. Stainless steel is another good material for woks, but never use highly reactive aluminum.

Infusing Aromatics

This simple method goes a long way when making soups or infusing any aromatics into stock: Use a mortar and pestle to bruise aromatics such as lemongrass, galangal, and lime leaves; this releases essential oils and decreases the density of the aromatics so that stock can penetrate better and extract more flavor. Pounding aromatics is much more effective then slicing them when it comes to extracting flavor—as an added bonus, it's also a great stress reliever.

Deep-Frying

Deep-frying refers to a method of frying in which the items being cooked are fully submerged in oil. A proper Asian wok, deep fryer, or appropriately sized pot are excellent vessels for deep-frying. If you deep-fry often, a countertop deep fryer may be a good investment; otherwise, a 6- to 8-quart pot with a sugar thermometer also works really well. Be sure to fill the pot only halfway, because the oil expands as it heats up and moisture from the ingredients you're frying causes it to bubble. It can get messy—even dangerous—if the oil starts to overflow.

It's also key not to overcrowd your vessel, as the ingredients will start to stick to each other and stew instead of deep-fry. Don't be intimidated by the quantities of oil called for in this book. You can easily deep-fry in batches using half the amount of oil, but make sure to use an appropriately sized vessel that's deep enough to fully submerge the item that you're frying. If you do that, keep the ingredients warm in the oven at 200°F, placed on a wire rack atop a baking sheet, until ready to serve.

Wok-Frying and Stir-Frying

Effective wok cooking is all about intense heat and fast, constant movement of your ingredients to prevent them from burning. Thin-sided woks made from carbon steel or cast iron are best for facilitating effective heat transfer and are absolutely crucial to making a top-notch stir-fry; because they have a rounded bottom, it's essential to use a wok ring for stability while you're cooking. As an aside, "gourmet" wok-shaped pans aren't really woks in my opinion—they're nothing more than thicker-sided, deeper pans.

Wok care is important. Always wash your wok with warm soapy water and rinse it well. Dry it thoroughly by heating it on the stove over medium-low heat—it should be bone dry when you put it away. If you're not planning to use it soon afterward, turn off the heat and rub a little vegetable oil into it with a paper towel before storing.

You'll also need both a wok spoon and a wok spade for stir-frying. The wok spoon helps you season, and the wok spade helps you flip your ingredients while simultaneously tossing them. Experienced chefs often dip their wok spoon in open pots of seasoning and use it to gauge taste, allowing them to be more efficient with their movements, as every second counts in wok-cooking.

While you're stir-frying, be mindful of what you're cooking: sear your sliced protein before adding your vegetables and curry paste. Don't toss your meat or seafood too much as you're searing it so that it has a chance to brown. Conversely, keep your vegetables moving as you're cooking them; this preserves their bright colors and prevents them from scorching or burning in the intense heat. Over time, a well-seasoned wok develops "wok breath," (page 71) adding a unique depth of flavor to the ingredients you're stir-frying.

A wok can also be used for deep-frying. Because of its rounded bottom, you don't need as much oil to get the same depth as you would if using a flat-bottomed pot. Be extra careful, though, because rounded woks are unstable; again, make sure you have a proper wok ring beneath it to secure the wok in place. Always use a wire-mesh spider to fish out the items you're frying, and shake off any excess oil before setting them aside to dry and cool on wire racks lined with paper towel. The paper towel helps absorb any excess oil, and the wire rack allows good air circulation to prevent your crispy food from getting soggy.

Grilling

Most of the grilling recipes in this book call for charcoal initially, but many of them can be prepared on gas grills and grill pans. Yet there's definitely something about cooking with charcoal that adds a rustic nature to your dishes, and I personally prefer charcoal grilling for the unique flavor and aroma that it imparts.

I use lump charcoal instead of briquettes, simply because briquettes are often laced with lighter fluid. If you're unfamiliar with charcoal grilling, it may take a couple of times to practice getting the heat right. Light your charcoal 30 minutes before cooking, and make sure that it's burning brightly before grilling to ensure that it's at the optimal temperature. I often pile my charcoal so that I have both a hot spot and a cool spot on the grill—this allows me to sear ingredients quickly and then move them to the cooler spot for cooking slowly, especially for thicker cuts of meat.

Snacks

Opposite page: Scallop Ceviche (page 15).

Introduction

LIKE MOST SOUTHEAST ASIANS, Thai people love to snack—the plethora of street vendors in Thailand definitely attests to this. Snack food also works great for appetizers as a fun, interactive way to start a meal, and I have the most fun developing these types of dishes for Maenam because they give me the most creative freedom. I remember coming up with our Spot-Prawn Crackers (page 20) as an accompaniment for a relish we served at one particular seasonal spot prawn dinner. Everyone was so delighted with how fluffy, light, and delicious the crackers turned out that we've continued making them as little snacks in the restaurant to this day.

In this chapter, I've included traditional dishes alongside playful modern riffs on how inventive and elegant a snack can be. Our Chicken Satay (page 29) is a perfect example of a traditional snack that almost everyone has already tried, whereas the Uni Sundae (page 47) is a nod to my more creative side. Whichever recipe style you gravitate toward, each creates a tasty way to break the ice at the beginning of a meal, or can be served as a beautiful standalone snack at a party. When left to my own devices, I love creating an entire meal built from lots of these little bites. I incorporate a variety of ingredients and tastes to make a collection of perfect little morsels that encourages people to eat with their hands and get more involved with their food.

Scallop Ceviche

SERVES 4 • PREP TIME: 30 MINUTES • ASSEMBLE TIME: 10 MINUTES

IT'S QUITE RARE TO FIND raw preparations of seafood in Thai cuisine, except in seaside villages where the ultra-fresh seafood is beautifully accented with *nahm jim*, thinly sliced garlic, and fresh coriander. I especially like this recipe because it shows off the beautiful shellfish available here on Canada's west coast; my absolute favorites are bay scallops from Qualicum Beach. These gorgeous plump scallops can grow up to 2 inches in size, and the shells are often larger than my hands. We prefer to buy them live and shuck them ourselves at the restaurant to ensure utmost freshness. If live scallops are unavailable, IQF (individually quick frozen) scallops from Hokkaido or Maine are also good.

4-8 large live bay scallops, or IQF scallops (see tip)

2-4 Tbsp Seafood Nahm Jim (page 132)

2 Tbsp finely sliced lemongrass, to garnish

2 Tbsp finely sliced fresh long-leaf coriander, to garnish

1 Tbsp finely julienned Makrut lime leaves, to garnish

Few sprigs of fresh coriander, to garnish

2-4 Tbsp cured salmon roe or sustainable caviar (see tip on page 48), to garnish (optional)

Edible flowers, to garnish (optional)

2 Tbsp Fried Shallots (page 235), to garnish

1. Clean the scallop shells with a brush to remove all sand and dirt. The shells will be used as presentation and serving pieces.

2. Using a flexible palette knife, pry open the two shells slightly, wide enough to stick in your thumb. The tension from the shells might feel uncomfortable, but it will be brief. Insert the palette knife and scrape the inside of the top flat shell until you separate the flesh from the shell. Open the flat top completely and flex the palette knife while scraping the bottom bowl-shaped shell. Once the flesh is completely dislodged from the shell, set it aside in a bowl on ice. Scrape the inside of the shells clean and wash them thoroughly; reserve for serving.

3. To trim the scallop meat, remove the outer mantle and the liver (black piece), keeping the flesh (muscle) and the roe (orange piece). For this recipe, only the muscle is needed; however, the roe is a tasty piece to incorporate into the ceviche should you feel adventurous.

4. Slice each scallop into four wedges. Place the scallop wedges back onto the shells and dress each with about ½ tablespoon nahm jim.

5. Garnish with lemongrass, long-leaf coriander, Makrut lime leaves, and coriander sprigs. I also like to serve it with cured salmon roe and an edible flower. Sprinkle the fried shallots on last for texture. Serve immediately.

æ When picking out live scallops from your local fishmonger, choose the heavier ones with closed shells. Scallops can vary in size, and picking the heavier ones increases your chances of finding ones with larger flesh (muscle). Test an open shell by squeezing it closed; it should bounce back and close by itself fairly quickly. If there's no tension and the scallop doesn't close its shell, that means it's dead. Avoid dead shellfish at all costs and never buy dead shellfish that is "on sale."

æ You can either discard the mantle, liver, and roe or make a quick broth with them for a simple hot sour soup, such as the one of clams and matsutake (page 87).

Recipe pictured on page 12.

Lobster Miang

SERVES 4 • PREP TIME: 30 MINUTES • COOK TIME: 1 HOUR, 15 MINUTES

MIANG IS A CLASSIC DISH, served by street vendors, wrapped with betel leaves into bite-size diamond-shaped gems. Though it can be served vegetarian, I really like it with shellfish. I wanted to serve a dish at Maenam that allowed guests to make their own wraps, so I took the traditional miang mix and combined it with grilled lobster. The result is both fun and delicious.

Lobster:

1 live lobster, about 2 pounds

2 stalks lemongrass, peeled

3 slices galangal

4 Makrut lime leaves

3 shallots

For the Lobster:

1. Kill and butcher the lobster (see sidebar on page 19).

2. Poaching is my preferred way of cooking lobster because it makes the meat more succulent and tender, while boiling tends to toughen it. To poach, in a large pot, bring water to a boil over high heat. Using a mortar and pestle, bruise the lemongrass, galangal, Makrut lime leaves, and shallots, and transfer to the boiling water. Cook for 15 minutes while maintaining a full rolling boil. Place the lobster into the boiling water and turn off the heat. Wrap the lid and top of the pot with plastic wrap to prevent the steam from escaping. Allow the steam to gently poach the lobster for 45 minutes to 1 hour.

3. Remove the lobster from the pot and, using kitchen scissors, cut off the bottom part of the tail, keeping the whole tail shell attached. Remove the head by twisting the tail while holding down the head firmly. Clean out the brain, gills, and innards. Remove the tail meat by cutting the tail in half, and devein if needed. Clean the meat from the claws and knuckles, and set aside on a cutting board. Dice all the lobster meat into ¾-inch cubes.

Miang Sauce:

6 slices galangal, roasted on grill

2 cloves garlic, roasted on grill

3 red Thai bird's eye chilies

1 Tbsp shrimp paste

1 Tbsp dried prawns

1 Tbsp roasted peanuts, skinned

Large pinch of coarse sea salt

1 cup palm sugar

⅛ cup water

¼ cup fish sauce

3 Tbsp Tamarind Water (page 233)

For the Miang Sauce:

1. Using a mortar and pestle, pound the roasted galangal, roasted garlic, chilies, shrimp paste, dried prawns, roasted peanuts, and salt into a paste.

2. In a saucepan over medium heat, simmer the palm sugar and water together for about 10 minutes, until the mixture thickens slightly but is not caramelized. Using a sugar thermometer, monitor the temperature to take it to a light-caramel stage, about 330°F. Add the fish sauce and tamarind water. Stir in the paste and cook for a few minutes, until the galangal is aromatic. Pour the sauce into a medium-size bowl and refrigerate until needed. You'll need about half a batch of the miang sauce for this recipe; store the remainder in the fridge until the next time you cook this dish, as it keeps for up to 1 month due to the high sugar content.

Recipe continued . . .

Miang Garnish:

1 pomelo

2 Tbsp finely diced shallots

1 Tbsp toasted grated coconut
(see tip on page 126)

1 Tbsp finely diced ginger

1 tsp diced lime, skin on

8-10 betel leaves

1 red Thai bird's eye chili,
finely sliced

Fresh coriander leaves

2 Tbsp Miang Sauce (see here)

Coarse sea salt, to taste

Black pepper, to taste

4 betel leaves

Few sprigs of fresh coriander,
to garnish (optional)

For the Miang Garnish:

1. Peel the pomelo by slicing off one end of it and scoring the thick skin and pith lengthwise with a paring knife, taking care not to pierce through to the flesh. Do so five times lengthwise around the pomelo. Use your hands to remove each section of skin and pith, trying to remove as much of the pith as possible from the flesh. Stick your thumb into the center of the pomelo and break it in half before segmenting it. To remove the pulp from the membrane, use a paring knife to slice open the edge of each segment, and peel away the membrane with your hands. Remove any seeds. Reserve 1 tablespoon of pomelo pulp for this recipe and dice it into ½- to 1-inch cubes.

2. In a large bowl, mix together the shallots, coconut, ginger, pomelo pulp, lime, betel leaves, chili, and coriander leaves, spooning in small amounts of the miang sauce to bind them together. You'll end up using about half a batch of the miang sauce. Do not overdress.

3. Add the diced lobster meat to the bowl with the miang garnish and mix until thoroughly combined. Taste for seasoning, and add salt and pepper if needed. To plate the dish, spoon the lobster mixture back into the lobster shell. Garnish with coriander if desired. Serve with betel leaves for making wraps.

æ When you buy a pomelo, choose one that feels heavy for its size—this indicates that it's juicy.

HOW TO PREPARE A LOBSTER

Choose a lobster that's between 1½ and 3 pounds. If it's any bigger, the meat can be tough and dry, while a smaller lobster just doesn't feel rewarding enough. Pick a lobster that's lively, with its tail flapping around and claws waving.

1. Using a heavy chef's knife, find the point on the lobster's head behind the eyes where it forms an upside-down "T." Stab your knife through its head in one motion to kill it quickly, and push the heel of the knife all the way through until the head is cut in half.

2. Cut the entire lobster in half by turning it over and piercing the underside first before crushing through the hard shell. It's always easier to cut through the softer abdomen because your knife could slide around dangerously if you cut down through the hard topside shell.

3. Do the same on the head and cut the entire lobster into two halves, often referred to as a "butterfly" cut.

4. Use a lobster cracker, nutcracker, meat mallet, or the back of your chef's knife to crack through the tough shells on the claws for ease of eating later on.

Another method for butchering the lobster, after you've stabbed it through the head, is to rip off the tail before turning the lobster on its back to slice through its soft underside. Split the head in half, crack the claws and knuckles, and cut the tail into medallions instead of butterflying them. A 2-pound lobster will give you four meaty 2-inch tail medallions—avoid slicing them any thinner than 2 inches or they'll overcook easily. This is the method used in the Lobster Clay Pot recipe (page 155).

Uni and Albacore Tuna on Spot-Prawn Crackers

SERVES 6 TO 8 • PREP TIME: 4 HOURS, PLUS DRYING • COOK TIME: 10 MINUTES

PRAWN CRACKERS WERE ONE of my favorite childhood snacks. The first time I experimented with making them, it brought me back to digging my little-kid hand into a bag for another fistful. And I'm not alone. Maenam staff used to fight over who got to eat the imperfect crackers that didn't make the cut for service. When I figured out that even the broken ones were an excellent garnish for other dishes, such as the Ahi Sashimi (page 31) and the Uni Sundae (page 47), I had to make extra so that we'd still have enough left over for snacking!

Spot-Prawn Crackers:

4 quarts canola oil (divided)

10 pounds prawn shells

2 Tbsp crushed ginger

2 Tbsp crushed garlic

6 quarts water

1 Tbsp fish sauce

2 cups Thai sticky rice, uncooked

Coarse sea salt (optional)

For the Spot-Prawn Crackers:

1. In a 4- to 6-quart stockpot over high heat, place 3 tablespoons canola oil and fry the prawn shells, ginger, and garlic until your kitchen is filled with a rich prawn aroma, about 10 to 15 minutes. Use a wooden spoon to crush the shells a bit before adding the water. Bring everything to a boil, then turn the heat down to medium-low and simmer for 3 hours. Remove from heat and let the stock cool before straining. Return the stock to a clean pot and cook over medium heat to reduce the stock by two-thirds; this will concentrate the flavor. You should have about 8 cups of stock remaining. Season with fish sauce.

2. In a large pot over medium-high heat, place the sticky rice and slowly add the stock while stirring. Simmer the rice for 25 minutes, stirring periodically to prevent it from sticking to the bottom of the pot. You want to overcook the rice so that it becomes a very loose risotto, thick and porridge-like in texture. Taste the rice and season with salt or more fish sauce if needed.

3. Preheat the oven to 100°F or, if available, set it to the dehydrate setting, or set a food dehydrator to 150°F. Line a baking tray with a silicone mat. Using a ring mold or by freestyling it, spoon the rice onto the silicone mat and spread it into ¼-inch-thick disks, about 1½ to 2 inches in diameter, ensuring an even thickness throughout. Don't overlap the rice disks, and bear in mind that they will decrease in size as they dehydrate. Place the disks in the oven or dehydrator, and cook for 12 to 16 hours, depending on quantity. The disks should be completely dry and hard throughout, with no soft spots in the middle or underside.

4. In a heavy 4-quart pot over medium-high heat, preheat the remaining canola oil to 375°F. Fry two or three rice disks at a time and wait until they puff up before flipping; they should puff up within 10 seconds if the oil is at the proper temperature. Cook until the crackers are light golden, airy, and crispy. Remove them from the oil and transfer the crackers to a baking rack lined with paper towel to absorb excess oil. Don't discard the smaller pieces—fry them and keep them as a garnish. Store any leftover prawn crackers in an airtight container at room temperature; they'll keep for up to 1 month.

Albacore Tuna Topping:

¼ pound albacore tuna, diced into ¼-inch cubes

1 Tbsp diced ginger

1 Tbsp finely diced shallots

1 small green Thai bird's eye chili, thinly sliced (optional)

2 Tbsp torn fresh coriander leaves

1 Tbsp sliced pak chi farang

1 Tbsp finely diced lime, skin on

3 Tbsp extra virgin olive oil

2 tsp coarse sea salt

Pinch of black pepper

For the Albacore Tuna Topping:

1. Mix the tuna with the ginger, shallots, and chili. Fold in the coriander, pak chi farang, and diced lime, then add the olive oil.

2. Season with salt and pepper.

Serving:

½ cup fresh sea urchin roe

2 Tbsp cured salmon roe

Few torn fresh coriander leaves, to garnish

For Serving:

1. Carefully place a spoonful of tuna onto each cracker and top it with a piece of uni, a small dollop of salmon roe, and coriander. Serve immediately.

æ During spot prawn season, most fishmongers have lots of extra shells in the freezer—they might even give them to you if you ask nicely. Flavoring stock for this recipe is a perfect way to use them up.

æ Notice that I opted to dice the lime in this recipe. In essence, this is a tuna tartare, so I added diced lime instead of lime juice or another acid. This way, the lime won't cure the tuna as quickly, but will still add acidity and freshness to the flavor profile. It also helps the crackers stay crispy for much longer!

Mini Cupcakes with Dungeness Crab

MAKES 30 TO 40 MINI CUPCAKES • PREP TIME: 30 MINUTES • COOK TIME: 10 MINUTES

THIS IS A BEAUTIFUL SNACK, big on taste and texture—one of my favorites to make and serve. The flavors are kind of nutty, rich with toasted coconut and peanut, and balanced with lots of freshness from the diced fresh lime, ginger, and shallots. It combines two classic snacks in Thailand: *kra tong thong* (often served with corn and minced chicken) and *miang* (betel-leaf wraps made with the same filling). Here we use the shell from kra tong thong and stuff it with miang mix (page 17). It's super-simple to make and combines the best elements of both dishes: crunch from the kra tong thong and the bright flavors of miang.

Kra Tong Thong Batter:

8 cups canola oil

3 cups rice flour

1 cup all-purpose flour

1 tsp coarse sea salt

1 cup Coconut Cream (page 205)

1 cup Limeized Water (see note on page 24)

For the Kra Tong Thong Batter:

1. In a heavy 4- to 6-quart pot over medium-high heat, preheat the oil to 350°F.

2. In a large bowl, mix the rice flour, all-purpose flour, and salt, then stir in the coconut cream until a dough forms. Slowly add the limeized water, stirring constantly until the mixture reaches the consistency of very thick cream. The batter should coat the back of a spoon easily to a thickness of $\frac{1}{16}$ to $\frac{1}{8}$ inch. Transfer the batter to a container that has enough depth to coat the mold (see tip).

3. Clean your kra tong thong mold well and dry it thoroughly. Once the oil has reached the correct temperature, place the mold in the hot oil for 2 to 3 minutes to warm it up and season it. All metal is porous to some degree, and heating it promotes better absorption of the oil for a more even coating.

4. When the mold is hot, remove it from the oil and dip it into the batter; the batter will sear onto the bottom of the hot mold. Place the coated mold back into the oil and fry until the cups are golden. If your mold is nicely seasoned, the cups should fall right off; if not, use a small toothpick or paring knife to gently push the cups off and onto a tray lined with paper towel. Repeat this process until you have 30 to 40 cupcakes. It's important to have extra batter in the bowl, as the cupcakes only work if the batter is deep enough to cover to the top of the mold.

Recipe continued . . .

Miang Garnish:

1 Tbsp toasted grated coconut (see tip on page 126)

1 tsp diced lime, skin on

1 Tbsp diced ginger

2 Tbsp diced shallots

½ cup loosely packed fresh coriander leaves

1 red Thai bird's eye chili, finely sliced

1 Tbsp pomegranate seeds

2 Tbsp Miang Sauce (page 17)

1 tsp coarse sea salt

Pinch of black pepper

Serving:

¼ cup Dungeness crabmeat

¼ cup cured salmon roe

¼ cup fresh coriander leaves

Sliced red Thai bird's eye chili, to garnish (optional)

For the Miang Garnish:

1. In a medium-size bowl and using a spatula, mix the coconut, lime, ginger, shallots, coriander leaves, chili, pomegranate seeds, miang sauce, salt, and pepper.

2. Fold in sauce until fully combined and not too wet. Don't mix too far ahead of assembling the cupcakes, as the lime will cause everything to sweat and you'll end up with soggy cupcakes. Set aside until ready to assemble.

For Serving:

1. Spoon about 1 tablespoon of the miang garnish into each of the cupcakes. Top them with a pinch of crabmeat, a small spoonful of salmon roe, coriander leaves, and chili. Serve immediately.

æ You'll need a kra tong thong mold, available at specialty Thai markets. If you can't track one down, you can use a small metal ladle instead (see Squid-Ink Cupcakes, page 25).

æ The bottoms of the cupcakes can be uneven, so it may be difficult to stand the pieces up on a serving platter. A trick we like to use is serving them in escargot dishes—the little cups of the dishes hold the cupcakes perfectly.

> To make limeized water, use a ratio of 1 teaspoon limestone paste (available at Asian supermarkets) with 4 cups water. Stir together and wait until the sediment settles to the bottom and the water appears clear. The limestone paste has a high alkalinity that, when mixed with water, allows the batter to brown more nicely when fried, giving you beautiful golden-brown cupcakes.

Squid-Ink Cupcakes

MAKES 6 TO 8 CUPCAKES • PREP TIME: 30 MINUTES • COOK TIME: 10 MINUTES

THESE ARE A SPINOFF of the mini cupcake recipe on page 23, but instead of using *kra tong thong* molds, we use a stainless-steel kitchen ladle to make the cups. Using a different mold and adding a spoonful of squid ink produces a completely different result, adding richness to this dish in both color and flavor.

Kra Tong Thong Batter with Squid Ink:

8 cups canola oil

3 cups rice flour

1 cup all-purpose flour

1 tsp coarse sea salt

1 tsp squid ink (see tip)

1 cup Coconut Cream (page 205)

1 cup Limeized Water (see note on page 24)

For the Kra Tong Thong Batter with Squid Ink:

1. In a heavy 4- to 6-quart pot over medium-high heat, preheat the oil to 350°F.

2. In a large bowl, mix the rice flour, all-purpose flour, and salt. Place the squid ink in a separate medium-size bowl, then stir in the coconut cream. Pour the liquid mixture into the dry ingredients and mix with a wooden spoon or spatula until a dough forms.

3. Slowly add the limeized water, stirring constantly until the mixture reaches the consistency of very thick cream. The batter should coat the back of a spoon easily to a thickness of $1/16$ to $1/8$ inch. Transfer the batter to a container that has enough depth to coat the back of a ladle. I prefer 2-ounce to 4-ounce ladles for a perfect snack-size cup.

4. Clean your ladle well and dry it thoroughly. Once the oil has reached the correct temperature, place the ladle into the oil for 2 to 3 minutes to warm it up and season it. When the ladle is hot, remove it from the oil and dip it into the batter; the batter will sear directly onto the bottom of the hot ladle. Place the coated ladle back into the oil and fry until the cups are golden. If your ladles are nicely seasoned, the cups should fall right off; if not, use a small toothpick or paring knife to gently push the cups off and onto a tray lined with paper towel. Repeat this process until you have 6 to 8 cupcakes. It's important to have extra batter in the bowl, as the cupcakes only work if the batter is deep enough to cover to the top of the ladle.

Recipe continued . . .

Tuna Filling:

¼ pound ahi tuna, diced into
¼-inch chunks

2 Tbsp Chili Jam Nahm Jim
(page 133)

1 Tbsp finely sliced lemongrass

1 Tbsp finely julienned Makrut lime
leaves

1 Tbsp finely sliced shallots

Serving:

6-8 sustainable prawns, blanched
and peeled

Pinch of coarse sea salt and black
pepper

3 Tbsp trout roe or sustainable
caviar (see tip on page 48),
to garnish

Few sprigs of fresh coriander,
to garnish

Edible flowers, to garnish (optional)

For the Tuna Filling:

1. Season the tuna with the chili jam nahm jim, lemongrass, Makrut lime leaves, and shallots. Mix until the ingredients are evenly distributed throughout the tuna mixture.

For Serving:

1. Divide the tuna filling evenly between the cups, and place a prawn on top of each. Season the prawns with salt and pepper and garnish with trout roe, coriander, and an edible flower. Serve immediately.

æ Squid ink is very common now and available from just about any fishmonger. It's a great ingredient to keep in the fridge or freezer for specialty pasta or pastry.

Chicken Satay

MAKES 12 TO 16 SKEWERS • PREP TIME: 30 MINUTES, PLUS REFRIGERATION • COOK TIME: 30 MINUTES

SATAYS ARE WONDERFUL Southeast Asian snacks. My favorite vendor in Thailand always serves pork skewers, but I prefer chicken thighs for juiciness and flavor. Sometimes, if my butcher is willing, I ask him to reserve the chicken oysters for me; these are from the small spot behind the hip socket that most people believe is the most succulent part of the bird. They're especially delicious when prepared satay style. This versatile marinade is nutty with turmeric and floral and fragrant with coriander seeds; it also works great on pork chops and grilled chicken.

Chicken Satay:

2 stalks lemongrass

3 Tbsp turmeric powder

4 Tbsp coarse sea salt (divided)

1¼ tsp white pepper (divided)

¼ cup granulated sugar

2 tsp coriander seeds

½ tsp cumin seeds

½ cup Coconut Cream (page 205)

4-6 boneless, skinless chicken thighs

Serving:

24 small bamboo skewers, presoaked overnight (see tip)

Small handful of fresh coriander leaves, to garnish (optional)

Cucumber Relish (page 231)

Peanut Sauce (page 232)

For the Chicken Satay:

1. To make the marinade, using a mortar and pestle, pound the lemongrass, turmeric powder, 3 tablespoons salt, ¼ teaspoon pepper, sugar, coriander seeds, and cumin seeds into a fine paste. Stir in the coconut cream. Check seasoning and adjust if necessary.

2. Dice the chicken thighs into ¾-inch cubes. Season with 1 tablespoon salt and 1 teaspoon pepper. Transfer the chicken cubes to a bowl. Add the marinade and toss well until evenly coated. Cover with plastic wrap and refrigerate for 1 hour.

For Serving:

1. Prepare a charcoal grill to medium heat 25 to 40 minutes prior to grilling (both a gas grill or grill pan on the stove at medium-high heat also work but are not preferred). Spread out the charcoal to achieve an even heat.

2. Once ready to cook, skewer the chicken evenly onto the presoaked bamboo skewers.

3. Grill the chicken skewers until they pick up a nice char on all sides and are cooked through, about 3 to 4 minutes per skewer depending on the thickness of your chicken. Garnish with coriander leaves if desired. Serve with cucumber relish and peanut sauce.

ə When grilling meat, presoaking bamboo skewers in a shallow dish of water overnight prevents them from burning on the grill.

Opposite page: Chicken Satay (top) and Fried Chicken Wings (bottom, page 30).

Fried Chicken Wings with Nahm Jim Jiao

SERVES 4 • PREP TIME: 10 MINUTES • COOK TIME: 7 MINUTES

FOR THE NEXT BIG GAME, try this recipe instead of ordering buffalo wings. I love the lightness of the batter—it gives the chicken wings an almost flaky texture.

4 quarts canola oil

12 chicken wings

2 tsp coarse sea salt, plus extra to taste

Pinch of white pepper

1 cup cornstarch

1½ cups water

½ tsp granulated sugar

½ tsp Toasted Chili Powder (page 234)

1 Tbsp finely sliced pak chi farang, to garnish

Nahm Jim Jiao (page 232), for serving

1. In a heavy 4- to 6-quart pot over medium-high heat, preheat the oil to 350°F.

2. Season the chicken wings with a pinch of salt and pepper. In a bowl, whisk the cornstarch and water together until they form a slurry resembling homogenized milk.

3. Dip each wing in the slurry until evenly coated and gently lower into the pot, one by one.

4. Fry for 7 minutes, until the wings are golden brown and crispy. Using a spider, remove them from the oil and transfer them to a rack lined with paper towel to absorb excess oil.

5. Season with the remaining salt and the sugar and toasted chili powder. Garnish with pak chi farang and serve with nahm jim jiao for dipping.

Recipe pictured on page 28.

Ahi Sashimi with Spot-Prawn Crackers

SERVES 4 • PREP TIME: 20 MINUTES • COOK TIME: 5 MINUTES

THIS DISH WAS THE DELICIOUS RESULT of a kitchen accident. One day while making Spot-Prawn Crackers (page 20) to use in canapés for a function, we spread the crackers too thinly as they were drying and they all fell apart when we fried them, turning into little cornflake-size bits. Culinary inspiration saved the day, and I decided to use the crunchy flakes on a sashimi special that night. I was especially drawn to the crackers' rich prawn flavor, and the crunch they offer is an excellent textural counterpoint to the delicate raw fish. It worked out really well, and I've been preparing the dish this way ever since.

¼ pound ahi tuna

¼ cup Seafood Nahm Jim (page 132)

¼ cup fresh coriander leaves

¼ cup fresh dill fronds

2 Tbsp finely sliced lemongrass

1 Tbsp finely julienned Makrut lime leaves

1 Tbsp finely sliced shallots

1 Tbsp finely sliced pak chi farang

1 Tbsp deseeded and julienned red chili pepper

¼ cup Spot-Prawn Crackers (page 20)

1 Tbsp sustainable caviar (see tip on page 48)

Pinch of flaked sea salt and black pepper

1. Using a sharp fish knife, slice the ahi tuna against the fibers of the fish into ¼-inch-thick pieces. Arrange the tuna slices neatly on a serving plate, cover with plastic wrap, and refrigerate for up to 2 hours until ready to serve.

2. Dress the tuna with the seafood nahm jim, and carefully sprinkle the coriander, dill, lemongrass, Makrut lime leaves, shallots, pak chi farang, and chili on and around the fish.

3. Finish by topping with the prawn crackers and caviar, and seasoning with salt and pepper. Serve immediately.

æ **When selecting sashimi-grade tuna, look for ahi tuna from Hawaii. These tuna are caught using long lines and are designated as sustainable.**

Crispy Fried Oysters

SERVES 3 TO 4 • PREP TIME: 15 MINUTES • COOK TIME: 5 MINUTES

I ABSOLUTELY LOVE OYSTERS! To my surprise, though, not everyone feels the same way. Many people are simply scared to try them, while others don't like the texture. I'm happy to say that this oyster dish is single-handedly responsible for converting many oyster unbelievers because of its crunchy texture and the delicious Seafood Nahm Jim dressing (page 132) that accompanies it.

Batter:

1 cup all-purpose flour

1 cup cornstarch

1 Tbsp baking powder

Pinch coarse sea salt

1 egg

1½ cups cold water

Oysters:

4 quarts canola oil

8-12 medium-size oysters, shucked (see sidebar)

Pinch of coarse sea salt

½ cup Seafood Nahm Jim (page 132)

¼ cup fresh coriander leaves, to garnish

For the Batter:

1. In a medium-size bowl, whisk together the flour, cornstarch, baking powder, and salt, then incorporate the egg and the cold water. Mix until the batter just becomes smooth, about the consistency of pancake batter. Keep cold in the fridge if not using right away.

For the Oysters:

1. In a heavy 6-quart pot, warm the canola oil over medium-high heat until it reaches 350°F.

2. Meanwhile, shuck the oysters (see sidebar).

3. Dip each oyster in the batter until evenly coated, then gently lower into the hot oil. Deep-fry for 2 to 3 minutes, until the oysters are golden with a crust that's crispy to the touch—do not overcook. Once done, use a spider to remove them from the fryer and transfer to a plate lined with paper towel. Season immediately with salt.

4. Serve with seafood nahm jim and coriander leaves as garnish.

HOW TO SHUCK AN OYSTER

When shucking oysters, make sure you have a shucking knife and dish towel handy. Do not attempt to do it freehand.

1. Clean your oysters well with a brush.

2. Oysters generally consist of a top shell and a bottom shell, with the bottom shell shaped more like a cup. Make sure that the flatter top shell is facing up so that the oyster liquor stays in the oyster once you remove the top shell.

3. Fold the dish towel over your left hand, almost like a baseball mitt. Place a single oyster cup-side down onto the towel, fold the towel over it so that both the top and bottom shells are covered, and hold it firmly. At the very tip of the oyster, there should be a seam where the top and bottom shells meet. Gently insert your shucking knife into this seam, but don't attempt to push the entire shucking knife through—this is a common mistake that'll cause you to stab the oyster itself. Instead, twist the tip of your knife at the seam until you hear a pop. Once the shell pops, slide your oyster knife along the top of the shell to dislodge the connective tissues, being careful to keep the oyster shell level to prevent the oyster liquor from spilling out.

4. Remove the top shell, inspect the rim of the bottom shell, and clean off any grit and broken bits of shell. The oyster should be nice and moist, surrounded with brine that smells fresh like the ocean. If the brine is at all on the funky side or is missing completely, toss out the oyster as this indicates that the oyster is dying.

5. Take the oyster knife and run it along the bottom shell to disconnect the same muscle; this enables you to slide the oyster out of its shell and eat it without a fork. Other people prefer to leave this muscle intact as proof that the oyster hasn't been pre-shucked, but you'll need to serve it with a fork to remove the oyster meat.

Fresh Oysters on the Half Shell

SERVES 3 TO 4 • PREP TIME: 10 MINUTES • ASSEMBLE TIME: 5 MINUTES

THIS RECIPE IS FOR PEOPLE who only eat their oysters raw. The Pacific oyster (*Magallana gigas*) is the variety that's readily available here in Vancouver. Their names may differ depending on size and exact point of origin, but they're all still the same species. I prefer medium-small to medium-size oysters, and Royal Miyagis, Golden Mantles, or Kusshis are my favorites to use for this recipe because they're the ideal size, brine, fat content, and minerality. Malpeques, Blue Points, and Beausoleils are delicious east coast alternatives.

Crushed ice or rock salt

12 medium-size oysters

½ cup Seafood Nahm Jim (page 132)

2 Tbsp fresh coriander leaves

2 Tbsp finely sliced lemongrass

1 Tbsp finely julienned Makrut lime leaves

1 Tbsp finely sliced shallots

1 Tbsp deseeded and julienned red chili pepper

1 Tbsp finely sliced pak chi farang

2 Tbsp Fried Shallots (page 235)

2 Tbsp cured salmon roe or sustainable caviar (see tip on page 48)

1. Prepare a serving platter by covering it with a layer of crushed ice or rock salt.

2. Scrub and shuck the oysters (see sidebar on page 33), taking care not to spill the oyster liquor, and place on the serving platter.

3. Once all the oysters are opened, spoon 1 to 2 teaspoons of the seafood nahm jim over each oyster. I personally prefer not to use too much, as it can overpower the delicately flavored raw oysters.

4. Carefully arrange the coriander leaves, lemongrass, lime leaves, shallots, chili peppers, and pak chi farang atop the oysters, placing the fried shallots and salmon roe on last. Serve immediately.

Prawn Cakes

SERVES 4 TO 6 • PREP TIME: 30 MINUTES • COOK TIME: 5 MINUTES

FRESHLY COOKED THAI FISH CAKES are one of my favorite snacks. In Thailand, they're typically made with catfish and red curry paste. I wanted to use prawns instead here because their silky, bouncy texture eliminates the fibrous quality that I find some fish cakes have. To enhance rather than overwhelm the delicate prawn flavor, I use a simple paste of garlic and chili rather than a curry paste. This recipe is delicious and easy to execute—great as a canapé or light appetizer.

4 quarts canola oil

1 garlic clove

1 red Thai bird's eye chili

Pinch of coarse sea salt

1 pound hand-minced prawn meat

½ cup diced long beans

2 Tbsp julienned Makrut lime leaves

2 Tbsp fish sauce

½ tsp white pepper

½ tsp granulated sugar

¼ cup Sweet Chili Sauce (page 233), for serving

1. In a deep fryer or large heavy pot over medium-high heat, preheat the canola oil to 350°F.

2. Using a mortar and pestle, pound the garlic, chili, and salt into a fine paste. Transfer the paste to a medium-size bowl together with the rest of the ingredients (excluding the sweet chili sauce). Using your hands, combine the ingredients thoroughly, then slap the mixture against the bowl until firm and sticky. Form the mixture into 16 to 20 balls, 1 to 1½ inches in diameter, or into 10 to 12 patties up to 2 inches wide and no more than 1 inch thick.

3. Test-fry one prawn cake in the fryer or pot, cooking it for about 2 minutes, until golden brown. The texture should be bouncy and lightly toothy. Depending on the size of your pot, fry them in one or two batches, then transfer to a plate lined with paper towel to drain any excess oil.

4. Serve with sweet chili sauce.

æ Proteins firm up while they're being worked with. Slapping the minced prawn mixture against the inside of the bowl by hand is just like kneading dough. Do this for 5 to 10 minutes, until you feel a firm bounce-back on the prawn meat.

Chiang Mai-Style Sausage

MAKES 12 TO 16 (5-OUNCE) SAUSAGES • PREP TIME: 1 HOUR, PLUS SOAKING • COOK TIME: 30 MINUTES

DEFINITELY ONE OF THE TASTIEST SNACKS you'll find in Chiang Mai. As a northern city, Chiang Mai has food that is rustic and full of robust flavors. These sausages can be eaten on their own, but they're absolutely wonderful when served with Pork Crackling (page 42) and Nam Prik Num (page 41). Like many other dishes in this book, they're better when grilled over charcoal, but can also be cooked in a grill pan on the stove. Your butcher is the best source for ordering natural hog sausage casings. They're usually either salted or kept frozen in plastic tubes—the latter is obviously easier to use, but both kinds come in bulk. Be prepared to freeze the unused casings for future use.

1 package natural sausage casing

10 long dry guajillo chilies

¾ cup chopped lemongrass

2 Tbsp ground long pepper

1 small piece cassia bark, grated (see tip)

¼ cup chopped galangal

1½ cups chopped shallots

1 cup chopped garlic

5 pounds fatty ground pork (30% fat)

1 Tbsp palm sugar

¾ cup light soy sauce

½ cup fish sauce

¼ cup julienned Makrut lime leaves

¼ cup fresh coriander leaves

1 banana leaf

½ cup grated coconut, for smoking

Pork Crackling (page 42), for serving

Nam Prik Num, for serving

1. In most cases, sausage casing is sold in a pack with lots of salt to preserve it. Soak the natural sausage casing in cold water for at least 2 hours before using. This will help rinse away both the salt and the smell of the casing. In a separate bowl, seed and soak the long dry chilies in water for a minimum of 1 hour.

2. Using a mortar and pestle (or a blender or food processor), grind the lemongrass, ground long pepper, and cassia bark before gradually adding the presoaked long chilies, galangal, shallots, and garlic, grinding them in with each addition until you achieve a fine paste.

3. In a large bowl, place the ground pork and mix in the paste. Grate the palm sugar directly into the meat mixture and slowly add the soy sauce and fish sauce until combined.

4. Sprinkle the Makrut lime leaves slowly into the mix to avoid clumping, and fold in the coriander leaves. Using your hands, slap the meat against the inside of the bowl a few times to emulsify the mix. Set aside in the fridge to chill for a minimum of 15 to 20 minutes until ready to stuff into the sausage casing.

5. If using a manual sausage stuffer, fill the stuffer with the chilled pork mixture and load the casing onto the tip. Slowly press the meat out until you can see it from the tip and tie a knot on the casing around the tip. Use your left hand to control the filling of the sausage and your right hand to operate the crank and control the speed at which the sausage comes out. Similarly, if using a motorized sausage stuffer attachment, you should use your left hand to control how tightly the sausage fills. Fill the sausage casing continuously and form the sausage into a ring. Alternatively, to hand-stuff the sausage casing, you can use a large piping bag with a large open tip to fill the casing. The sausages can be kept raw in the fridge for 3 to 4 days or in the freezer for up to 2 months.

6. Before you grill the sausages, use a cake tester to prick holes in the casings so that the steam can escape. This prevents the sausages from bursting while they're cooking.

7. Prepare a charcoal grill to medium heat 25 to 40 minutes prior to grilling. Spread out the charcoal to achieve an even heat.

8. Once the grill is heated, find a spot where the heat is subtle and constant. Place a banana leaf on the grill and lay the sausages on it; this allows them to cook slowly without bursting. Sprinkle grated coconut onto the coals to smoke the sausage for about 10 minutes, then turn the sausage over and cook for another 5 minutes. Once the sausages are cooked, remove the banana leaf from underneath and place them onto the hottest part of the grill for 2 minutes per side to sear on some grill marks. Set aside.

9. Let the sausages rest for 5 minutes before slicing them on a 45-degree bias. Serve with pork crackling and nam prik num.

æ Though not ideal, whole cinnamon sticks are an okay substitute for whole cassia bark in this particular recipe. Sourcing ingredients from Chinatown or specialty Asian grocery stores will definitely lead you to whole cassia bark that has a more subtle, well-rounded flavor than cinnamon.

Nam Prik Num

SERVES 4 TO 6 • PREP TIME: 1 HOUR, PLUS CURING AND DEHYDRATING • COOK TIME: 45 MINUTES

NAM PRIK NUM IS MY FAVORITE RELISH from Chiang Mai. Its smoky aromas and robust, rustic flavors are an excellent way to awaken your palate at the start of a meal. Pork crackling is one of the best things to serve with it. You can use store-bought crackling, but I think it's more worthwhile to make your own. Nam prik num doesn't keep well, so prepare it in small batches and store it for up to 3 days in the fridge.

Nam Prik Num:

2-4 bamboo skewers

6 medium-size shallots, unpeeled

12 large cloves garlic

4 green Anaheim peppers

4 hot green banana peppers

8 slices galangal

1 Tbsp coarse sea salt

¼ cup fish sauce

1 Tbsp freshly squeezed lime juice

1 Tbsp palm sugar (optional)

1 Tbsp Fried Garlic (page 235),
to garnish

1 Tbsp sliced green onions,
to garnish

For the Nam Prik Num:

1. Preheat a charcoal grill to high heat 45 minutes to 1 hour prior to grilling. While the grill is preheating, presoak bamboo skewers in warm water.

2. Keeping the skin on the shallots, skewer them onto the bamboo skewers. Skewer the garlic cloves on a separate skewer to ensure easier grilling.

3. Once the grill is heated, place the green Anaheim peppers and hot green banana peppers on the grill and char for about 5 minutes, turning them occasionally to ensure the skins are evenly blistered. Remove them from the grill and place them in a bowl. Cover them with plastic wrap until the skin softens, then peel off the blackened skins.

4. Grill the skewered shallots until the shallot skins are charred. Grill the garlic and galangal until they are lightly charred with nice grill marks. Remove from the grill, place them in a bowl, and cover them with plastic wrap until the residual heat steams them through and softens the centers. Peel off and discard the charred skins.

5. Using a mortar and pestle, pound the shallots, garlic, and galangal into a paste, using the coarse sea salt as an abrasive. Slice the roasted Anaheim and banana peppers into chunks, add them to the mortar, and continue pounding into a rough paste. Fold in the fish sauce and lime juice, then check the seasoning. The relish should taste smoky, salty, and spicy. If sour, add the palm sugar for balance; if sweet, add lime juice. Garnish with fried garlic and green onions.

Recipe continued . . .

Pork Crackling:

1 pound pork back or belly skin
(see tip)

1 cup coarse sea salt

1 cup dark soy sauce (optional)

8 cups canola oil

Coarse sea salt, for finishing

For the Pork Crackling:

1. Trim any excess fat from the underside of the pork skin, and clean thoroughly. Rub the skin with the salt and let it cure in the fridge for 12 hours.

2. The next day, rinse the salt off the skin under cold running water. Fill a 6- to 8-quart pot with water and boil the pork skin over high heat. The pork skin will swell up as it cooks, so you'll need a lot of water and room in your pot. I like adding some dark soy sauce to give the pork crackling a rich golden color, but this is strictly optional. Boil the skin for about 2 hours, until the skin is so soft that it falls apart at the touch. Carefully remove the skin from the pot with a spider, and cut it into strips that are 1½ inches wide by 3 inches long. Sometimes I like to leave the pork skin whole and let guests break it apart as they eat it.

3. Preheat the oven to 100°F or, if available, set it to the dehydrate setting, or set a food dehydrator to 150°F. Line a baking tray with parchment paper. Dehydrate the skin pieces for 12 hours. The skins should be completely dry and contain no moisture; if the skins are still soft or pliable, dry them some more. Once dried, you can keep your dehydrated skins in the fridge for up to 2 weeks until you need to fry them.

4. To fry the skins, preheat the canola oil in a 4-quart pot to 375°F to 400°F. Line a tray with paper towel and put it beside the stove. When the oil comes to temperature, fry the skins a few pieces at a time. The skins will expand a lot as they're frying, so don't overcrowd the pot. Once the crackling pieces puff up, turn them over a few times to ensure even cooking, then remove them from the oil and place them on the paper towel-lined tray to drain well. Season with sea salt.

Serving:

Soft-boiled eggs

Cucumbers

Green beans

Chiang Mai-Style
Sausage (page 38) (optional)

For Serving:

1. Serve the nam prik num in a dish alongside a platter of crudités with soft-boiled eggs, cucumbers, green beans, and pork crackling. It's also great with smoked sausage (page 38).

æ Ask a good butcher to sell you some pork skin, preferably from the back or belly. The skin needs to have lots of collagen for it to puff up nicely, so leg skin doesn't work as well. Depending on your butcher, the skin may be ready to go from the point of purchase; however, you often have to trim and clean off the excess fat from the underside of the skin.

Shrimp and Salmon Betel-Leaf Wraps

SERVES 4 TO 6 • PREP TIME: 20 MINUTES • COOK TIME: 5 MINUTES

THIS IS A REALLY QUICK AND EASY RECIPE that's always a party favorite. You can replace the salmon with hamachi or kingfish; I also like using tuna for this recipe. The strong bright flavors of the chili jam in the dressing pair better with oilier-fleshed fish that are a bit stronger tasting than delicate white fish.

¼ pound sockeye salmon fillet

4-6 sidestripe prawns, or other smallish shrimp

4-6 betel leaves

4 cups water

2 Tbsp granulated sugar

¼ cup Chili Jam Nahm Jim (page 133)

3 Tbsp finely sliced lemongrass

1 Tbsp finely julienned Makrut lime leaves

1 Tbsp finely sliced pak chi farang

1 Tbsp finely diced shallots

1 Tbsp Fried Shallots (page 235)

Pinch of coarse sea salt and black pepper

Juice of 1 Makrut lime

1 tsp grated Makrut lime zest

2 Tbsp finely shaved fennel

¼ cup fennel tops, to garnish

¼ cup fresh coriander leaves, to garnish

2 Tbsp cured salmon roe, to garnish (optional)

1. Skin your salmon fillet and dice the flesh into small cubes. In a medium-size pot of salted boiling water, blanch the sidestripe prawns with the shell on for 30 seconds. Remove immediately and cool in an ice bath or in a bowl under cold running water. Peel the prawns and set aside.

2. To prepare the betel leaves, remove their stems, as they are tough to digest. Place the water and sugar in a bowl, then add the leaves and soak for 10 minutes. Transfer the soaked leaves to paper towel to dry. The sugar firms up the betel leaves and gives them a gentle bittersweet flavor.

3. In a small mixing bowl, combine the salmon and the chili jam nahm jim. Add the lemongrass, Makrut lime leaves, pak chi farang, diced shallots, fried shallots, salt, and pepper. Mix until well combined. Season with the Makrut lime juice and zest. The mixture should taste rich with chili jam yet balanced with perfumes of lemongrass and Makrut lime. Gently fold in the shaved fennel.

4. Place a nice spoonful of the salmon mixture onto each betel leaf. Carefully place a sidestripe prawn atop each salmon quenelle and garnish with fennel tops, coriander leaves, and salmon roe. Serve immediately.

Hamachi Crudo

SERVES 4 • PREP TIME: 10 MINUTES • ASSEMBLE TIME: 5 MINUTES

IN CERTAIN PARTS OF THAILAND where fresh seafood is abundant, they serve this dish with a little dressing and some freshly sliced herbs and aromatics. I like to add fresh hearts of palm—they offer great texture and add a delicate, sweet roundness to balance out the sharp, tangy flavors. You'll want your guests to enjoy this dish immediately after you dress it, so it's important to preslice the fish and refrigerate it while preparing the rest of the recipe.

¼ pound fresh hearts of palm (see tip)

Squeeze of lime juice

1 pound boneless hamachi or Mediterranean sea bass fillet

¼ cup Seafood Nahm Jim (page 132)

1 tsp grated Makrut lime zest

3 Tbsp finely sliced lemongrass

2 Tbsp finely julienned Makrut lime leaves

2 Tbsp finely sliced shallots

1 Tbsp finely sliced pak chi farang

1 Tbsp deseeded and julienned red chili pepper (optional)

½ cup fresh coriander leaves

1 Tbsp cured salmon roe or sustainable caviar (see tip on page 48), to garnish (optional)

1. Slice the hearts of palm across the grain into ⅛-inch-thick pieces. Set aside in a bowl of cold water with a squeeze of lime juice. The lime juice prevents the hearts of palm from browning and enhances their refreshing flavor.

2. With a very sharp fish knife, cut the hamachi against the grain into ¼- to ½-inch-thick slices. Fan out the slices on a plate, cover with plastic wrap, and refrigerate for up to 2 hours until ready to serve.

3. Once you're ready to serve the crudo, remove the fish from the fridge. Spoon the nahm jim on top, then grate the Makrut lime zest over it. Sprinkle evenly with the lemongrass, Makrut lime leaves, shallots, pak chi farang, chili, and coriander leaves. Finish with the sliced hearts of palm and salmon roe.

ə When buying fresh young hearts of palm, look for ones that aren't fibrous and dry. The flesh should be tender, juicy, and creamy white.

Uni Sundae

SERVES 4 TO 6 • PREP TIME: 45 MINUTES, PLUS OVERNIGHT FREEZING • ASSEMBLE TIME: 10 MINUTES

THERE'S A THIN LINE between sweet and savory in Thai cooking. I often play with that line, as I don't have much of a sweet tooth and I like my desserts more on the savory side. This dish is a neat little starter; we serve it as a canapé or amuse-bouche to kick-start a meal. I've always had a fondness for uni, or sea urchin, but its texture and flavor are challenging for many people. Making an ice cream with it is a more subtle introduction.

Uni Ice Cream:

2 cups full-fat milk

2 cups whipping cream

1 cup granulated sugar

8 egg yolks

1 cup fresh sea urchin roe (see tip)

For the Uni Ice Cream:

1. To make over direct heat, pour the milk and whipping cream into a 2-quart saucepan and bring to a simmer over medium heat, about 5 minutes. Meanwhile, in a large bowl, whisk together the sugar and egg yolks until pale and fully combined. While whisking, slowly drizzle the hot-cream mixture into the egg-yolk mixture. If you pour in the cream all at once, it will cook the egg yolks. Once whisked, return the mixture to the saucepan and whisk constantly over medium-low heat until it thickens, about 5 minutes. Do not overcook the mixture as it will scramble the eggs; it should be thick enough to coat the back of a spoon with a consistency of loose porridge.

If you're uncomfortable making the ice-cream custard over direct heat, you could use the more forgiving double-boiler method instead. Place the cream-and-egg mixture into a large bowl and rest it atop a pot of simmering water over medium heat. Whisk the mixture over the simmering water until the mixture thickens.

2. Prepare two mixing bowls: one large bowl with ice and one medium-size bowl that rests on top of the ice. Pour the hot ice-cream base into the medium-size bowl on ice—a crucial step to stop the cooking process. When the mixture has cooled, blend in the sea urchin roe with a hand blender until the liquid is velvety smooth. Transfer to an ice-cream and sorbet maker and freeze according to the manufacturer's instructions. Once the ice cream is ready, remove it from the machine and freeze it overnight before using.

3. Place four to six small serving bowls in the freezer prior to assembling; this allows the ice cream to stay chilled when you're ready to serve.

Recipe continued . . .

Serving:

½ pound Dungeness crabmeat

2 Tbsp Spot Prawn Cracker bits
(page 20) or shrimp crackers or
puffed rice

2 Tbsp julienned young coconut
meat

½ cup fresh sea urchin roe

¼ cup cured salmon roe or
sustainable caviar (see tip)

Sprigs of fresh dill, to garnish

Sprigs of fresh coriander, to garnish

Gold flakes, to garnish (optional)

Flaked sea salt, to garnish (optional)

Edible flower petals, to garnish
(optional)

For Serving:

1. Spoon two to three small scoops of uni ice cream into each bowl. Place an equal amount of the Dungeness crabmeat atop the ice cream in each bowl and sprinkle with spot prawn cracker bits for texture.

2. Finish with the young coconut meat, sea urchin roe, salmon roe, and sprigs of dill and coriander. You can add gold flakes, along with a few sprinkles of flaked sea salt and edible flower petals, for extra texture and flavor contrast. Serve immediately.

æ When making this recipe, ask your seafood supplier if they have sea urchin paste for the uni ice cream. Sea urchin paste is made from the broken roes that are left after processing; dealers often keep and freeze them for sauces. It's a much cheaper way to make a large batch of ice cream.

æ Although beluga sturgeon is an endangered species, a number of sustainable caviar options have been developed in recent years. Some are harvested through aquaculture, while others are sourced from sustainable fisheries—do your research before buying. Two Canadian purveyors of note who now produce sustainable caviar are Acadian Sturgeon and Caviar and Northern Divine.

Steamed Mussels with Lemongrass and Thai Basil

SERVES 4 TO 6 • PREP TIME: 10 MINUTES • COOK TIME: 5 MINUTES

ONE OF MY FAVORITE THINGS to eat oceanside in Thailand is freshly steamed shellfish. Here in Vancouver, we're blessed with beautiful mussels and clams from the pristine waters surrounding Vancouver Island. I love using mussels from nearby Salt Spring Island for their thick, velvety texture and buttery flavor. They're widely available across the country, as are Prince Edward Island mussels, a delicious alternative from the opposite coast. We feature this dish, known as *Hoi Malaeng Puu Bai Horapha*, on the menu at Maenam to proudly showcase our local shellfish, as the aromatics really enhance the mussels' natural nectar.

3 stalks lemongrass, sliced into 3-inch chunks

6 Makrut lime leaves

2 Tbsp sliced shallots

4-6 red Thai bird's eye chilies

2 pounds mussels, cleaned and debearded

12 tomatoes, quartered

Small handful of fresh Thai basil leaves, plus extra to garnish

1 cup Seafood Nahm Jim (page 132)

1 Tbsp fish sauce

¼ cup chicken stock or Master Stock (page 61)

Finely sliced lemongrass, to garnish

1. Using a mortar and pestle, pound the lemongrass, Makrut lime leaves, shallots, and chilies until bruised.

2. Transfer the mixture to a large 12-inch skillet, then add the mussels, tomatoes, Thai basil, seafood nahm jim, and fish sauce. Add the stock last to prevent splashing. Cover with a lid and steam over high heat until all the mussels open, about 5 minutes.

3. Transfer the mussels to a large serving bowl and garnish them with Thai basil and sliced lemongrass.

ə If you don't end up using all the broth, save it in the fridge as a wonderfully fragrant base for Caesar cocktails.

> One of my favorite things to do with leftover mussels is to lightly pickle them: Reserve some of the cooking liquid in the pan and mix it with equal parts of water and apple cider vinegar or white wine vinegar. Whisk in 2 tablespoons sugar and 1 teaspoon salt. Bring this brine mixture to a simmer, then pour it into a bowl and allow it to cool. Meanwhile, remove the remaining mussels from their shells. Once the brine has cooled, add the mussels to the bowl, cover tightly with a lid or plastic wrap, and marinate in the fridge. These lightly pickled mussels will last for up to 1 week if kept in the fridge.

Recipe pictured on the title page.

Northern-Style Grilled Hen

SERVES 4 TO 6 • PREP TIME: 20 MINUTES, PLUS OVERNIGHT MARINATING • COOK TIME: 45 MINUTES

GAI YANG, A TRADITIONAL CHARCOAL-GRILLED HEN, is a street-food favorite in northern Thailand. Restaurant after restaurant in Chiang Mai offers their own version, whether it's split or butterflied over a charcoal grill or cooked on a rotisserie. And the marinades also vary, ranging from a really simple rub of fish sauce and garlic, to ones with greater complexity of spices. This recipe is a sweeter version of a classic Thai coconut marinade. When you're ready for grilling, make sure to brush the excess marinade off the chicken to prevent the sugar and cream from burning.

2 free-range chickens, 1½ to 2 pounds each

1 cup palm sugar

1 cup granulated sugar

2 cups fish sauce

2 cups Coconut Milk (page 205)

1 cup garlic cloves

1 Tbsp dark soy sauce (optional) (see tip)

Pinch of white pepper

Nahm Jim Jiao (page 232), for serving

1. Using a cleaver or large chef's knife, butterfly each chicken by cutting through the backbone and leaving the breastbone attached. Press down to slightly break the breastbones so that the chickens lie flat on your cutting board. Place chickens in a large stainless-steel bowl.

2. Place the palm sugar, granulated sugar, fish sauce, coconut milk, garlic, dark soy sauce (if desired), and white pepper in a blender and blend until thoroughly combined. Pour the marinade over the chickens, ensuring that each bird is thoroughly coated. Cover the bowl with a lid or wrap tightly with plastic wrap, and marinate the chickens in the fridge overnight.

3. Prepare a charcoal grill to medium heat 45 minutes prior to grilling. When the grill is at the desired temperature, spread out the charcoal to achieve an even heat. Make sure to adjust the height of the grill rack so that it's 6 to 8 inches above the charcoal, or smother the charcoal with some grated coconut to prevent the chicken skin from burning.

4. Once the flames subside, grill the chickens over the coals until golden, cooking for about 15 minutes on each side depending on the size of your hens. The chickens should cook slowly and evenly while the skin is being crisped; if the charcoal is too hot or the grill is too close to the coals, the chickens will burn before the meat is cooked through.

5. Place cooked chickens on a large serving platter and serve with a small bowl of nahm jim jiao for dipping.

æ If using a rotisserie oven like we do at one of our restaurants, Freebird Chicken Shack, keep the chicken whole and simply immerse it in the marinade overnight. Clean off the excess marinade the next day to prevent burning, skewer through for the rotisserie oven, and roast at 375°F for 45 minutes.

æ Though totally optional, adding a tablespoon of dark soy sauce to the marinade gives the chicken a rich, dark skin. If you're not careful during the cooking process, however, you may end up burning the chicken because the skin becomes so dark in color.

Salmon Crackling with Caviar

SERVES 4 • PREP TIME: 30 MINUTES, PLUS SOUS-VIDE COOKING AND OVERNIGHT DEHYDRATING • COOK TIME: 20 MINUTES

MY FRIEND JENICE, who owns a fish plant, always has a lot of extra salmon skin and asked me if I could use it for something. Since we've been making pork crackling at the restaurants for years, why not make salmon crackling too? Ask your fishmonger if they have salmon skin—chances are you might even get it for free! After a bit of trial and error, the salmon crackling turned out quite nicely: puffy, airy, crunchy, and light in texture. The trick is using both a food-saver machine and a sous-vide cooker—the latter is definitely necessary, and I wouldn't make this recipe without one. A few years ago, I probably wouldn't have included this recipe in this book, but now that sous-vide cooking is more easily accessible to home cooks, I figured why not!

Salmon Crackling:

4-5 pieces salmon skin (see tip)
1 cup kosher salt
4 quarts canola oil

For the Salmon Crackling:

1. Clean the salmon skin by using a thin filleting knife to scrape the skin free of scales, fat, and flesh. Wash the skin with water, rub it with the kosher salt, and lay it out on a baking tray to cure for 1 hour.

2. Preheat your sous-vide circulator to 162°F. Rinse the salt off the skin under cold running water and carefully lay it flat in one or two food-saver bags. Note that the pieces of skin will stick together if they overlap or get folded over during the vacuum-packing process. Seal the salmon skin at 100% vacuum and let it cook in the circulator for 12 hours. By cooking the skin slowly at this temperature, we're activating the collagen without overcooking it.

3. Once the salmon skin is almost cooked, preheat your oven to 150°F or prepare your dehydrator according to the manufacturer's instructions, and prepare an ice bath. When the skin is cooked, transfer the bag(s) from the circulator to the ice bath. Remove the skin from the bag(s) and transfer to a nonstick silicone baking mat. Leave in the preheated oven or food dehydrator overnight.

4. When fully dried, the salmon skin will be hard and crispy; carefully remove it from the oven or food dehydrator. If you're not cooking the salmon crackling immediately, wrap it in paper towel and store in an airtight container. It will keep for up to 2 days on the counter in a cooler part of your kitchen, or 1 week in the fridge.

5. In a heavy 6-quart stockpot over medium-high heat, preheat the canola oil to 400°F. Once the oil comes to temperature, fry the dried salmon skin pieces one at a time. As the skin puffs up, use tongs to submerge it in the oil for 10 to 20 seconds and ensure it's fully cooked through. Remove from the oil and transfer the cooked skin to a baking sheet lined with paper towel to absorb excess oil. Set aside at room temperature until ready to serve.

Salmon Relish:

1 small bamboo skewer, presoaked in warm water for 2 hours

3 cloves garlic

2 red Thai bird's eye chilies

3 slices galangal

1 shallot, unpeeled

¼ pound sockeye salmon fillet

2-3 Tbsp fish sauce

1 tsp palm sugar

2-3 Tbsp freshly squeezed lime juice

Pinch of white pepper

1 Tbsp finely sliced pak chi farang

Serving:

¼ pound sliced cold-smoked salmon

⅛ cup thinly sliced baby cucumber

Few fresh coriander leaves

1 Tbsp sustainable caviar (see tip on page 48)

For the Salmon Relish:

1. Preheat a charcoal or gas grill to medium heat. Place the garlic and chilies together on the presoaked bamboo skewer. Grill them along with the galangal slices and shallot for 5 minutes, or until they're charred and cooked through, and set aside. Place the salmon fillet on the grill skin-side down and cook it for 5 minutes, then turn it over and cook it flesh-side down for another 3 minutes until fully cooked through. Remove from heat to rest until you assemble the canapés.

2. Using a mortar and pestle, pound the garlic, chilies, galangal, and shallot together into a fine paste. Remove the skin from the grilled salmon fillet and flake the flesh into the mortar. Gently pestle the mixture while simultaneously folding with a spoon or spatula until the salmon and aromatics are well incorporated. Season with fish sauce, palm sugar, lime juice (if serving right away), and white pepper before stirring in the pak chi farang. The relish should taste smoky, hot, sour, and salty. The relish can be stored in an airtight container in the fridge for a few days; however, once you season it with lime juice, you should eat it the day it's prepared because the flavor won't be as bright and fresh thereafter.

For Serving:

1. When ready to serve, break the crackling into canapé-size portions. I generally like to prepare this dish as a two-biter, so crackling pieces are about 1 by 2 inches. Fold a slice of cold-smoked salmon onto the skin. Spoon a dollop of the salmon relish onto the smoked salmon.

2. Garnish with one or two slices of baby cucumber, a few coriander leaves, and caviar. Serve immediately.

ꝏ Any fatty fish skin would work for this dish as the skins are usually high in collagen.

Coconut-Cream Relish of Fermented Pork and Spot-Prawn Tomalley

SERVES 4 • PREP TIME: 30 MINUTES • COOK TIME: 10 MINUTES

THIS IS AN IRRESISTIBLE COCONUT CREAM-BASED RELISH, known as *lon naem*, that makes a fantastic party appetizer. I love this dish because it showcases our local spot prawns and it gives people a good recipe for using the prawn heads.

Coconut-Cream Relish:

1 cup Coconut Cream (page 205)

½ cup chicken stock

3 Tbsp cooked Spot-Prawn Tomalley (page 54)

½ cup minced fermented Thai sausage

2 Tbsp palm sugar

2 Tbsp Tamarind Water (page 233)

2 Tbsp fish sauce, or to taste

Small pinch of white pepper

1 Tbsp mandarin orange juice (see tip)

¼ cup chopped fresh raw spot prawn meat

2 Tbsp sliced shallots

2 Tbsp fresh coriander leaves

1 Tbsp finely sliced pak chi farang

For the Coconut-Cream Relish:

1. In a saucepan over medium heat, simmer the coconut cream with the stock for 5 minutes. Season with the cooked spot-prawn tomalley. Add the sausage, and cook for an additional 3 to 5 minutes.

2. Turn off the heat and season with the palm sugar, tamarind water, fish sauce, and white pepper. Freshen the coconut cream by stirring in the mandarin orange juice.

3. To finish, stir in the chopped raw spot prawn meat, shallots, coriander leaves, and pak chi farang.

Suggested Accompaniments for Serving:

Radishes

Cucumber slices

Endive leaves

Pieces of blanched endives

Starfruit slices

Fresh white peeled turmeric slices (optional)

Cha-om fritters

Spot-Prawn Crackers (page 20)

Edible flower petals (optional)

For Serving:

1. Serve the relish immediately alongside a platter of suggested crudités and spot-prawn crackers for dipping.

æ When squeezing fresh mandarin orange juice, reserve the orange peel and dry in the sun or in a dehydrator on the medium setting overnight. Homemade dried orange peels are far better to use than store-bought ones that often smell musty and are rather bland in flavor.

Grilled King-Crab Relish

SERVES 4 • PREP TIME: 25 MINUTES, PLUS SOAKING OF SKEWERS • COOK TIME: 5 MINUTES

NAM PRIK IS AN INTENSELY ROBUST Thai relish that's often enjoyed with raw or cooked vegetable crudités as a bright, refreshing flavor balance. Grilled prawns are most commonly used with this recipe, but it works well with any grilled crustaceans or rich oilier fish such as salmon or mackerel. I made this version one day with some leftover grilled king crab legs, and the meatiness complements the sharp flavors really well. The trick is to play around with the accompanying vegetables, mixing textures and tastes for a refreshing counterpoint.

4 bamboo skewers, presoaked for 2 hours

3 shallots, unpeeled

5 cloves garlic

4 red Thai bird's eye chilies

5 slices galangal

2 king crab legs

Zest and juice of 1 Makrut lime

1 Tbsp coarse sea salt

2 tsp palm sugar

Pinch of white pepper

¼ cup freshly squeezed lime juice

2-3 Tbsp fish sauce

1 Tbsp finely sliced pak chi farang

Few sprigs of coriander

Suggested Accompaniments for Serving:

⅛ cabbage, blanched

⅛ head cauliflower, separated into florets and blanched

8 okra, blanched

8 cucumber slices

8 long beans, cut into 2-inch lengths

1 starfruit, sliced

1 cup peeled and sliced fresh white turmeric, if available

1. Prepare a charcoal grill to medium heat 25 to 40 minutes prior to grilling. Spread out the charcoal to achieve an even heat.

2. Keeping the skin on the shallots, skewer them on a presoaked bamboo skewer for ease of grilling. Do the same with the garlic, chilies, and galangal so there'll be less handling on the grill.

3. Grill your king crab legs along with the skewers, ensuring a nice char and imparting smoky flavor—no more than 5 minutes, flipping once. Keep in mind that all king crab legs are precooked and frozen; we're merely grilling them to impart the smoky charcoal flavor. Remove the other skewers once charred. If the centers of the shallots are still firm to the touch, place the shallots in a bowl and cover them with plastic wrap to let them steam through, about 5 minutes. Peel the shallots once they're soft throughout. If you wait until the roasted shallots cool off, the charred skin tends to stick to the flesh and it'll be more difficult to peel them.

4. Peel the king crab legs, remove the meat, and set aside.

5. Using a large mortar and pestle, pound the Makrut lime zest until it breaks down. Add the salt, peeled shallots, and grilled garlic, chili, and galangal; pound into a fine paste. Add the king crabmeat and continue to pound lightly while mixing and folding in the crabmeat with a spoon. Don't overwork the crab—maintain a relatively coarse texture for the crabmeat while incorporating it thoroughly with the grilled mixture.

6. Season with the palm sugar, white pepper, lime juice, fish sauce, and Makrut lime juice. Taste the nam prik; it should be bold, intense, and equally hot and sour. Finish with the pak chi farang and coriander.

For Serving:

1. Serve the relish in a small bowl alongside a plate of suggested vegetables and fruit.

Noodles and One-Bowl Meals

Opposite page: Hot Sour Pork Soup (page 67).

Introduction

THE NOTION OF STREET FOOD was brought to Thailand by Chinese immigrants, which means many Thai street-food delicacies are Chinese in origin. Pad Thai (page 74), now thought of as a quintessential Thai food, is a perfect example of this Chinese influence: stir-fried rice noodles with tamarind, Chinese chives, bean sprouts, and preserved radishes. And *khao man gai*, or Hainanese Chicken on Rice (page 61), is identical to a dish served in China's Hainan province.

Noodles and one-bowl meals are just one spectrum of street food. Quick to prepare and easy to eat, these dishes are enjoyed for breakfast and lunch, as well as early-afternoon or late-night snacks in Thailand. Very rarely would you entertain friends for dinner over these types of dishes. Although delicious, they're meant for quick-stop meals before heading back to work or onto the next adventure.

I've always been especially fascinated by family-owned street stalls and small storefronts that have specialized in making one single dish over and over for decades. People tend to connect deeply with their neighborhood comfort-food joints, and I greatly admire how their recipes remain consistent through the years. For these two reasons, we've been trying to focus our newer business ventures along those lines. We offer smaller, more focused menus at our two noodle spots, Fat Mao Noodles and Sen Pad Thai, enabling us to be more consistent across all the dishes and facilitating a higher turnover ratio—this translates into prepping our menu items fresh daily. And these limited but specialized menu offerings that riff off of typical dishes by Thailand's street-food vendors are our way of paying homage to them.

Hainanese Chicken on Rice

SERVES 6 • PREP TIME: 30 MINUTES • COOK TIME: 4 HOURS, PLUS OVERNIGHT REFRIGERATION AND REST TIME

HAINANESE CHICKEN, KNOWN AS *KHAO MAN GAI* in Thailand, is the ultimate comfort food for any Asian. Tracing its origins to China's Hainan province, this dish was introduced to Thailand by early Chinese immigrants. To make a dish of only two components—chicken and rice—you have to start with the best-quality chicken. Cooks in China often source a top-notch yellow-skinned free-range chicken; I use an organic free-range chicken that's air chilled after processing. Air-chilled chickens have more intense flavor, lower water content, and better texture. The second secret to success is having a good master stock. I'm giving you a basic chicken stock recipe to use in making your chicken rice, but keep this stock and top it up with water each time you make this dish. The broth will become stronger and more fully flavored over time.

Master Stock:

3-pound chicken carcass

8 quarts cold water

¼ cup thinly sliced ginger

2-3 coriander roots, roughly chopped

1 pandan leaf

1 Tbsp white peppercorns

2 star anise

Chicken:

1 (1½- to 2-pound) free-range chicken (see recipe introduction)

¼ cup coarse sea salt

1 Tbsp white pepper

1 tsp ground star anise

6 quarts Master Stock (see here) or chicken stock

¼ cup sliced ginger

3 coriander roots, roughly chopped

1 pandan leaf

1 Tbsp Fried Shallots (page 235)

For the Master Stock:

1. Using a heavy cleaver, break apart the chicken carcass into 3-inch chunks, or ask your butcher to do it for you. Give the pieces a quick rinse with cold water and transfer them to a stockpot filled with the cold water. If you have any cubes of previously frozen master stock, add them to the pot.

2. Using a mortar and pestle, bruise the ginger, coriander, and pandan leaf, then add them to the stock. Bring the stock to a boil over medium-high heat. As the stock comes to a boil, skim off any impurities, or you'll have a difficult time skimming the stock without removing the spices. Turn down the heat to a low simmer and add the white peppercorns and star anise.

3. Simmer the stock on low for 2 to 3 hours. If you simmer it for too long, you'll start to taste the bitterness of the bones rather than the sweetness of the chicken. Strain the stock through cheesecloth and set aside until needed. This should yield between 6 to 7 quarts of master stock. If you're not using it right away, cool the stock in a large bowl over an ice bath. Store in the fridge for up to 3 days or freeze. I suggest either freezing it in ice-cube trays or 2-cup freezer-safe plastic containers.

For the Chicken:

1. Trim the excess skin and fat off the chicken, usually around the neck and tail. Save the excess skin and fat for the chicken rice. In a small bowl, mix the salt together with the white pepper and star anise and generously rub the chicken with the seasoned salt mix, both inside the cavity and the outside. Refrigerate uncovered overnight.

Recipe continued . . .

2. In a 10-quart pot, combine the stock, ginger, coriander roots, pandan, and fried shallots, and bring to a boil over high heat. Once the stock comes to a rolling boil, gently lower the whole chicken into the stock. Bring the stock back to a simmer (about 5 minutes), then cover the pot with a lid and turn off the heat. Let the chicken sit in the stock at room temperature until it's cool enough to touch (at least 2 hours). This method ensures that the chicken is cooked very gently, leaving the breast meat silky and the legs and thighs buttery. I like to put the whole pot in the fridge to chill completely until serving; this allows a flavorful jelly to form between the skin and meat.

Chicken Rice:

½ cup chicken neck fat and skin, from your local butcher

2 cloves garlic, crushed

2 Tbsp crushed ginger

2 coriander roots, roughly chopped

3 cups jasmine rice

3¾ cups Master Stock (see here) or chicken stock

1 Tbsp coarse sea salt

1 tsp white pepper

1 Tbsp crushed Fried Shallots (page 235)

1 pandan leaf

2 cups water

Serving:

¼ cup Ginger-Scallion Sauce (page 231) or Fermented Soybean Sauce (page 231) (optional)

For the Chicken Rice:

1. Dice the chicken neck fat and skin into 1-inch chunks. In a 4-quart Dutch oven over medium heat, gently sweat the diced fat and skin. Once the fat is fully rendered from the skin (about 2 tablespoons), cook the chicken skin until it turns golden brown. Leave the chicken bits in the pot (it's worth it!), add the garlic, ginger, and coriander roots, and sweat until they become aromatic.

2. Add the jasmine rice and toss to ensure that each grain of rice is well coated with chicken fat. Add the stock, salt, white pepper, fried shallots, and pandan leaf, and bring to a boil. Once the rice boils, turn the heat down to low and cook, covered, for 15 to 20 minutes, until all the stock has been fully absorbed. Turn off the heat and let the rice rest for 5 minutes before you fluff it for serving. Reserve the remaining chilled stock to create a master stock.

For Serving:

1. Remove the cold chicken from the pot, debone it, and reserve the bones. Thinly slice the meat.

2. Serve the sliced chicken atop a bed of chicken rice accompanied by ginger-scallion sauce or fermented soybean sauce.

Chiang Mai Curried Chicken and Noodle Soup

SERVES 4 • PREP TIME: 1 HOUR • COOK TIME: 1 HOUR, 15 MINUTES

KNOWN IN THAILAND AS *KHAO SOI*, this dish is believed to be a derivative of Burma's *khao swè*, which means "noodles." There's a significant Burmese population in northern Thailand, which explains the Burmese influence in this dish. I've been hooked on it since I first tasted it in Chiang Mai—it became my lunch choice every day of that trip! There's something especially comforting about chicken soup and noodles, and this version is particularly delicious: while most varieties are made with powdered dry spices, ours is flavored by a curry paste made with fresh aromatics, including shallots and turmeric. For me, it's essential to use fresh turmeric and to braise the chicken in the broth, enabling the soup to pick up flavor from the chicken and vice versa.

Soup:

2 cups Khao Soi Curry Paste (page 203)

1 cup Cracked Coconut Cream (page 206)

¼ cup palm sugar, plus extra to taste

4 chicken legs

¼ cup light soy sauce, plus extra to taste

1 Tbsp dark soy sauce, plus extra to taste

1 cup Coconut Cream (page 205)

1 cup Coconut Milk (page 205)

3 cups chicken stock or Master Stock (page 61)

8 cups canola oil

2 bundles wonton noodles, for frying

Serving:

4 bundles wonton noodles

¼ cup sliced mustard greens, to garnish

3 cups bean sprouts, to garnish

½ cup sliced spring onions, to garnish

½ cup fresh coriander leaves, to garnish

4 lime wedges, to garnish

Toasted Thai dried bird's eye chili, to garnish (optional)

Chili Oil (page 230)

For the Soup:

1. In a wok or frying pan over medium-high heat, fry the curry paste in the separated coconut cream until pungent, about 10 minutes. Season with palm sugar and add the chicken legs.

2. Lightly stir-fry the chicken legs for 5 minutes, then add in the light and dark soy sauces, coconut cream, coconut milk, and stock. Turn the heat down to medium-low and simmer until the chicken is fork-tender, about 45 minutes to 1 hour. The soup should taste salty with a sweet finish. Season with light soy sauce and more palm sugar if necessary; if needed, add additional dark soy to enhance the soup's richness of color.

3. In a heavy 6-quart pot or Dutch oven over medium-high heat, preheat the canola oil to 350°F. Line a baking tray with paper towel and set aside.

4. Separate the wonton noodles into four to six batches to avoid clumping. Using a pair of tongs, gently place the individual noodles into the hot oil and fry each batch for about 1 minute; the noodles will puff up and turn golden brown. Transfer the fried noodles to the lined baking tray and drain well; keep at room temperature until ready to serve.

For Serving:

1. Bring a large pot of water to a rolling boil and cook the wonton noodle bundles for 1 minute, until al dente. Distribute the cooked noodles evenly into four bowls. Ladle the soup over the noodles and give the noodles a shake so they don't stick together. Place a chicken leg atop each bowl and garnish evenly with the mustard greens, bean sprouts, spring onions, coriander leaves, fried wonton noodles, lime wedges, and toasted chili. Serve with chili oil in a small side dish.

Opposite page: Braised Duck Noodle Soup (left, page 66) and Chiang Mai Curried and Chicken Noodle Soup (right).

Braised Duck Noodle Soup

SERVES 4 • PREP TIME: 30 MINUTES, PLUS OVERNIGHT SOAKING • COOK TIME: 2 TO 3 HOURS

WE VISIT THAILAND ALMOST EVERY YEAR to see family and to keep researching new recipes, and the first thing we usually eat is this duck noodle soup from a small shop outside our house. According to Kate, this shop has been owned by the same family since her high school days. The shopkeepers braise whole duck and ask if you want breast or leg meat. They also ask which kind of noodles you prefer: wide rice (*sen yai*), thin rice (*sen lek*), vermicelli (*sen mi*), or wonton noodles (*sen jin*). My favorite combination, reflected in this recipe, is duck leg with wide rice sheets.

Broth:

4 duck legs

¼ cup sliced galangal

4-5 Chinese mushrooms, presoaked overnight (see tip)

2 stalks lemongrass

2 pods Thai cardamom

2 star anise

2 cloves

1-2 pandan leaves

1 small piece cassia bark

1 strip dried orange peel (see tip on page 54)

1 vanilla bean

2 Tbsp rock sugar or palm sugar

1 tsp white peppercorns

4-5 Tbsp light soy sauce

3 Tbsp dark soy sauce

For the Broth:

1. In a heavy 6-quart pot, place the duck legs in 12 cups of water and bring to a boil over medium-high heat, then turn the heat down to a low simmer. Periodically skim off any impurities as they appear at the surface. Once the stock is clear, add the rest of the ingredients and simmer over medium-low heat for 2 to 3 hours, until the duck legs are tender.

2. Remove the duck legs and mushrooms and set aside. Taste the stock; if the flavors need to be intensified, simmer for another 15 minutes or so. Otherwise, remove the stock from the heat and set aside.

Serving:

4 cups (1½ pounds) fresh rice sheets

3 Tbsp Fried Garlic Oil (page 235)

Small handful of fresh coriander leaves, to garnish

½ cup sliced Asian celery, to garnish

¼ cup sliced pak chi farang, to garnish

4 Tbsp Fried Garlic (page 235), to garnish

4 tsp Toasted Chili Powder (page 234), to garnish

4 Tbsp Chili Vinegar (page 230), to garnish

3 cups bean sprouts, to garnish

For Serving:

1. Quickly blanch the rice sheets in a pot of boiling water for 30 seconds. Divide the rice sheets equally into four bowls and season with some garlic oil to separate the noodles and prevent them from clumping.

2. Place a duck leg and mushrooms atop the rice sheets in each bowl, pour the hot broth over them, and garnish each serving with all the herbs and seasonings. Serve immediately.

æ Soak dried mushrooms in cold water, preferably overnight, to reconstitute them. The soaking liquid is often used to enhance taste. Adding a cup of the mushroom liquid to your master stock for this recipe will bump up its depth of flavor.

Recipe pictured on page 64.

Hot Sour Pork Soup

SERVES 6 • PREP TIME: 2 HOURS, PLUS SOAKING • COOK TIME: 5 MINUTES

THERE'S A LADY WHO DRIVES BY our house in Bangkok on a scooter every morning. She honks, and we bring bowls outside so she can make soup to order for us right there on the spot. She always has a wide variety of noodles for us to choose from—including instant noodles (known as *mama*) because Thai people love the texture of instant noodles—and I always choose one of my favorites: rice noodles or vermicelli. No matter which noodles you prefer, this is one of the simplest noodle dishes you can make, and the effort-to-taste ratio is fantastic!

Pork Stock:

2 pounds pork bones

Thumb-size knob of ginger, bruised

Soup:

6 single-serving packages vermicelli noodles or fresh rice noodles

1 cup ground pork

¾ cup fish sauce

¾ cup Chili Vinegar (page 230)

¾ cup Sweet Vinegar (page 230)

¾ cup Chili Oil (page 230)

For the Pork Stock:

1. In a large pot over medium-high heat, cover the pork bones with water, bring them to a boil, then strain and wash off any coagulated solids from the bones under cold running water.

2. Cover the bones again, this time with a gallon of water, return the pot to the heat, and bring to a boil. Add the ginger, reduce the heat to medium-low, and simmer for 2 hours.

3. Strain the pork stock; it should yield 12 cups of stock. Set aside.

For the Soup:

1. Meanwhile, place the vermicelli into a 6-quart pot and pour in enough cold water to cover it. Let the vermicelli sit for 1 hour.

2. In a 2-quart saucepan over medium heat, cook the ground pork with the pork stock for 3 to 5 minutes. Use a slotted spoon to remove the ground pork to a bowl once it's cooked. Season the pork stock with fish sauce, chili vinegar, sweet vinegar, and chili oil. It should taste sharp, hot, and sour.

Recipe continued . . .

Serving:

½ pound BBQ pork, thinly sliced

2 Tbsp garlic oil

4 cups bean sprouts, to garnish

½ cup sliced Asian celery
(stems and leaves), to garnish

½ cup sliced pak chi farang,
to garnish

½ cup sliced spring onions,
to garnish

½ cup fresh coriander leaves,
to garnish

6 lime wedges, to garnish

6 Tbsp Fried Shallots (page 235),
to garnish

6 Tbsp roasted peanuts, skinned
and crushed, to garnish

2 Tbsp black pepper, to garnish

1 Vietnamese pork roll (fried),
quartered and thinly sliced (see tip)

For Serving:

1. In a separate pot over high heat, boil the vermicelli in water for 1 minute, strain, then divide it evenly among six bowls. Distribute the BBQ pork evenly atop the noodles, then ladle the soup over the vermicelli, add the ground pork, finish with garlic oil, and evenly split the garnishes between the bowls. Serve immediately along with the sliced pork roll.

æ Vietnamese pork rolls are available at any specialty Southeast Asian market. At the restaurant, we buy our pork rolls from a really good *banh mi* shop around the corner that makes them in-house for their sandwiches. Vietnamese pork roll is kind of like a bouncier pâté, almost like a giant deep-fried pork meatball.

Recipe pictured on page 58.

Boat Noodles

SERVES 6 • PREP TIME: 45 MINUTES • COOK TIME: 10 MINUTES

BOAT NOODLES, OR *GUAY DIEW RUA*, are delicious little bowls of noodles served in dark broth by street vendors. They were originally made aboard the tiny boats of Thailand's floating markets. When you order boat noodles from a Thai street stall, you have a choice of beef or pork as well as your preferred type of noodle. I almost always pick beef with sen yai (wide rice noodles) because I prefer the richer flavor of beef over pork, and the silky texture of the wide rice noodles over all other kinds. The secret ingredient for this delicious soup is BLOOD! Make sure you find a good butcher you can trust, and ask them to save you the beef blood for this recipe—it's definitely worth it!

Broth:

6 star anise

1 small piece cassia bark

4 cloves

4 pods Thai cardamom

Dried peel of 1 orange (see tip on page 54)

2 long peppers

4 quarts chicken stock, beef stock, or Master Stock (page 61)

¼ cup fish sauce

Serving:

2 pounds fresh rice sheets or rice noodles

4 cups bean sprouts, plus extra to garnish

1 cup sliced spring onions, plus extra to garnish

1 cup fresh coriander leaves, plus extra to garnish

½ cup sliced pak chi farang, plus extra to garnish

½ cup water spinach, plus extra to garnish

¼ cup fried Thai baby garlic (see tip on page 235), plus extra to garnish

For the Broth:

1. In a small frying pan over medium heat, toast your dry spices, orange peel, and long peppers for at least 5 minutes, until fragrant.

2. In a 6-quart stockpot, add the stock, toasted spices, and fish sauce, and simmer over medium-low heat for 30 minutes, until the flavors of the spices have been released. Periodically skim off any impurities as they appear at the surface.

For Serving:

1. Meanwhile, if you're using fresh rice sheets, gently separate them and split them equally between six bowls. If the rice sheets are cold, or if they're the rehydrated variety, boil them in water for 10 seconds first. Top each of the noodle bowls with equal portions of the bean sprouts, spring onions, coriander leaves, pak chi farang, water spinach, and fried garlic, reserving some of each for garnish. Top equally with fish sauce, sweet vinegar, white pepper, and toasted chili powder. This is the traditional Thai way: seasoning the bowl prior to adding the soup.

2. After 30 minutes, simmer the minced steak and the meatballs in the broth for no more than 5 minutes, carefully separating the minced beef into smaller chunks. It's common to leave the larger spices in the broth; most people know not to chew on them if they pop up.

Recipe continued . . .

Serving (continued):

½ cup fish sauce, or to taste

2-3 Tbsp Sweet Vinegar (page 230), to taste

1-2 tsp white pepper, to taste

1-2 tsp Toasted Chili Powder (page 234), to taste

1 pound hanger steak, hand-minced

1 pound beef meatballs

1¼ cups beef blood

1 cup freshly fried Pork Crackling (page 42)

3. Once the beef is cooked, right before serving, carefully temper the beef blood by pouring 1 cup of hot broth into the blood before pouring the tempered mixture back into the soup; this enables you to smoothly emulsify the soup with the beef blood. If you add the blood directly into the simmering broth, you'll run the risk of coagulating the blood and making the soup grainy.

4. When the beef blood is completely incorporated, heat the soup at medium heat until it darkens and thickens slightly. Don't boil the soup, as it will separate. Ladle the soup, minced steak, and meatballs into the seasoned noodle bowls, garnishing them with more fried garlic, bean sprouts, spring onions, coriander leaves, water spinach, and pak chi farang before serving immediately along with freshly fried pork crackling. Check the seasoning—I like mine hot and sour, rich with beef flavor. Condiments are often served with boat noodles, and most Thais would season with some sugar to balance the flavors.

ə I prefer to hand-mince the beef in this recipe for better texture and a charmingly rustic inconsistency—and because, in all honesty, that's how they do it in Thailand. Using ground beef would make the soup muddier and eliminate the beef's toothy bite.

ə When it comes to the beef blood and meatballs, find a good butcher in Chinatown who makes them fresh regularly. You'll definitely notice a difference in flavor and texture compared to the frozen ones.

ə Beef offal is often served as part of this dish in Thailand; if you're a fan, I highly recommend using tripe and liver for the soup, adding them to cook together with the minced beef.

Pad Si Ew

SERVES 1 LARGE SINGLE SERVING, OR 2 FAMILY STYLE • PREP TIME: 30 MINUTES, PLUS REFRIGERATION
• COOK TIME: 5 MINUTES

SIMPLE, QUICK, AND DELICIOUSLY PERFUMED by the smoky flavor of a well-seasoned wok, this is my go-to lunch in Thailand, and I definitely prefer it made with fresh rice noodles instead of dried. Fresh noodles don't need water to cook; hence, they pick up better wok flavor ("wok breath") and have far better texture. When selecting fresh noodles, make sure you choose the thin and chewy ones, which are often mixed with tapioca, rather than the thick Chinese soft rolls.

"Wok breath" refers to the deep smokiness that a well-seasoned wok imparts to food. Dry noodle dishes such as *pad si ew* are especially enhanced by this flavor. It's important to preheat your wok well so that the food hits the hot wok with a sizzle, and you have to keep the wok moving constantly to prevent the food from overcooking while giving it enough time to pick up the wok breath. But make sure the wok isn't so smoking hot that the oil burns as soon as you pour it into the pan—the smell of burning oil is hugely undesirable and adds unwanted bitterness to your food.

Pickled Chilies:

1 cup water

1 cup white vinegar

1 cup granulated sugar

Pinch of coarse sea salt and white pepper

½ cup sliced rings of mixed peppers

Pad Si Ew:

1 cup wide rice noodles/sheets, preferably fresh

1 Tbsp dark soy sauce

3 Tbsp canola oil

¼ cup minced or sliced beef (pork or chicken can also be used)

1 garlic clove, crushed into a paste

¼ cup sliced gai lan

1 egg, lightly beaten

Pinch of white pepper

1 Tbsp Thai sweet soy sauce (see tip)

1 tsp oyster sauce

1 tsp fish sauce

For the Pickled Chilies:

1. In a medium-size saucepan, combine the water, vinegar, sugar, salt, and white pepper, and bring to a boil over medium heat. Turn off the heat and allow the pickling liquid to cool down.

2. Meanwhile, place the sliced mixed peppers in a large glass jar. Pour the cooled pickling liquid over the peppers, and store in the fridge for up to 2 weeks. You can use this condiment to accent any noodle dish.

For the Pad Si Ew:

1. Gently separate your fresh rice noodles/sheets by hand. If using dried rice noodles, soak them in cold water for 1 hour to rehydrate before separating them. Coat the rice noodles/sheets with the dark soy sauce to prevent them from sticking together and to add richness in color.

Recipe continued . . .

2. In a wok over high heat, preheat the canola oil until smoking hot, then add the beef and cook for about 1 to 3 minutes, until caramelized. Add the garlic and stir-fry until fragrant. Add the gai lan and make a well in the center before adding the egg, using the back of your wok spoon to scramble the egg so it doesn't mix with the rest of the ingredients too much—we're not making an omelet here.

3. Add the rice noodles, toss to incorporate thoroughly, and toast the noodles until they turn opaque. Stir in the white pepper, sweet soy sauce, oyster sauce, and fish sauce, and let the noodles pick up some of the "wok breath" (see recipe introduction).

Serving:

Fried Garlic (page 235)

Chili Vinegar (page 230)

Pickled chilies

For Serving:

1. Transfer to a serving dish, garnish with fried garlic, and serve with a side of chili vinegar and pickled chilies.

ə̇ℓ Sweet soy sauce is soy sauce with added molasses. It's generally dark in color and syrupy in texture, readily available at any Asian supermarket.

Pad Thai

SERVES 1 LARGE SINGLE SERVING, OR 2 TO 4 FAMILY STYLE • PREP TIME: 30 MINUTES • COOK TIME: 5 MINUTES

PAD THAI IS, BY FAR, one of the most popular dishes in Thai cuisine because its sweet-and-sour flavor profile appeals to Western palates—perhaps it's the sweet-and-sour pork of Thai food! It's also the Thai dish that's probably been modified the most from its traditional version; of its countless variants, we specialize in three different iterations of it at our restaurant Sen Pad Thai. One thing's for sure: when done right, it's absolutely delicious. I've seen pad thai recipes that call for ketchup and dried rice noodles—that's dead wrong. Tamarind and fresh rice noodles are the secrets to making this dish, along with a screaming hot wok.

Pad Thai Sauce:

1 cup Tamarind Water (page 233)

1 cup granulated sugar

¼ cup fish sauce

¼ cup water

1 pandan leaf

For the Pad Thai Sauce:

1. In a medium-size pot, whisk the tamarind water, sugar, fish sauce, water, and pandan leaf together and bring to a simmer over medium heat. Ensure the sugar is melted and not burned to the bottom of the pot. Continue to simmer for 5 minutes more, then remove from heat to cool. This dish will require ½ cup pad thai sauce; you can store any remaining sauce in an airtight container in the fridge for up to 2 weeks.

Pad Thai:

⅛ cup peanut oil

½ shallot, sliced

½ cup firm tofu, cut evenly into matchsticks

1 Tbsp preserved radish

3-4 wild or sustainably farmed prawns

1 egg, lightly beaten

2 cups fresh pad thai noodles (see tip)

Pinch of Toasted Chili Powder (page 234)

4-6 Tbsp fish sauce

½ cup Pad Thai Sauce (see here)

½ cup bean sprouts, plus extra to garnish

¼ cup chopped Chinese chives, plus extra to garnish

1 spoonful crushed peanuts, to garnish

1 lime, cut into wedges, to garnish

For the Pad Thai:

1. Preheat a wok over medium heat, then add the peanut oil and stir-fry the shallots and tofu together for about 30 seconds, until caramelized but not too dark. Add the radish and prawns, and continue stir-frying for another 15 seconds. Stir in the egg until it has coagulated, then add the noodles. Toast the noodles until they turn white, about 15 seconds. DO NOT LET THEM BURN.

2. Add 1 cup of water, toasted chili powder, and fish sauce. Toss the noodles to coat them, then turn down the heat to medium and allow the noodles to absorb the liquid for 3 to 5 minutes. The noodles should be pliable and slightly chewy but not firm. Pour ½ cup of the pad thai sauce over the noodles, turn the heat up to high, toss together to coat the noodles evenly, and allow the syrup to reduce and caramelize. Your pad thai should be darker in color; have a slightly nutty aroma and, texturally, should be pliable but not mushy.

3. Stir in the bean sprouts and Chinese chives. Transfer the pad thai to a serving platter. Garnish with more bean sprouts, Chinese chives, crushed peanuts, and lime wedges.

ᴂ Use fresh noodles, as they stay nicely al dente. Noodles that require rehydrating always end up in a gooey mess.

Soups

Opposite page: Hot Sour Soup of Sablefish, Clams, and Turmeric (page 79).

Introduction

THOUGH MOST PEOPLE ARE FAMILIAR with *tom yum goong*, a popular version of Thai hot sour soup, they probably don't realize just how many variations there are. They tend to be distinguished regionally, reflecting differences in geography and availability of local ingredients. Heartier, more rustic soups from landlocked northern Thailand are typically flavored with tamarind instead of lime, while piquant, deeply spiced soups from southern Thailand can be fragranced by turmeric and often feature fresh seafood due to this region's coastal proximity. Case in point: the Hot Sour Chicken Soup with Chanterelles (page 89) inspired by northern Thailand, versus the southern-influenced Hot Sour Soup of Sablefish, Clams, and Turmeric (page 79). No matter the region, fresh hot sour soup is incredibly easy to make, and I've included recipes for straight-up Hot Sour Base (page 102) as well as for Hot Sour Coconut Base (page 102).

Each soup recipe is authentic in both flavor and spirit. What's being served regionally in Thailand I've chosen to serve seasonally in North America because of the four distinct seasons we have. To reflect changes in weather and temperature, I like to serve lighter-bodied soups from the south in the summer, but prefer serving heartier-flavored soups from the north in the fall and winter through to early spring. And I especially enjoy playing around with ingredients that reach their peak at particular times of the year, like fresh tomatoes when they're at their sweetest in the summertime. Hot weather lends itself to lighter-bodied soups with flavor bases like turmeric, while colder days are perfect for fuller-flavored ingredients like coconut milk and roasted pork shoulder, which both add richness. Fall is the only time that we make the Hot Sour Soup of Clams and Matsutake (page 87) at Maenam; it's when the mushrooms are in season, and the weight of this soup makes it ideal for the transitioning weather. When you're building your own soup, definitely look to seasonality for your flavor cues.

Hot Sour Soup of Sablefish, Clams, and Turmeric

SERVES 4 • PREP TIME: 30 MINUTES • COOK TIME: 10 MINUTES

THIS IS A BEAUTIFUL SOUP. I tasted it for the first time en route to Hua Hin at a seafood restaurant where they served it with whole Indian mackerel, head on and guts in. The turmeric's sharpness worked really well with the mackerel's oiliness, and I wanted to recreate that same flavor profile when I returned to Vancouver. I tried making this soup with whole sardines first—no success. Then I decided to use clams, for their brininess, together with sablefish, for its rich flavor yet delicate texture. I finished it with dill, not an herb typically used in that part of Thailand, but I found it balanced the soup nicely.

½ pound clams

2 Tbsp peeled and roughly chopped fresh turmeric

2 Tbsp roughly chopped galangal

3 garlic cloves

4 cups Hot Sour Base (page 102)

8-10 small slices fresh hearts of palm, cut against the grain

½ cup hand-shredded oyster mushrooms

4 red Thai bird's eye chilies

½ cup sliced sablefish, ½-inch thick

¼ cup fish sauce

¼ cup freshly squeezed lime juice

¼ cup sliced pak chi farang

Small handful of fresh dill

1. Clean the clams (see page 169).

2. Using a mortar and pestle, pound the turmeric as fine as possible, ensuring there aren't any chunks remaining. Add the galangal and garlic and pound into a fine paste.

3. In a 6-quart pot over medium heat, infuse the hot sour base with the aromatic paste. Bring to a gentle simmer, stirring well to incorporate completely. Add the hearts of palm, oyster mushrooms, chilies, and clams. Simmer for about 4 minutes. If any clams haven't opened by the 6-minute mark, discard them, as they're likely dead. Add the sablefish and cook for an additional 30 seconds to 1 minute (depending on the size of the fish), or until the fish is done.

4. Season with the fish sauce and lime juice; the soup should taste equally hot, sour, and salty. Fold in the pak chi farang and dill. Be careful when serving the sablefish to avoid breaking apart its delicate flesh.

Recipe pictured on page 76.

Southern-Style Grilled Fish Soup

SERVES 4 • PREP TIME: 10 MINUTES • COOK TIME: 25 MINUTES

ALSO KNOWN AS *DOM GATI*, this soup from the southern part of Thailand is typically served with smoked fish and coconut milk. The smoky flavor really penetrates through the coconut and is balanced by sour fruits and tamarind. Instead of smoked fish, though, I like to use grilled salmon. Salmon's natural oiliness is ideal for grilling, and I typically throw some grated coconut on the coals to smoke the fish and give it more aroma. Within seconds of adding the salmon to the freshly made soup, its grilled smokiness delicately perfumes the broth.

Broth:

4 red Thai bird's eye chilies

1 stalk lemongrass

3 thin slices galangal

2 shallots

2 Makrut lime leaves

4 cups Hot Sour Coconut Base (page 102)

Salmon:

2 Tbsp Coconut Cream (page 205)

1 Tbsp fish sauce

Pinch of white pepper

½ pound sockeye salmon fillet

¼ cup grated coconut, for smoking

For the Broth:

1. Using a mortar and pestle, bruise the chilies, lemongrass, galangal, shallots, and Makrut lime leaves. Add them to a medium-size pot along with the hot sour coconut base and bring to a simmer over medium heat.

2. Simmer for about 10 minutes, giving the flavors enough time to infuse gently before making the dom gati. Turn the heat off until the salmon is cooked.

For the Salmon:

1. Prepare a charcoal grill to medium-high heat 25 to 40 minutes prior to grilling (both a gas grill or grill pan on the stove at medium-high heat also work but are not preferred).

2. In a small bowl, stir together the coconut cream, fish sauce, and white pepper. Marinate the salmon fillet in the mixture for 5 minutes.

3. When the grill is at the desired temperature, spread out the charcoal to achieve an even heat. Cook the salmon skin-side down for 4 to 5 minutes, until the skin is crispy. During the grilling process, sprinkle the grated coconut through the grill directly onto the charcoal and cover to create smoke. Finish cooking the salmon on the flesh side for 1 minute. Remove promptly from the grill and set aside until ready to serve. The salmon will continue to cook while resting; I like to serve my salmon at medium-rare to medium. If you desire it more well-done, you can leave it on the grill for about 3 more minutes to cook it medium-well, bearing in mind that it will also cook further when added to the soup.

Recipe continued . . .

Dom Gati:

½ cup hand-shredded oyster mushrooms

½ cup cherry tomatoes (halved optional)

3 Tbsp Tamarind Water (page 233)

½ cup fresh tamarind leaves

¼ cup finely sliced pak chi farang

¼ cup fresh coriander leaves, plus extra to garnish

¼ cup fish sauce

3 Tbsp freshly squeezed lime juice

½ cup julienned sour green mangoes

1 large dried guajillo chili, deseeded and fried, plus extra to garnish

1 Tbsp Chili Oil (page 230), plus extra to garnish

1 Tbsp cured salmon roe, to garnish (optional)

For the Dom Gati:

1. Once the salmon is cooked, bring the broth back up to a gentle simmer over medium heat, then add the oyster mushrooms, tomatoes, and tamarind water. Stir in the tamarind leaves, pak chi farang, and coriander.

2. Season with the fish sauce and lime juice, and add the sour green mangoes last. Pour the soup into a large bowl, then slice the grilled salmon into two or three pieces and carefully place them skin side up into the soup. Garnish with more coriander, and fried guajillo chili, and finish with chili oil. The optional salmon-roe garnish can be placed atop the grilled salmon skin.

Hot Sour Soup of Spot Prawns

SERVES 4 • PREP TIME: 45 MINUTES • COOK TIME: 10 MINUTES

SPOT PRAWNS ARE ONE OF OUR LOCAL SEAFOOD GEMS, found in the Pacific Ocean from California all the way up to Alaska, and they're now widely available at fish markets across North America. When in season, they're an absolute must-have. I love using their rich heads and shells to enhance the broth. For the spot-prawn tomalley, peel away the head and reserve only the pink tomalley; don't use any dark ones. Keep the tomalley in the freezer, and gradually add to it piece by piece until you have enough to make this beautiful west coast version of the ever-so-popular tom yum goong.

Spot-Prawn Tomalley:

2 cups prawn tomalley, picked
(see recipe introduction)

¼ cup garlic cloves

¼ cup chopped ginger

¼ cup canola oil

¼ cup palm sugar

¼ cup Tamarind Water (page 233)

½ cup Coconut Cream (page 205)

Fish sauce, to taste

¼ cup Chili Oil (page 230)

Soup:

2 red Thai bird's eye chilies

4 cups Hot Sour Base (page 102)

1½ cups hand-shredded oyster mushrooms

2 Tbsp chili jam

8 medium-size spot prawns
(see sidebar)

⅓ cup fish sauce

⅓ cup freshly squeezed lime juice

½ cup finely sliced pak chi farang

½ cup fresh coriander leaves

2 Tbsp Chili Oil (page 230) or prawn tomalley oil, or 1 Tbsp of each if available

For the Spot-Prawn Tomalley:

1. Place the tomalley in a bowl and purée with a hand blender until smooth.

2. Using a mortar and pestle, pound the garlic and ginger into a smooth paste. In a frying pan over medium heat, pour the canola oil and heat until shimmering before frying the paste until golden. Stir in the tomalley and cook until the raw "brain" smell disappears and the mixture has a rich prawn fragrance.

3. Season with palm sugar and tamarind water, stir in the coconut cream, and season with fish sauce. Stir in the chili oil to add color and help preserve the tomalley's freshness. Reserve 1 tablespoon of the prawn tomalley, and 1 tablespoon of the oil that has separated if available, and set aside at room temperature until ready to plate. The balance of the tomalley can be stored in the fridge for 1 week or in the freezer for 2 months.

For the Soup:

1. Using a mortar and pestle, bruise the chilies. In a medium-size pot, combine the chilies, hot sour base, and mushrooms, and bring to a boil over medium-high heat. Once the soup boils, stir in the chili jam and the reserved tomalley until fully incorporated, and return the soup to a low boil.

2. Cut the prawns in half lengthwise. Pick the prawn brains out, add them to the soup, and cook for 2 minutes. Add the prawn halves and cook for a maximum of 30 seconds. Remove the soup from the heat and season with the fish sauce, lime juice, pak chi farang, and coriander leaves. Drizzle with chili oil and/or prawn tomalley oil to finish. The soup should be equally hot, sour, and rich with prawn flavor.

Recipe continued . . .

HOW TO SOURCE SPOT PRAWNS

Most seafood stores carry spot prawn heads when they're in season because there are always customers who prefer to buy them with the heads removed. You can buy the heads, or you might be able to get them for free depending on your relationship with your local fishmonger. If you can't source fresh spot prawns, try to find sustainably fished wild prawns rather than farmed prawns from Asia.

1. Do not store live prawns in the fridge, as they won't keep for more than half a day out of the tank. If you're not cooking the prawns right away, steam them for 45 seconds to 1 minute; this enables you to keep the cooked spot prawns in the fridge for up to 2 days.

2. When cleaning spot prawns, keep only the heads that are clear and free of dark blemishes; discard any black or significantly discolored ones, as they're likely to cause illness. Be especially mindful when working with spot prawn heads, as the tips are razor sharp.

3. The reserved tomalley will keep in the fridge for up to 1 week. You can use it as an accent for hot sour soups.

Hot Sour Soup of Clams and Matsutake

SERVES 4 • PREP TIME: 10 MINUTES • COOK TIME: 35 MINUTES

THIS CANADIAN TAKE ON A CLASSIC THAI SOUP is a perfect example of Maenam's food. A version I had in Hua Hin, a beach town just south of Bangkok, is a favorite of mine. It embodies simplicity, a perfect balance of the clam nectar's savory flavors and the citrus aroma of the holy basil. I wanted to reinvent the soup by adding the subtle pine notes of BC matsutake mushrooms into the mix to complement the clams and holy basil. If you can't track down holy basil, both lemon basil and sweet basil can be substituted in a pinch; however I find that Thai basil overpowers the delicate matsutakes. The final dish ends up being very Canadian, yet still very Thai in both spirit and flavor.

Soup:

6 cups chicken stock or Master Stock (page 61)

½ pound B-grade matsutake mushrooms, finely sliced (see note)

3 stalks lemongrass

6 slices galangal

3 coriander roots, roughly chopped

4 shallots, unpeeled

5 Makrut lime leaves

3-7 red Thai bird's eye chilies, to taste

Pinch of coarse sea salt

For the Soup:

1. In a 2- to 3-quart pot, over low heat, infuse the stock with the flavor of the matsutake mushrooms by gently simmering them together for about 20 minutes.

2. Using a mortar and pestle, bruise the lemongrass, galangal, coriander roots, shallots, Makrut lime leaves, and chilies with a pinch of salt as an abrasive. Stir all the aromatics into the stock and continue simmering for about 10 minutes, until the broth becomes fragrant with aromas of galangal and lemongrass and hints of pine from the matsutake mushrooms.

> Matsutakes or white pine mushrooms are one of the most expensive mushrooms you can buy. They can be sourced from specialty Korean and/or Japanese grocers, or from individual pickers at local farmers' markets. I prefer the latter, as their mushroom quality and price are often much better. A-grade matsutakes are smaller mushrooms that haven't opened yet and have a more intense aroma and flavor. B-grade matsutakes are slightly larger mushrooms with caps that have already blossomed and, thus, a less concentrated taste. When choosing matsutakes, try to select the smaller uncapped mushrooms, because these have more intense flavors. Gently squeeze the mushroom stems and check that they are fairly pale, dry, and very firm. Stay away from any matsutakes that are soft and wet, as they most likely have worms.

Recipe continued . . .

Serving:

1 pound littleneck clams

2 ounces A-grade matsutake mushrooms, thinly sliced (see tip)

2 cups fresh holy basil leaves (see recipe introduction)

½ cup sliced pak chi farang, to garnish

½ cup freshly squeezed lime juice

½ cup fish sauce

For Serving:

1. Clean the clams (see page 169).

2. Returning to the pot of soup, turn the heat up to high and cook the clams in the soup until the clams open, about 5 to 6 minutes. If any clams haven't opened by the 6-minute mark, remove them from the soup and discard them as they're likely dead. Add the A-grade matsutake mushrooms. Turn off the heat and stir in the holy basil and pak chi farang—the holy basil's citrus aroma accents the matsutake mushrooms perfectly.

3. Season with the lime juice and fish sauce; the soup should taste equally hot and sour, then salty, and should not be sweet at all. Serve immediately.

Hot Sour Chicken Soup with Chanterelles

SERVES 4 • PREP TIME: 1 HOUR • COOK TIME: 5 MINUTES

CHANTERELLES AREN'T TYPICAL THAI MUSHROOMS, but I find that their earthy flavor matches perfectly with the rustic flavors imparted by tamarind and fresh tamarind leaves. Chicken and tamarind soup is quite popular in the northern part of Thailand, traditionally prepared by chopping raw free-range chicken into chunks and simmering it directly in broth with aromatics before the soup is seasoned with herbs. I've opted to poach the chicken first and then shred the meat for a more refined presentation. There's a certain rustic charm to this dish, and I think that chanterelle mushrooms really elevate it.

Poached Chicken and Chicken Broth:

5 quarts chicken stock or Master Stock (page 61)

1 free-range chicken

6 stalks lemongrass

1 cup sliced galangal

Large bunch of coriander stems or roots

20 Makrut lime leaves

10 large shallots

4 red Thai bird's eye chilies

For the Poached Chicken and Chicken Broth:

1. In an 8-quart stockpot over medium-high heat, bring the stock to a low rolling boil, then add the whole chicken and turn the heat down to low. Ensure the chicken is completely submerged, and keep the temperature at very low heat until the chicken is cooked through, about 30 to 45 minutes. It's key that there's very little temperature change in the stock while the chicken is poaching; if it boils, it will dry out the chicken meat. Turn off the heat and let the chicken cool down in the broth before removing it from the pot and setting it aside.

2. Using a mortar and pestle, bruise the lemongrass, galangal, coriander stems, Makrut lime leaves, shallots, and chilies and add them to the braising stock, bringing it to a simmer again over low heat for 15 minutes. Reserve 2 cups, and freeze the rest in ice-cube trays to create a master stock for your next soup.

3. Once the chicken has cooled, hand-shred the meat into chunks about a finger-width thick. Set aside 1 cup of shredded chicken meat for the soup. The rest will store in the fridge for 2 to 3 days and would be perfect for the Hot Sour Chicken Soup with Tamarind Leaves and Bamboo (page 93).

Recipe continued . . .

Soup:

2 cups Hot Sour Base (page 102)

8 cherry tomatoes, halved

4 red Thai bird's eye chilies

Pinch of Fried Garlic (page 235)

Pinch of Fried Shallots (page 235)

1 cup fresh chanterelle mushrooms

1 cup shredded Poached Chicken
(see here)

¼ cup fish sauce, or to taste

2 Tbsp Tamarind Water (page 233),
or to taste

2 tsp granulated sugar, or to taste
(optional)

½ cup fresh tamarind leaves

¼ cup freshly squeezed lime juice,
or to taste

½ cup fresh Thai basil leaves,
to garnish

½ cup sliced pak chi farang,
to garnish

For the Soup:

1. In a 6-quart pot, combine 2 cups of the reserved chicken broth with the hot sour base. Add the cherry tomatoes, chilies, fried garlic, and fried shallots. Bring the soup to a simmer over medium heat, then add the chanterelle mushrooms. Cook for 3 to 5 minutes, until the mushrooms are cooked through, then add the reserved shredded chicken meat. Don't overboil the poached chicken, as it will dry out.

2. While the soup is simmering, season to taste with the fish sauce, tamarind water, and a touch of sugar (if needed). Stir in the tamarind leaves; these impart lots of sour flavor. Turn off the heat and add the lime juice to taste just before serving to balance the earthiness and saltiness of the soup; you may not need all of it. The final product should taste equally hot and sour with earthiness from both the tamarind leaves and chanterelle mushrooms. Garnish with the Thai basil and pak chi farang immediately before serving.

æ Whenever you're braising or simmering meat, don't remove the meat from the braising or simmering liquid while it's still warm. Any steam that escapes from the meat causes it to dry out by the time it cools down. Instead, keeping meat in the liquid during the cooling process greatly helps retain its moisture.

Hot Sour Chicken Soup with Tamarind Leaves and Bamboo

SERVES 4 • PREP TIME: 10 MINUTES • COOK TIME: 20 MINUTES

MY FIRST TASTE OF THIS HEARTY TRADITIONAL SOUP from northern Thailand immediately evoked a childhood memory: I was with my family in Taiwan, hiking along trails through a bamboo forest near my dad's friend's house. We harvested fresh young bamboo and started a campfire in the woods to make a chicken soup with it. What really makes this dish is the rustic flavor of tamarind combined with the licorice notes of Thai basil. The freshness of the bamboo shoots lifts the dish beautifully.

Soup:

2 cups Chicken Broth (page 89)

2 cups Hot Sour Base (page 102)

8 cherry tomatoes, halved

4 red Thai bird's eye chilies

Pinch of Fried Garlic (page 235)

Pinch of Fried Shallots (page 235)

2 fresh bamboo shoots, sliced

1 cup shredded Poached Chicken (page 89)

Serving:

6 Tbsp fish sauce, or to taste

2 Tbsp Tamarind Water (page 233), or to taste

Pinch of granulated sugar, or to taste (optional)

½ cup fresh tamarind leaves

¼ cup freshly squeezed lime juice, or to taste

¼ cup sliced pak chi farang, to garnish

2 Tbsp fresh Thai basil leaves, to garnish

For the Soup:

1. In a 6-quart stockpot, combine the chicken broth, hot sour base, cherry tomatoes, chilies, fried garlic, and fried shallots. Bring to a simmer over medium heat, then add the sliced bamboo.

2. Cook over medium to medium-high heat for 5 to 10 minutes, until the bamboo is cooked through, then add the shredded poached chicken and simmer for another minute to heat through. Don't overboil the poached chicken, as it will dry out.

For Serving:

1. Remove the soup from heat and season to taste with the fish sauce, tamarind water, and pinch of sugar (if needed). Add the tamarind leaves gradually; keep in mind that they will impart lots of sourness.

2. Add the lime juice to taste just before serving to balance the earthiness and saltiness of the soup; you may not need all of it. The final product should taste equally hot and sour with earthiness from the tamarind leaves. Garnish with the pak chi farang and Thai basil before serving.

ℛ Leftover soup mellows out in the fridge overnight, so you'll probably have to reseason it with a little more fish sauce, tamarind water, and lime juice when you reheat it on the stove the next day. And definitely throw in more fresh herbs just before you eat it.

Clear Soup of Roasted Duck and Winter Melon

SERVES 4 • PREP TIME: 3 HOURS, PLUS REDUCING • COOK TIME: 20 MINUTES

CLEAR SOUP, OR *GENG JEUT*, is subtle in flavor compared to typical soups—definitely a Thai dish with Chinese DNA. Soups in Thailand are generally more intense and sharper in flavor, while this is subtle and cleansing, homey and comforting. It's the kind of soup you crave when you have a cold, and is a favorite of kids and older people. It's also a nice early summer soup, refreshing and meant to relieve your palate from fiery fare. The young coconut juice really comes through, which is cooling but doesn't overpower the rich duck flavor.

1 whole Chinese BBQ duck

1 white onion, sliced in half

4 quarts water

2 cloves garlic

6 black peppercorns

1 cross-section of cut winter melon (page 260), cut into 1½-inch cubes

6 shiitake mushrooms

2 Tbsp Fried Garlic (page 235)

2 Tbsp oyster sauce, or to taste

2 Tbsp light soy sauce, or to taste

Pinch of granulated sugar

½ cup julienned young coconut meat

½ cup young coconut water

1 cup fresh Thai basil leaves

2 Tbsp thinly sliced spring onions

Small handful of fresh coriander leaves, to garnish

Few drops sesame oil, to garnish

Pinch of white pepper, to garnish

1 Tbsp deseeded and julienned red chili pepper

1. Debone the BBQ duck carefully, keeping the meat and the bones separate. Break down the bones into 3-inch cubes. Slice the duck meat and set aside.

2. In a frying pan over medium-high heat, sear the onion halves until the cut sides are blackened. Add the blackened onions to a 6-quart stockpot along with the duck bones, water, garlic, and peppercorns. Bring to a boil over high heat, then reduce the heat to medium-low and simmer for 3 hours.

3. Strain the stock and discard all the solids. Turn the heat down to a low simmer, and reduce the liquid until about 8 cups of stock remain, about 1 to 2 hours.

4. Add the winter melon to the duck stock and continue simmering. Meanwhile, quarter the shiitake mushrooms. Add the mushrooms to the soup along with the sliced duck meat. Turn up the heat to medium and cook the soup for 10 to 15 minutes more, until the winter melon becomes translucent and tender while still holding its shape.

5. Season with fried garlic, oyster sauce, soy sauce, and sugar. It should taste rather refreshing and not overly seasoned. To finish, add the coconut meat, coconut water, Thai basil, spring onions, and coriander. Garnish with a few tiny drops of sesame oil, a tiny pinch of white pepper, and chili peppers.

Northern-Style Hot Sour Pork Soup with Tamarind

SERVES 4 TO 6 • PREP TIME: 15 MINUTES • COOK TIME: 50 MINUTES

THE RUSTIC NATURE OF NORTHERN THAI CUISINE is something I've always been drawn to. Cooking this hearty soup brings back memories of the small village in northern Thailand where I was lucky enough to stumble upon it. There are hundreds of variations of hot sour soup, most of which are very regional and specific. This is my interpretation of that beautiful soup I had up north. Stewing the pork tendons for hours allows the collagen to break down into the broth, giving it an incredible richness.

Pork:

2 pounds pork ribs, cut into 2-inch cubes (see tip)

1 pound pork tendon (see tip)

Pinch of coarse sea salt

6 stalks lemongrass

1 cup sliced galangal

Large bunch of coriander stems or roots

20 Makrut lime leaves

10 large shallots

4 red Thai bird's eye chilies

3 Tbsp roasted peanuts, skinned

Soup:

3 cups Hot Sour Base (page 102)

½ cup straw mushrooms

6 cherry tomatoes, halved

3 dried Thai bird's eye chilies, hand-broken into pieces

1 Tbsp Fried Garlic (page 235)

1 Tbsp Fried Shallots (page 235)

1 tsp granulated sugar

3 Tbsp Tamarind Water (page 233)

4-6 Tbsp fish sauce, to taste

4-6 Tbsp freshly squeezed lime juice, to taste

¼ cup sliced pak chi farang

¼ cup fresh Thai basil leaves

For the Pork:

1. In a 4- to 6-quart stockpot, place the pork ribs and pork tendon, fill the pot with enough water to cover, and add a pinch of salt. Bring to a boil over medium heat, then drain off the liquid and wash the pork thoroughly until it is completely free of blood and coagulation. Top with fresh water again and simmer over medium-low heat.

2. About 30 minutes into the simmering process, using a large mortar and pestle, bruise the lemongrass, galangal, coriander, Makrut lime leaves, shallots, chilies, and peanuts, and add them to the braising stock. Continue simmering for another 15 minutes, until the ribs are tender and the tendon is soft and almost mushy. Total cooking time for the ribs shouldn't be longer than 45 minutes; if the tendon isn't done by this point, remove the ribs from the braising liquid and simmer the tendon further. Some Asian cultures prefer a crunchy texture for tendons, but I personally like them when they melt in your mouth.

For the Soup:

1. In a separate 6-quart pot, add 3 cups of the pork braising stock, hot sour base, the tendon, and the ribs. Stir in the straw mushrooms, cherry tomatoes, dried chilies, fried garlic, fried shallots, sugar, and tamarind water. Bring to a simmer over medium heat and continue simmering for 5 minutes, until the tomatoes soften. Turn off the heat and season to taste with the fish sauce, lime juice (if needed), and herbs. The soup should taste equally hot and sour with added depth from the Thai basil and fried garlic paired with a slight hint of sweetness.

æ Source your pork tendon from a very good specialty butcher; I suggest going to Chinatown or an Asian market, where tendon is quite common. Ask your butcher to cut your ribs into 2-inch cubes if they're not precut for stewing.

Hot Sour Soup of Braised Beef Shin

SERVES 4 TO 6 • PREP TIME: 15 MINUTES • COOK TIME: 3 HOURS

I LOVE THIS SOUP because of its weight—light but rich, refreshing yet earthy. Beef shin provides heaps of flavor and complexity, and the Asian celery balances it so well with herbaceous notes and refreshing aromas. This soup is ideal for a chilly fall or winter day.

Soup:

1 pound boneless beef shin

¼ pound beef tendon (optional)

2 Tbsp coarse sea salt

6 cups chicken stock or Master Stock (page 61)

2 Tbsp roughly cut ginger

1 pandan leaf

6 Tbsp sliced galangal

3 stalks lemongrass

6 Makrut lime leaves

3 shallots, unpeeled

4-6 red Thai bird's eye chilies

1 cup hand-shredded oyster mushrooms

½ cup cherry tomatoes, halved

6-8 Tbsp fish sauce, to taste

6-8 Tbsp freshly squeezed lime juice, to taste

Serving:

½ cup sliced Asian celery stems, to garnish

½ cup Asian celery leaves, to garnish

3 Tbsp sliced pak chi farang, to garnish

2 Tbsp whole fried dried Thai bird's eye chilies

2 Tbsp Fried Garlic Oil (page 235)

1 Tbsp Fried Garlic (page 235)

For the Soup:

1. Dice the beef shin into 2-inch cubes and the tendon into 1-inch chunks. Rub the shin and tendon pieces with salt. Place the beef shin and tendon into a 6-quart pot. Top with water and bring to a boil over medium heat. Once boiled, discard the liquid and quickly rinse off the beef tendon and shin under running water to get rid of any impurities, giving you a cleaner broth.

2. Return the beef shin and tendon to the pot. Add the stock, ginger, and pandan leaf. Bring to a boil over medium heat, then lower the heat to a gentle simmer. Cook for 2 to 3 hours, until the shin and tendon are tender.

3. Using a mortar and pestle, bruise the galangal, lemongrass, Makrut lime leaves, shallots, and chilies before stirring them into the soup. Simmer on low heat for 10 more minutes.

4. Add the oyster mushrooms and tomatoes and cook for another 5 minutes. Remove from heat and season to taste with the fish sauce and lime juice. The soup should be sour, hot, and rich with robust beef flavor.

For Serving:

1. Ladle the soup into a serving bowl; garnish with Asian celery stems and leaves and pak chi farang.

2. Top with fried chilies, fried garlic oil, and fried garlic to finish.

æ Ask your butcher for boneless beef shin, also called "golden coin" by Chinese butchers because it's often served sliced into medallions in Chinese cuisine. Beef osso buco is a good substitute if you're finding it difficult to track down boneless beef shin—it's essentially the same thing as the golden coin and is the shin strip from this cut of meat. The osso buco's bone marrow will give this dish a welcome fattiness.

Hot Sour Soup of Halibut and Thai Basil

SERVES 4 TO 6 • PREP TIME: 30 MINUTES • COOK TIME: 15 MINUTES

IF THEY'RE AVAILABLE, I enjoy using halibut cheeks for this recipe, but halibut fillets are an easy substitute. Halibut cheeks have a texture that's similar to chicken and a distinctive flavor that stands out nicely. This is a wonderfully simple dish to make; the soup's clean flavor profile is punctuated by a hint of licorice from the Thai basil and rustic depth from the fried garlic.

2 stalks lemongrass

¼ cup sliced galangal

2 shallots

4-6 red Thai bird's eye chilies

6 Makrut lime leaves

3 coriander roots, roughly chopped

4 cups chicken stock or Master Stock (page 61)

¼ pound cleaned halibut cheeks

1 cup hand-shredded oyster mushrooms

¼ cup fish sauce

¼ cup freshly squeezed lime juice

1 Tbsp Fried Garlic (page 235)

1 tsp Fried Garlic Oil (page 235)

¼ cup sliced pak chi farang

1 cup fresh Thai basil leaves

1. Using a mortar and pestle, bruise the lemongrass, galangal, shallots, chilies, Makrut lime leaves, and coriander roots. In a 6-quart pot over medium heat, bring the stock to a simmer, then stir in all the bruised aromatics and continue simmering over medium heat for about 10 minutes to infuse the broth with their flavors.

2. Meanwhile, clean the halibut cheeks by removing the silverskin, and cut them into 2-inch cubes.

3. Once the broth has been infused, add the oyster mushrooms to the soup base and simmer for 3 to 5 minutes before adding the halibut cheeks. Simmer for another 3 minutes, then remove from heat and season with fish sauce, lime juice, fried garlic, and fried garlic oil. The soup should taste hot, sour, and aromatic from the fried garlic. Stir in the pak chi farang and Thai basil to finish.

Soup Bases

MAKES ABOUT 4 CUPS EACH • PREP TIME: 10 MINUTES • COOK TIME: 10 MINUTES

ALTHOUGH INFUSION MIXES ARE AVAILABLE at a typical grocery store, making good hot sour soup is very simple, and all it takes is six to seven key ingredients. The most important thing comes from the infusion of the six aromatics: lemongrass, galangal, Makrut lime leaves, coriander roots, shallots, and Thai bird's eye chilies. With these, you have a good backbone for any hot sour soup. Hence, we've highlighted it as a base to start most of the hot sour soups listed.

Hot Sour Base:

5 cups chicken stock

4 stalks lemongrass, peeled

Handful of galangal

6-8 Makrut lime leaves

4 coriander roots, roughly chopped

3 medium-size shallots

2 red Thai bird's eye chilies

Hot Sour Coconut Base:

3 cups Coconut Milk (page 205)

2 cups Coconut Cream (page 205)

4 stalks lemongrass, peeled

Handful of galangal

6-8 Makrut lime leaves

4 coriander roots, roughly chopped

3 medium-size shallots

2 red Thai bird's eye chilies

For Both Hot Sour Soup Bases:

1. In a 2-quart pot, bring the liquids to a simmer over medium heat. While waiting for the pot to simmer, using a mortar and pestle, bruise all the aromatics.

2. Once the liquid has come to a simmer, add the bruised aromatics to the pot and continue simmering for 10 minutes. Do not overcook.

3. In Thailand, it is very common to leave the aromatics in the soup as it indicates that the soup is freshly made. However, you can strain them out and use only the stock if desired. Bear in mind that these soup bases are meant to be used right away. If frozen, their freshness disappears.

æ The most important thing to remember when making the soup base is not to overcook it. Overcooking creates a stew-like flavor—definitely not how a Thai soup should taste. Instead, infuse all the aromatics for 10 to 15 minutes maximum, to capture the intensity and sharpness of galangal, lemongrass, and Makrut lime leaf.

Salads

Opposite page: Green Papaya Salad (page 107).

Introduction

GROWING UP IN CANADA, I'd go over to my school friends' homes for dinner, where they'd serve meat and vegetables with potatoes on the side. This took me a little getting used to, because the opposite happens in Asian cultures, where rice comes first and all the other dishes are side dishes. Everything put on the table for a Thai meal is meant to encourage you to eat more rice, and the same holds true for salads.

One of my first tasks as a Thai cook was helping to make the salad dressings, which are characteristically fresh and intense, with sharp, bright flavors. The first time I tasted a complete, dressed Thai salad, I was captivated. And it wasn't just the dressing; it was the salad itself. It was like having a million different things going on in my mouth at once, balanced in not only flavor but texture too. The bright, verdant contrast of fresh herbs with the hearty depth of fried garlic and shallots all accented the grilled meat and gave the salad so much life—it was like nothing I'd ever experienced before. This was the defining moment that made me fall in love with Thai food.

Traditional Thai salads are different from what most Westerners' idea of a salad is: lettuce and other fresh vegetables tossed in dressing. *Larp* is a perfect example of how Thai salads differ from those in North America: minced meat served with herbs, versus lettuce and other fresh vegetables tossed in dressing. The focus of a Thai salad is often on a protein and its flavoring, whereas a Western salad usually highlights the greens and fresh vegetables. At restaurants in Chiang Mai, there's typically a table in the center with fresh herbs from which you pick your own bouquet to accompany your meal. And typically, Thai salads are generously dressed compared to their Western counterparts because they're meant to be consumed with rice at the same time. Keep this in mind when you prepare the heavily seasoned salads in this chapter, and make sure to pair them with a healthy serving of rice. You can serve them as a side dish if you'd like, or perhaps with a little less dressing, but this would run counter to the traditional way of eating Thai salads.

Green Papaya Salad

SERVES 1, OR 2 TO 3 AS AN APPETIZER • PREP TIME: 5 MINUTES • ASSEMBLE TIME: 5 MINUTES

GREEN PAPAYA SALAD IS, by far, the most popular dish among Thai people. It's most commonly portioned for one person, but is also easily shared as an appetizer between two or three. The simplicity, robust flavors, sharpness, and balance of this salad make it a perfect ambassador for Thai cuisine, and it highlights the full spectrum of Thai flavors: hot, sour, sweet, and salty. There are countless regional variants of this dish, but this is the classic version, also known as *som dtam thai*.

2-3 red Thai bird's eye chilies

1-2 garlic cloves

Pinch of coarse sea salt

2 Tbsp palm sugar

2 Tbsp dried prawns

1 Tbsp roasted peanuts, skinned

1 Tbsp Tamarind Water (page 233)

1 Tbsp freshly squeezed lime juice

Fish sauce, to taste

1 cup shredded green papaya

⅛ cup sliced long beans, cut into 1-inch lengths

4 cherry tomatoes, halved

2 Tbsp shredded carrot

1. Using a mortar and pestle, pound the chilies and garlic together into a fine paste, using a pinch of salt as an abrasive. Add the palm sugar, dried prawns, and roasted peanuts, and pound everything together until it becomes a coarse paste. Add the tamarind water, lime juice, and fish sauce to complete the dressing, and stir with the pestle until fully incorporated.

2. Add the green papaya, long beans, cherry tomatoes, and carrot and pound lightly to bruise and soften them so they can absorb the dressing, then toss to combine with the paste. Alternatively, if your mortar and pestle isn't large enough to handle all the ingredients, you can use a pestle with a large mixing bowl for the vegetables. The finished salad should taste sour, salty, lightly sweet, and hot.

ə It's common for most Thai kitchens to have more than one kind of mortar and pestle. For this recipe, look for a clay mortar with a wooden pestle or a wooden mortar and pestle combination. They're commonly used by Thai street vendors specifically for making green papaya salad, and they prevent you from overpounding the vegetables while still bruising them enough to absorb the dressing.

Recipe pictured on page 104.

Heirloom Tomato Salad

SERVES 4 • PREP TIME: 5 MINUTES • ASSEMBLE TIME: 5 MINUTES

TRADITIONALLY, SOM DTAM THAI is a simple Green Papaya Salad (page 107). It has since branched out into regional variants that include *som dtam laos, som dtam gapi, som dtam plah rah*—the list goes on. I've come across some som dtam salads that use very little papaya, focusing instead on tomatoes, corn, or even squash. This version is one of my favorite salads to make. It calls for ripe mixed heirloom tomatoes, which we get from Milan Djordjevich of Stoney Paradise when they're at their peak a few weeks a year. Handpicked on the morning they're delivered, Milan's tomatoes and grapes (page 222) are the best in the world. It's no exaggeration to say that he has a cult following among Vancouver chefs, and you have to be in his good books for him to sell to you. The simplicity of this salad highlights the gorgeous gems he drops off at our kitchen doors at the end of every summer.

1-2 pounds ripe mixed heirloom tomatoes (see tip)

4 red Thai bird's eye chilies

2 garlic cloves

Pinch of coarse sea salt

2 Tbsp roasted peanuts, skinned

2 Tbsp dried prawns, plus 1 Tbsp to garnish

¼ cup shredded green papaya

2 Tbsp long beans, cut into 1-inch lengths

1 Tbsp shredded carrot

1 Tbsp palm sugar

3 Tbsp freshly squeezed lime juice

2 Tbsp fish sauce, or to taste

1 Tbsp Tamarind Water (page 233)

1. Using a sharp knife, slice the tomatoes into random and creative shapes, making sure to preserve their texture. I love the randomness as the beautiful colors complement each uniquely shaped piece. Place the sliced tomatoes into a bowl and set aside.

2. To make the dressing, using a mortar and pestle, pound the chilies, garlic, and salt until crushed. Add the peanuts and dried prawns, and continue pounding into a coarse paste. Add the green papaya, long beans, and shredded carrot; pound until bruised. Season with the palm sugar, lime juice, fish sauce, and tamarind water. The dressing should taste sour, salty, sweet, and hot.

3. Carefully fold the tomatoes into the dressing with a spatula, and gently bruise them with the pestle. Do not pound the tomatoes, as we are trying to preserve their delicate texture.

4. Transfer the salad to a plate, and spoon the leftover dressing in the mortar onto the salad. Garnish with dried prawns and serve immediately.

æ Try visiting farmers' markets during the summer—the vine-ripened tomato varietals you'll find there are far better than anything in a supermarket. When purchasing heirloom tomatoes, I don't like squeezing them to test for ripeness, as this can bruise their delicate flesh. Instead, I like to smell them for flavor. A ripe tomato should have beautiful aromas of tomatoes and vines. Be creative in your selection: I like to mix it up for different levels of sweet and tart. Always start with a pint of Sungolds and add some Cherokee Purples, Green Zebras, or Carolina Golds; the ratio doesn't matter—you can't go wrong. Store your tomatoes in a closed paper bag; paper is porous and still allows the tomatoes to breathe while keeping bugs at bay.

Roasted Pork Salad with Chili Jam

SERVES 4 TO 6 • PREP TIME: 10 MINUTES • COOK TIME: 10 MINUTES

NECESSITY IS THE MOTHER OF INVENTION—I first put this recipe together when I had pork roast leftovers, and it's a great way to use up leftover grilled or roasted meats. Alternatively, this salad is excellent with Chinese BBQ pork; HK BBQ Master is my favorite spot to pick it up locally, as it serves what's arguably some of the best Chinese BBQ in North America. I usually order medium-fat and extra-burned BBQ pork to get the best texture and flavor.

1 lime

½ cup young lotus stems or fresh hearts of palm (see tip)

2-3 pounds slow-roasted pork shoulder or Chinese BBQ pork

1 cup Fried Shallots (page 235) (divided)

½ cup peeled and thinly sliced lemongrass

2 Tbsp sliced Makrut lime leaves

½ cup sliced Asian celery stems

½ cup Asian celery leaves

½ cup fresh mint leaves

½ cup fresh coriander leaves

¼ cup sliced pak chi farang

¼ cup Chili Jam Nahm Jim (page 133)

1. Preheat the oven to 350°F.

2. In a large bowl, squeeze the juice of a whole lime into 8 cups of cold water.

3. Add the sliced young lotus stems or fresh hearts of palm to the acidulated water to keep them from oxidizing.

4. Place the pork on a baking sheet lined with parchment paper and warm it in the oven for 10 minutes. Slice the pork into bite-size pieces and transfer to a serving bowl along with all but 2 tablespoons of the fried shallots, as well as the lemongrass, Makrut lime leaves, Asian celery stems and leaves, mint, coriander, and pak chi farang. Drizzle in the chili jam nahm jim and toss to incorporate fully.

5. Remove the lotus stems or hearts of palm from the water, dry the pieces well, and toss into the salad. Finish the salad by topping it with 2 tablespoons fried shallots. Serve immediately.

æ Before cleaning the young lotus stems, check to see if their membranes are thick and require peeling. If the exposed stems are white and fresh, there's no need to peel them; however, if they're grayish brown, peel them by breaking off a small piece and carefully stripping away the outer layer of the stem to expose the tender white stem. Slice the young lotus stems thinly. If using fresh hearts of palm, peel away some of the tough dried outer pieces and slice them thinly against the grain.

Larp Duck Salad

SERVES 4 • PREP TIME: 30 MINUTES, PLUS SOAKING OF SKEWERS • COOK TIME: 5 MINUTES

LARP IS ONE OF MY FAVORITE THAI SALADS. Popular in the Isan region, this delightful salad originated in Laos. It's a rustic dish characterized by rich, robust spices and intensely spicy heat, and it's often paired with local specialty herbs such as Vietnamese mint, pak chi farang, and sour leaf. Some call it the "minced-meat" salad, but the best larps are ones that contain both meat and offal. If available, I highly recommend fresh chopped duck liver in this recipe; my favorite version has crispy duck intestines, but those are harder to track down. Offal gives this salad more depth and character.

Larp Spice Mix:

2 Tbsp mah kwan

5 long peppers

3 pods Thai cardamom

2 tsp black peppercorns

1 tsp white peppercorns

2 blades mace

1 star anise

2 Tbsp galangal powder mix (see note)

For the Larp Spice Mix:

1. In a frying pan over medium heat, toast all the whole spices while tossing them repeatedly to prevent them from burning. The trick is to not turn the heat up high, as this burns the outside of the spices before they're fully warmed through. Done properly, you'll smell the nutty flavors being released from the spices and see a nice sheen, which indicates that the essential oils have been properly released.

2. Remove from heat and transfer the toasted whole spices to a mortar and pestle. Grind all the toasted whole spices first, then add the galangal powder and combine thoroughly. Reserve 2 teaspoons for the salad. Refrigerate any unused larp spice mix in a small airtight container; it will keep well for 1 to 2 months, beyond that, the flavor won't be nearly as fresh and strong.

Roasted Shallot Paste:

4 shallots, unpeeled

6 cloves garlic

3-4 bamboo skewers, presoaked in warm water for 2 hours

6 slices galangal, ¼-inch thick

Pinch of coarse sea salt

For the Roasted Shallot Paste:

1. Prepare a charcoal grill to high heat 25 to 40 minutes prior to grilling (both a gas grill or grill pan on the stove at medium-high heat also work but are not preferred). Spread out the charcoal to achieve an even heat.

2. Once the grill is heated, roast the shallots with the skin on, turning them occasionally until charred. Place the roasted shallots in a small bowl, cover them with plastic wrap, and let their natural steam cook them through. Skewer the garlic cloves on the presoaked bamboo skewers and char them on the grill, then set aside. Grill the slices of galangal, turning them occasionally until they're charred, then use a mortar and pestle to pound them with a pinch of salt.

Recipe continued . . .

3. Peel the roasted shallots while they're still warm to the touch. If you wait until the roasted shallots cool off, the charred skin tends to stick to the flesh and it'll be more difficult and messier to peel them. Add the peeled shallots and roasted garlic to the mortar, and pound everything together into a fine paste. Reserve 1 tablespoon for the salad. The roasted shallot paste can be kept in a bowl at room temperature for up to 2 hours. If you're not using it right away, it will keep in the fridge for up to 1 week, or the freezer for up to 4 weeks.

Larp Salad:

½ cup chicken stock or Master Stock (page 61)

2-3 Tbsp fish sauce (divided)

¾ cup hand-minced duck breast

2 tsp Larp Spice Mix (see here)

1 Tbsp Roasted Shallot Paste (see here)

1-2 tsp chili powder, to taste

2 Tbsp freshly squeezed lime juice

Dash of mangda fish sauce (page 117) (optional)

Small pinch of granulated sugar (optional)

¼ cup fresh Vietnamese mint leaves

¼ cup fresh mint leaves

¼ cup fresh coriander leaves

3 Tbsp finely sliced pak chi farang

2 Tbsp sliced spring onions

2 Tbsp sliced shallots

1-2 Tbsp Toasted Rice Powder (page 117), to taste

⅓ cup Pork Crackling (page 42) or duck crackling, broken into pieces (optional)

3 Tbsp Fried Shallots (page 235)

Fried red Thai bird's eye chilies (optional)

1 lime, cut into wedges

For the Larp Salad:

1. In a frying pan over medium heat, stir together the stock and 1 tablespoon of fish sauce. Add the minced duck, 2 teaspoons larp spice mix, and 1 tablespoon roasted shallot paste. Mix until incorporated thoroughly and cook until the duck is done, signaled when it releases the stock back into the pan. Allow some of the liquid to cook off and make sure the duck isn't too wet, then season with 1 to 2 more tablespoons of fish sauce, chili powder to taste, and lime juice. The duck should taste salty and spicy with just a hint of sour that doesn't overpower the salty and spicy components.

2. Add the mangda fish sauce if desired, and the sugar only if needed to balance the flavors, as the duck shouldn't be sweet at all.

3. In a medium-size bowl, mix the Vietnamese mint, mint, coriander leaves, pak chi farang, spring onions, and shallots together. Add the rice powder. Add the crackling and the duck to the bowl, and toss all the ingredients together until well combined. Transfer to a serving platter, sprinkle the fried shallots and fried chilies on top, and serve with lime wedges.

Galangal powder mix is equal parts galangal powder, Makrut lime leaf powder, and lemongrass powder. While these powders can be purchased at a specialty Asian grocer, you can also make it easily: thinly slice the fresh galangal and lemongrass, and dehydrate them in a dehydrator or oven set to 100°F overnight. Once the ingredients have cooled, grind them into a fine powder with a grinder or mortar and pestle.

Larp Tartare of Beef

SERVES 4 • PREP TIME: 15 MINUTES • ASSEMBLE TIME: 5 MINUTES

I FIRST TRIED THIS RAW BEEF DISH in Thailand at a roadside stall in my wife's hometown near Saraburi. The vendor used a special fermented sauce made from cow's stomach to give it a distinct bitter flavor. Although he hand-chopped each order of tartare salad on the spot to ensure freshness, his lack of refrigeration made me worry just the opposite! I tried the salad reluctantly and was absolutely blown away. It was deep and complex, just like a larp, and the freshly chopped beef was tender and delicious. I wanted to recreate this dish, but didn't have any success with sourcing the hard-to-find fermented stomach seasoning. So I turned to the tried-and-true roasted shallot paste and achieved the bitter richness I was looking for, combining the bittersweetness from roasted shallots and garlic with the smokiness from grilled galangal. My version is another way for you to serve this dish, a unique marriage of Thai larp and French beef tartare.

¼ pound beef tenderloin (see tip)

¼ cup Roasted Shallot Paste (page 111)

1-2 Tbsp Larp Spice Mix (page 111)

2-3 Tbsp fish sauce

1-2 tsp chili powder

1 Tbsp Fried Shallots (page 235)

1 tsp Fried Garlic (page 235)

2 Tbsp Toasted Rice Powder (page 117) (divided)

2 Tbsp freshly squeezed lime juice

Small pinch of granulated sugar (optional)

1 Tbsp fried red Thai bird's eye chilies, plus extra to garnish

¼ cup fresh Vietnamese mint leaves

¼ cup fresh mint leaves

¼ cup fresh coriander leaves

3 Tbsp finely sliced pak chi farang

2 Tbsp sliced spring onions

2 Tbsp sliced shallots

1 raw egg yolk (optional)

⅓ cup Pork Crackling (page 42) (optional)

Dash of mangda fish sauce (page 117) (optional)

1 lime, cut into wedges

1. Clean the beef tenderloin by using a small paring knife to peel off the silverskin, chain, connective tissue, and excess fat before cutting it into a small dice for the tartare. Keep the meat cold by working in a shallow bowl chilled on ice.

2. Mix the roasted shallot paste and larp spice mix in with the meat, then season with the fish sauce, chili powder, fried shallots, and fried garlic. Add 1 tablespoon of toasted rice powder, the lime juice, and a pinch of sugar if needed. Mix until combined; the tartare should taste smoky, spicy, and fragrant.

3. In a separate mixing bowl, toss the fried chilies, Vietnamese mint, mint, coriander, pak chi farang, spring onions, shallots, and 1 tablespoon of toasted rice powder, and arrange them on a serving platter as a bed for the tartare. Carefully spoon the tartare mixture over the herbs. Finish with an egg yolk atop the tartare along with some pork crackling, more fried chilies, and the mangda fish sauce. Serve immediately with wedges of lime.

æ Most butchers will sell cleaned beef tenderloin as filet mignon. Ask for tenderloin ends—the uneven ends that butchers can't portion for steak. They're usually half the price of filet mignon and offer much greater food value for the dollar, given that you'll be cutting them up for tartare.

Grilled Beef Salad

SERVES 1, OR 2 TO 3 FAMILY STYLE • PREP TIME: 10 MINUTES, PLUS OVERNIGHT SOAKING AND DEHYDRATING • COOK TIME: 15 MINUTES

NAHM DTOK IS ONE OF MY FAVORITE DISHES TO EAT—it's simple yet has a bright sharpness. Toasted rice powder is the secret ingredient here: easy to make, it adds texture and a subtle nutty flavor to any dish. My preferred variant of this salad is a northern Thai version that's seasoned with a fish sauce made with "mangda"— waterbugs that live in the rice fields. Mangda fish sauce has a distinct nose that ranges from petrol to floral, which elevates the salad's flavors.

Toasted Rice Powder:

1 cup Thai sticky rice

1 tsp galangal powder (see note on page 112)

1 tsp lemongrass powder (see note on page 112)

Salad:

½ pound Wagyu beef striploin

6 Tbsp freshly squeezed lime juice

¼ cup fish sauce

Small dash of mangda fish sauce (see recipe introduction) (optional)

Pinch of Toasted Chili Powder (page 234)

1 tsp granulated sugar, or to taste

½ cup fresh coriander leaves

½ cup fresh mint leaves

2 shallots, sliced

2 Tbsp sliced pak chi farang

1 Tbsp Toasted Rice Powder (see here)

æ You can substitute the beef striploin with grilled pork, roasted chicken, or even grilled fish.

For the Toasted Rice Powder:

1. Soak the sticky rice in water overnight.

2. Strain the rice and dry it in a food dehydrator at medium setting, or spread evenly on a baking sheet and dry it in an oven set to the lowest temperature, 100°F to 150°F, for 1 day. Don't set the temperature too hot or the rice will start cooking before it dries thoroughly. When the rice is bone dry, toast it in a wok over low heat or in an oven at 350°F until golden brown with toasty aroma.

3. Using a mortar and pestle, grind the toasted rice into a fine powder. Mix in the galangal and lemongrass powders to give it extra fragrance. Reserve 1 tablespoon for this recipe. Store in an airtight container in the pantry for up to 2 months; beyond that, the flavor may fade.

For the Salad:

1. Prepare a charcoal grill to high heat 25 to 40 minutes prior to grilling (both a gas grill or grill pan on the stove at medium-high heat also work but are not preferred). Spread out the charcoal to achieve an even heat.

2. Grill the beef until rare to medium-rare, about 2 to 4 minutes per side depending on the thickness of your cut of meat. Transfer to a plate to rest for 10 minutes.

3. To make the dressing, in a medium-size bowl, whisk together the lime juice, fish sauce, and mangda fish sauce, then add the toasted chili powder and sugar. The dressing should be aromatic with the toasted chili powder and taste hot, sour, and salty. Mix in more sugar to balance the flavors if needed, but it shouldn't have a detectable sweet taste.

4. Slice the beef as thinly as possible against the fibers. Place in a large salad bowl together with the coriander, mint, shallots, and pak chi farang; mix well. Drizzle in the dressing and toss until incorporated. Sprinkle the toasted rice powder over the salad to finish.

Crispy Soft-Shell Crab and Sour-Mango Salad

SERVES 3 TO 4 • PREP TIME: 30 MINUTES • COOK TIME: 10 MINUTES

Crispy Soft-Shell Crabs:

3-4 soft-shell crabs

2 Tbsp fish sauce

4 quarts canola oil

1 cup cornstarch

1 cup water

For the Crispy Soft-Shell Crabs:

1. To clean soft-shell crabs, flip the crab so the shell is on the top. Holding the crab on either side of the shell, flip open the shell to reveal the gills on the body. Use a paring knife to remove the gills on both sides of the crab and rinse under cold running water to clean.

2. Place the cleaned soft-shell crabs in a bowl with fish sauce and marinate for 2 minutes.

3. In a heavy 6-quart pot over medium-high heat, preheat the canola oil to 350°F.

4. In a separate bowl, whisk the cornstarch and water together until the slurry is the consistency of thick cream. Dredge the crabs in the slurry until completely coated, then gently lower into the hot oil, deep-frying them until golden brown and crispy. Carefully remove them from the oil and transfer to a rack with paper towel beneath it to absorb excess oil.

Sour-Mango Salad:

1 cup julienned sour green mangos

½ cup fresh coriander leaves

½ cup fresh mint leaves

2 Tbsp roasted cashews

1 Tbsp finely sliced shallots

1 Tbsp finely sliced pak chi farang

1 Tbsp peeled and finely sliced lemongrass

1 Tbsp finely julienned Makrut lime leaves

1 Tbsp Fried Garlic (page 235)

¼ cup Orange-Chili Nahm Jim (page 132)

For the Sour-Mango Salad:

1. In a large bowl, mix the green mangos together with the coriander, mint, cashews, shallots, pak chi farang, lemongrass, Makrut lime leaves, and fried garlic.

2. Toss the salad with the orange-chili nahm jim and serve it atop the crispy soft-shell crabs.

æ If you can't track down sour green mangos, use green apples as a substitute.

Spot-Prawn Salad with Chili Jam

SERVES 4 • PREP TIME: 30 MINUTES • COOK TIME: 15 MINUTES

SPOT PRAWNS, OR SPOTTED PRAWNS, are one of my favorite things to eat when in season here on the west coast; they remind me of wild king river prawns from Thailand. This salad's bright, fresh flavors always mark the arrival of summer for me, and they beautifully accent the spot prawns' natural sweetness. Though I recommend grilling the prawns for this dish, it also works well if you decide to serve them raw or blanched.

2 pounds live spot prawns (see tip)

1 cup Fried Shallots (page 235)

1 cup peeled and thinly sliced lemongrass

1 cup julienned Makrut lime leaves

1 cup fresh mint leaves

1 cup fresh coriander leaves

½ cup sliced pak chi farang

Chili Jam Nahm Jim (page 133), to taste

1. Prepare a charcoal grill to medium heat 25 to 40 minutes prior to grilling (a gas grill also works but isn't preferred). Spread out the charcoal to achieve an even heat.

2. Grill the prawns for about 45 seconds per side on the hottest part of your grill—don't overcook them or they'll become mushy.

3. Once all the spot prawns are grilled, split each one in half down the belly with a sharp knife while keeping the head on, and transfer them to a large bowl. Toss in the fried shallots, lemongrass, Makrut lime leaves, mint, coriander, and pak chi farang. Season to taste with the chili jam nahm jim.

æ When buying spot prawns from your local fishmonger, be sure to check that they are all alive and swimming. Their heads must be clear and free of dark marks. You should cook your spot prawns as soon as you get home because they won't last more than 3 hours in your fridge. If you bought too many spot prawns, be sure to remove their heads before refrigerating the extra ones. The heads release an enzyme that causes the flesh to deteriorate at a faster rate when the prawns are dead and increases the probability of getting sick due to spoilage.

Steamed Clam Salad with Orange-Chili Dressing

SERVES 4 • PREP TIME: 15 MINUTES • COOK TIME: 5 MINUTES

THIS IS A BEAUTIFUL SALAD, typical of seaside Thailand. The trick to making it well is using the freshest clams possible, and keeping some of their nectar after steaming to add into the salad. Very little prep is needed to highlight the fresh sweetness of seafood picked right out of the ocean—often you need nothing more than a quick stir-fry, steam, or grill before serving atop fresh aromatics and herbs tossed in a sharply flavored dressing.

Clams:

1 pound Manila clams

¼ cup water

2 Tbsp sliced shallots

1 stalk lemongrass, peeled and bruised

5 Makrut lime leaves

Salad:

½ cup fresh mint leaves

½ cup fresh coriander leaves

2 Tbsp roasted peanuts, skinned

2 Tbsp toasted grated coconut (see tip on page 126)

Meat of ¼ young coconut, sliced into strips

2 Tbsp sliced shallots

2 Tbsp peeled and sliced lemongrass

1 Tbsp finely julienned Makrut lime leaves

2 Tbsp sliced pak chi farang

5-6 cherry tomatoes, halved

¼ cup Orange-Chili Nahm Jim (page 132)

For the Clams:

1. Clean the clams (see page 169).

2. In a covered wok over medium-high heat, steam the clams with the water, shallots, lemongrass, and Makrut lime leaves until the clams open, about 5 to 6 minutes. If any clams haven't opened by the 6-minute mark, discard them, as they're likely dead. Remove the opened clams from the wok and set aside in a bowl. Reserve the clam nectar in a bowl at room temperature until you're ready to plate the salad.

For the Salad:

1. In a large serving bowl, toss the mint, coriander, roasted peanuts, toasted coconut, young coconut, shallots, lemongrass, Makrut lime leaves, and pak chi farang together. Drizzle in some of the clam nectar and add the cherry tomatoes.

2. Add the clams; gently toss everything together until well incorporated, taking care not to bruise the tomatoes. Serve immediately with orange-chili nahm jim.

Opposite page: Grilled Squid (left, page 124) and Steamed Clam (right).

Grilled Squid with Sour Mango and Banana Blossom Salad

SERVES 4 • PREP TIME: 20 MINUTES • COOK TIME: 5 MINUTES

IT'S VERY COMMON IN THAILAND to pair crisp sour fruit such as starfruit or pomelo with smoky grilled fish, prawns, shellfish, or squid—I'm especially partial to tart green mango. The banana blossoms give this salad a unique bitterness, while the coconut cream balances it out by adding a bit more richness to the dressing. You can replace the squid with just about any grilled seafood to make this quick and simple salad.

Grilled Squid:

½ pound squid

¼ cup fish sauce

Pinch of white pepper

For the Grilled Squid:

1. Prepare a charcoal grill to high heat 25 to 40 minutes prior to grilling (both a gas grill or grill pan on the stove at medium-high heat also work but are not preferred). It's important to have a hot grill so that the squid doesn't stick or cook for too long and shrink. Spread out the charcoal to achieve an even heat.

2. To clean the squid, pull the cartilage and peel off the skin and wings. Cut off the head and tentacles from the body. If the squid has an ink sac, be careful to keep it intact while removing it. Rinse both the tube and the head thoroughly under cold running water and dry them with paper towel.

3. Marinate the squid in a bowl with the fish sauce and white pepper for 5 minutes.

4. Grill the squid to medium doneness, about 2 minutes. The squid should be soft to the touch but not rubbery, and have beautiful grill marks but not be burned. Remove from heat and set aside on a plate to rest.

Salad:

½ medium-size banana blossom

1 Tbsp white vinegar

1 Tbsp coarse sea salt

¼ cup Orange-Chili Nahm Jim (page 132)

2 tsp Coconut Cream (page 205)

Zest of ½ Makrut lime or ½ mandarin orange (optional)

½ cup peeled and julienned sour green mango

½ cup fresh coriander leaves

½ cup fresh mint leaves

2 Tbsp peeled and finely sliced lemongrass

2 Tbsp roasted peanuts, skinned

1 Tbsp finely sliced shallots

1 Tbsp sliced pak chi farang

1 Tbsp finely julienned Makrut lime leaves

For the Salad:

1. Bring a 4-quart pot of water to boil over medium-high heat. Meanwhile, peel away and discard the outer layers of the banana blossom until you're left with the lighter, pale-colored inner layers. Slice the inner layers across the grain into ¼-inch strips, then place them in a bowl of cold water with some white vinegar to prevent them from discoloring. Add salt and the sliced banana blossoms to the pot of boiling water and cook for 3 to 5 minutes, until tender. Rinse under cold running water to cool.

2. To make the dressing, in a small bowl, combine the orange-chili nahm jim with the coconut cream. Add the Makrut lime zest to give the dressing more fragrance.

3. In a serving bowl, mix the sour green mango together with the coriander, mint, lemongrass, roasted peanuts, shallots, pak chi farang, and Makrut lime leaves. Toss the banana blossoms into the salad, then drizzle in the dressing and toss once more until thoroughly incorporated. Slice the grilled squid into 1- to 2-inch strips and toss with the salad before serving. Serve immediately.

Recipe pictured on page 122.

Salad of Grilled Sockeye Salmon

SERVES 4 • PREP TIME: 40 MINUTES • COOK TIME: 10 MINUTES

THERE ARE FIVE DIFFERENT SPECIES of salmon in the Pacific Ocean here on Canada's west coast: sockeye, coho, chum, pink, and spring. My favorite of them all is sockeye, as its lean flesh is full of flavor. I love grilling it for this recipe, although spring or coho also work well. I've been spoiled by the bounty of our local waters, so much so that I flatly refuse to eat farmed salmon. If you can't track down sockeye salmon, steelhead trout is a good replacement.

½ pound sockeye salmon fillet

1 Tbsp fish sauce

Pinch of white pepper

1 cup fresh coriander leaves

1 cup fresh mint leaves

½ cup freshly grated young coconut meat

2 betel leaves, torn

¼ cup Orange-Chili Nahm Jim (page 132)

¼ cup peeled and toasted Thai peanuts

2 shallots, sliced

1 Tbsp toasted grated coconut (see tip)

3 Tbsp Fried Shallots (page 235), to garnish

2 Tbsp cured salmon roe, to garnish

1. Prepare a charcoal grill to medium heat 25 to 40 minutes prior to grilling (both a gas grill or grill pan on the stove at medium-high heat also work but are not preferred). Spread out the charcoal to achieve an even heat.

2. Meanwhile, remove the sockeye salmon from the fridge and let it sit for about 30 minutes so it comes to room temperature. Using a paper towel, thoroughly dry the fish skin.

3. Season the salmon with the fish sauce and a pinch of white pepper. Oil the grill lightly. Grill the salmon skin-side down until medium-rare, about 4 to 6 minutes depending on the thickness. If your grill is too hot, the fish skin will burn instead of becoming crispy, so play around with the temperature. In the final 30 seconds, flip the fish over to cook the flesh slightly and achieve medium-rare doneness. Remove the fish from the grill and let it rest for 3 to 5 minutes while preparing the salad.

4. While the salmon is resting, place the coriander, mint, young coconut, and betel leaves in a bowl, toss with the orange-chili nahm jim, then mix in the peanuts and shallots. Slice the fish on a bias into 1½-inch-thick pieces and carefully fold it into the salad. Transfer the salad to a serving platter. Garnish with the toasted grated coconut, fried shallots, and cured salmon roe.

> Although pre-toasted grated coconut is readily available in most supermarkets, it's very rewarding to make your own. Preheat the oven to 350°F. Carefully crack open a large coconut, scrape out the white coconut meat, and grate it with a grater. Spread the grated coconut meat on a baking sheet and toast it in the oven until golden, 10 to 15 minutes. You can store the toasted grated coconut in an airtight container in the pantry for up to 2 weeks.

Roasted Duck Salad

SERVES 4 • PREP TIME: 15 MINUTES • COOK TIME: 20 MINUTES

BANGKOK'S CHINATOWN IS WHERE I FIRST TASTED this Chinese-inspired salad that's punctuated by BBQ duck, soy, and sesame. It's a super-quick and simple but delicious recipe. Just go to a really good Chinese BBQ shop and buy half a roasted duck—or, if you're like me, get a whole duck and eat the other half on the way home.

Dressing:

¼ cup chicken stock

2 Tbsp palm sugar

2 Tbsp light soy sauce

1 Tbsp Tamarind Water (page 233)

Pinch of white pepper

3 Tbsp sesame seeds

2 Tbsp Fried Shallots (page 235)

For the Dressing:

1. Preheat the oven to 350°F.

2. In a small pot over medium heat, add the chicken stock and palm sugar; the palm sugar will melt in the stock as it's warming. Once it comes to a simmer, stir in the light soy sauce, tamarind water, and white pepper; bring it back up to a simmer and remove from heat.

3. Toast the sesame seeds in the oven for 10 to 15 minutes, until golden. Reserve 1 tablespoon for the salad. Using a mortar and pestle, grind the rest of the sesame seeds together with the fried shallots and combine them in the dressing.

Salad:

½ roasted duck, deboned

6 lychees, peeled and pitted

½ cup fresh coriander leaves

½ cup Thai basil leaves

2 Tbsp toasted Thai peanuts

2 Tbsp Fried Shallots (page 235)

2 Tbsp Fried Garlic (page 235)

1 Tbsp sliced green onions

For the Salad:

1. Keep the oven at 350°F.

2. In a shallow roasting pan, warm the duck slightly in the oven for 5 to 10 minutes.

3. In a large serving bowl, mix together the lychees, coriander, Thai basil, Thai peanuts, fried shallots, fried garlic, green onions, and the reserved toasted sesame seeds. Remove the duck from the oven; it should be warm to the touch, but not hot. Slice the duck into ½-inch-thick pieces and add the meat and all the nice bits of crispy skin to the salad mix. Toss with the dressing until thoroughly incorporated, and serve immediately.

Chicken with Blood-Orange Salad

SERVES 4 • PREP TIME: 1 HOUR • COOK TIME: 10 MINUTES

ALTHOUGH BLOOD ORANGES AREN'T COMMONLY FOUND IN THAILAND, their full-bodied bittersweet flavor is a delicious accent for most roast poultry. This simple salad is an ideal way of using up leftover roast chicken or turkey, and it's especially refreshing the day after decadent holiday feasting.

6 baby beets

Pinch of coarse sea salt

½ roasted chicken or leftover turkey, about 1½-2 cups of meat

2 blood oranges

1 cup fresh coriander leaves

1 cup fresh mint leaves

½ cup sliced pak chi farang

½ cup Asian pennywort (see tip)

¼ cup Blood-Orange Nahm Jim (page 133)

1 Tbsp peeled finely sliced lemongrass

1 Tbsp finely julienned Makrut lime leaves

¼ cup Fried Shallots (page 235)

1. Preheat the oven to 350°F.

2. Place the baby beets on a baking sheet, sprinkle with a pinch of salt, cover in aluminum foil, and roast for 45 minutes, or until they're soft. Remove the beets from the oven and allow them to cool before peeling carefully with a paring knife.

3. If you're using leftover chicken or turkey, pop it into the oven for about 10 minutes to warm up slightly while you're preparing the blood oranges.

4. Using a vegetable peeler, remove the skin from the blood oranges, being careful not to include any of the bitter white pith. Cut the peeled skins into a fine julienne, and segment the rest of the oranges by removing the white pith and slicing out the individual orange segments.

5. In a large serving bowl, toss the baby beets and chicken together with the sliced blood oranges and the rest of the ingredients, finishing the salad with the fried shallots and julienned orange zest. Serve immediately.

æ Asian pennywort is a swamp green that's common throughout Southeast Asia. It has a distinct bittersweet flavor with a thin but sturdy leaf and is great for salads. You can find it at specialty Asian markets.

Dressings

PREP TIME: 15 TO 20 MINUTES • MAKES ABOUT 1½ CUPS EACH

IN THAI, *NAHM JIM* MEANS "DRESSING." There are many versions, but the standard *nahm jim talay* refers to a version that we like for seafood. It's great for all seafood applications—whether raw, grilled, boiled, or steamed—and is probably the most common nahm jim. Over the years, we've created different nahm jims for different salads, adding certain ingredients like blood orange to highlight elements of the proteins that we're serving it with. However, we also use a lot of standard nahm jims, such as the Chili Jam Nahm Jim that's commonly served with grilled prawns.

Seafood Nahm Jim

¼ cup sliced galangal

5 green Thai bird's eye chilies

2 red Thai bird's eye chilies

8 cloves garlic

¼ cup chopped coriander root

Pinch of kosher salt

2 red chili peppers, deseeded

⅓ cup granulated sugar

⅔ cup freshly squeezed lime juice

½ cup fish sauce

Zest and juice of 1 Makrut lime

Orange-Chili Nahm Jim

10 green Thai bird's eye chilies

6 garlic cloves

¼ cup chopped coriander root

Pinch of kosher salt

3 orange chili peppers, deseeded

⅓ cup granulated sugar

⅔ cup freshly squeezed lime juice

½ cup fish sauce

Zest and juice of 1 mandarin orange

Chili Jam
Nahm Jim

½ cup sliced galangal

7 green Thai bird's eye chilies

3 red Thai bird's eye chilies

8 garlic cloves

¼ cup chopped coriander root

Pinch of kosher salt

¼ cup granulated sugar

2 Tbsp chili jam

⅔ cup freshly squeezed lime juice

½ cup fish sauce

Zest and juice of 1 Makrut lime

Blood-Orange
Nahm Jim

¼ cup sliced galangal

5 green Thai bird's eye chilies

6 garlic cloves

¼ cup chopped coriander root

Pinch of kosher salt

2 red chili peppers, deseeded

⅓ cup granulated sugar

⅔ cup freshly squeezed lime juice

½ cup fish sauce

Zest and juice of 1 blood orange

When you make any Thai dressing, always use a stone mortar and pestle. The following method will work with each one of these recipes.

1. Place the hardest ingredients in the mortar first, such as galangal slices, Thai bird's eye chilies, garlic, coriander root, and fruit zest. Always add a pinch of kosher salt to the mortar—it acts as an abrasive and helps break down the fibers. Pound the ingredients with the pestle; the technique isn't just up-and-down pounding or grinding, but a combination of both motions. You want to strike one side of the mortar with the pestle and grind it back to the other side, using your wrist and the momentum of the pestle only. If you're doing this correctly, it should take you only a minute or two to break down the hardest ingredients. Most importantly, never overcrowd the mortar.

2. Slice the deseeded chili pepper flesh so that it's easier to break down. Add it to the mortar and continue to pound. Be very careful not to look directly into the mortar while you're pounding as bits of chili may splash up into your eye. Cover the top of the pestle with one hand if needed to prevent the ingredients from splashing out, as the mixture will become quite wet. Make sure that the chili pepper skins are pounded into fine pieces; after this point, they won't break down any further.

3. Add the sugar (and chili jam, if required) to the mortar. The sugar will absorb the moisture; instead of pounding, grind it into the mixture with the pestle to further develop a fine paste. The finer your paste, the smoother your dressing will be.

4. Stir in the liquids: lime juice, fish sauce, and Makrut lime or other fruit juice. Mix with the pestle until the liquids are well incorporated, and let the dressing sit for 5 minutes before tasting it; such strong flavors often need time to get to know each other. Adjust to taste if needed. Most of the salad dressings that include fresh lime should be served immediately; however, if you have a little extra left over, you can keep it in the fridge for a couple of days without losing too much freshness. Bear in mind that freshly squeezed lime juice oxidizes very quickly and can't be kept for long periods of time.

Stir-Fries

Opposite page: Stir-Fried Chanterelles and Baby Corn (page 163).

Introduction

GROWING UP IN ASIA, I always had a wok kitchen in my home. When my family moved to Canada, we had a custom wok burner built on the back porch and used it extensively. I especially love using a well-seasoned wok rather than a sauté pan for stir-frying because of the smoky aromas that it imparts as well as its ability to cook something in a very short amount of time while preserving the color, integrity, and flavor of vegetables and beautifully and quickly searing small cuts of meat. Stir-Fried Chanterelles and Baby Corn (page 163) is a perfect example of a dish with pristine ingredients that greatly benefit from the speed and efficiency of cooking in a wok, and are enhanced by the smoky "wok breath."

Wok-cooking is hot and fast over intense direct heat, and you need to have the proper tools for it (see page 10). Dishes like Eight-Spiced Whole Fish (page 141) are made to order in Thailand, where the cooks are experts in the art of wok-cooking. The wok's blistering heat requires fast and careful handling of both food and seasoning. This takes practice, but don't be intimidated.

Stir-fries should be super-simple, and I'm admittedly guilty of making them a little more complicated than they need to be—but for good reason. The Stir-Fried Beef Shin with Holy Basil (page 146) and Dry Curry Stir-Fry of Crispy Pork Belly (page 149) are two such examples. They're typical street dishes that are cooked to order—traditionally made with minced beef and pork belly slices respectively—but instead I braise and deep-fry these meats first to add richness and tenderness before frying them. These extra steps build layers of flavor and add depth. Take ribs, for example: I always braise them first and wait until they cool down before frying them. I could very easily just use slices of beef—a good steak cut works well if I'm stir-frying from raw. But I definitely prefer to get the best of both worlds by combining cooking techniques: tenderness from braising or crispness from deep-frying, accented by depth of flavor from stir-frying.

Black-Pepper Crab

SERVES 4 • PREP TIME: 20 MINUTES • COOK TIME: 20 MINUTES

BLACK-PEPPER CRAB is a very popular dish from Yaowarat, Bangkok's Chinatown district. I first made it on a dare from a Singaporean friend—he was reminiscing how it's one of his hometown favorites and didn't think that the Thai version could be nearly as good. The predominant difference is that Singaporeans cook it with butter, while Thais make it more saucy with oyster sauce. My own version ended up somewhere between the two by emulsifying butter into the oyster sauce to add richness. What started out as a dare has since become one of the signature dishes at Maenam!

Black-Pepper Sauce:

6 Tbsp black peppercorns

2 Tbsp white peppercorns

½ cup unsalted butter

3 cloves garlic

3 red Thai bird's eye chilies

3 Tbsp canola or peanut oil

¼ cup oyster sauce

2 Tbsp fish sauce

1 Tbsp granulated sugar, or to taste

½ cup chicken stock

1 Tbsp cornstarch (optional)

For the Black-Pepper Sauce:

1. In a small frying pan over medium heat, lightly toast the black and white peppercorns, tossing them for about 5 minutes, until aromatic. Ensure that the peppercorns smell nutty and peppery instead of coffee-like, which would mean that they're overcooked. Add the butter. Without burning the butter, continue to toast the peppercorns, stirring often, until the mixture becomes fragrant. Spoon the peppercorns and melted butter into a mortar and pestle. Grind the peppercorns and butter into a paste, then transfer to a small bowl and set aside.

2. Wipe down the mortar and pestle with paper towel. Add the garlic and chilies and pound into a paste. Return the same frying pan to the stove over medium heat. Add the cooking oil and garlic-chili paste; fry until fragrant. Add the peppercorn paste and stir to combine, cooking until smoky. Stir in the oyster sauce, fish sauce, and sugar and mix until well combined before incorporating the chicken stock. Simmer for 2 to 3 minutes and taste for seasoning; if it's too spicy, decrease the heat level by adding sugar incrementally. Check the consistency: if the sauce doesn't coat the back of a spoon well, add cornstarch to thicken and bring to a simmer to activate the cornstarch. Remove pan from heat and reserve sauce for serving.

Crab:

1 live Dungeness crab, 2-3 pounds (see tip)

4 quarts peanut oil

1½ cups cornstarch

1½ cups water

½ cup diagonally sliced green onions

¼ cup julienned ginger

½ cup fresh coriander leaves

For the Crab:

1. Kill and butcher the crab (see sidebar on page 139).

2. In a deep fryer or a 6- to 8-quart Dutch oven over high heat, preheat the peanut oil to 350°F. In a large mixing bowl, whisk the cornstarch and water together until the slurry is the consistency of thick cream. Gently toss the crab legs in the cornstarch slurry until coated thoroughly, then slowly place them into the hot oil to avoid splattering. Fry for 4 to 5 minutes, until

Recipe continued . . .

the slurry on the crab shell is crispy and firm to the touch and the flesh at the thickest part of the meat on the body is white rather than translucent. Remove the crab legs and transfer them to a baking sheet lined with paper towel to absorb excess oil.

3. Heat a wok or skillet over medium-high heat. Transfer the deep-fried crab legs directly into the hot wok together with the black-pepper sauce, green onions, ginger, and coriander, and toss or ladle all the ingredients together until well combined. Stir-fry for 5 minutes, until heated through. Serve immediately.

æ When I'm buying live crab from just about any fishmonger, they always ask me if I need it killed and cut up. My answer to that is definitely no! I firmly believe that shellfish should be kept live right up to the minute you'll be cooking it to ensure utmost freshness. Choose a good-size crab that's lively—if you pick it up (carefully!), its legs should spring back and forth as it fights to be back in the water. My grandmother's tried-and-true method is to squeeze the legs; if they feel hollow and soft, it indicates that the crab may die soon. Ideally, the crab's legs should feel firm and tight and be full of movement. Avoid crabs that are missing limbs.

HOW TO PREPARE A CRAB

1a.

1a. Before butchering the live crab, submerge it in a large covered stockpot of water for 15 minutes. As most Thai people are Buddhist, they have a hard time killing crab and lobster, and they believe that drowning them in fresh water is a less cruel way to dispatch them.

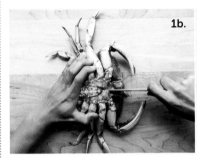  

1b. Alternatively, lay the crab abdomen-up on a large cutting board. Stab the point of your knife into its abdomen above the triangular stomach flap, and rapidly slice down to cut through the mouth of the crab. This is the quickest and most humane way to kill it.

2. Remove the stomach flap with a twist-and-pull motion.

3. This should reveal a small slot into which you can fit your thumb, enabling you to pull the shell off the body. Keep the yellowish crab tomalley in the shell.

4. Next, remove the two tooth-like flaps (mouth) and gills on either side of the body, and discard them along with the stomach flap.

5. Cut the body in half.

6. Insert your knife between the crab legs and split the body into six to eight pieces.

Eight-Spiced Whole Fish

SERVES 4 TO 6 • PREP TIME: 30 MINUTES • COOK TIME: 15 MINUTES

MY BROTHER-IN-LAW INTRODUCED ME to this dish, called *plah tort samun plai*, on my first visit to Thailand. After eating it at a restaurant, he declared that his was much better. So he cooked his own delicious version that very evening—sourcing better-quality fish and palm sugar made all of the difference. Sure enough, he was right—and I've used his recipe ever since. This versatile dish works with whole fish, fillets, or fish chunks.

Fish:

4 quarts peanut oil

1 whole 2-pound Mediterranean sea bass or sea bream, gutted and scaled (see tip)

1 cup cornstarch

2 cups water

Bamboo skewer

For the Fish:

1. In a deep fryer or a 6- to 8-quart Dutch oven over high heat, preheat the peanut oil to 350°F. Ensure that there will be enough oil to cover the fish completely.

2. Meanwhile, score the fish, two to three cuts per side. Using a large sharp chef's knife, cut through the meat to the backbone on a 45-degree angle intermittently down the length of the fish; if your fish is 6 to 10 inches long, score it every 1½ to 2 inches. Slice through to the bone to ensure fast, even cooking and provide more surface area for the fish to become crispy. In a large shallow mixing bowl, whisk together the cornstarch and water until the slurry is the consistency of thick milk.

3. Secure the fish in a "C" shape with a bamboo skewer, allowing the fish to stand up for unique presentation. Dredge the fish in the cornstarch slurry and coat it well, then lower it carefully into the hot oil to prevent splattering. Fry the fish for about 15 minutes, until fully cooked and the exterior is golden brown and crispy. Remove the fish from the oil and transfer to a plate lined with paper towel to absorb excess oil.

Eight-Spice Sauce:

1 cup Caramelized Tamarind Sauce (page 234)

1 Tbsp peeled and fried lemongrass

1 Tbsp fried green peppercorns

1 Tbsp fried dried red Thai bird's eye chilies

1 Tbsp fried galangal

1 Tbsp Fried Shallots (page 235)

1 Tbsp Fried Garlic (page 235)

10 Makrut lime leaves, halved lengthwise and fried

For the Eight-Spice Sauce:

1. In a wok or skillet over medium heat, bring the caramelized tamarind sauce to a simmer. Add the rest of the ingredients and toss to combine, then bring to a rolling simmer.

2. Add the fish to the wok and baste with the sauce until evenly coated. Remove the fish from the wok and user the skewer to stand it upright on a platter. Drizzle the remaining sauce atop the fish and serve immediately.

æ If your fishmonger hasn't already scaled your fish, place it in a plastic bag and use the back of a large chef's knife to scrape off the scales. Pay extra attention to hard-to-reach areas like around and beneath the fins. Remove your fish from the plastic bag, rinse it under cold running water, and dry the skin thoroughly.

Stir-Fried Venison with Black Pepper and Oyster Sauce

SERVES 4 • PREP TIME: 10 MINUTES • COOK TIME: 5 MINUTES

I USE VENISON FOR THIS QUICK AND EASY STIR-FRY, but you can easily substitute the red meat of your choice. Beef tenderloin or any steak cut would work particularly well, as the meat is tender and quick to cook.

Garlic-Chili Paste:

3 cloves garlic

3-5 red Thai bird's eye chilies

Pinch of coarse sea salt and white pepper

2 red chili peppers, deseeded and sliced

Stir-Fry:

2 red chili peppers, halved and deseeded

1 small sweet onion, cut into wedges

¼ cup sliced baby corn

3 Tbsp julienned grachai

2 stalks fresh green peppercorns

3-4 Makrut lime leaves

¼ cup canola oil

½ pound venison loin, cleaned and cut into 1-inch cubes

2 Tbsp oyster sauce

1 Tbsp fish sauce

1 Tbsp black pepper

1 Tbsp granulated sugar

3 Tbsp chicken stock or water (optional)

½ cup fresh Thai basil leaves

½ cup fresh holy basil leaves

Nahm Plah Prik (page 232)

For the Garlic-Chili Paste:

1. Using a mortar and pestle, pound the garlic, chilies, salt, and white pepper into a paste. Add the red chili peppers to the mortar and lightly bruise them. Set the paste aside.

For the Stir-Fry:

1. In a separate bowl, mix together the chili peppers, sweet onion wedges, baby corn, grachai, green peppercorns, and Makrut lime leaves.

2. Heat the canola oil in a wok over high heat. When the oil starts smoking, add the cubed venison and sear for about 90 seconds to get some color. Add the garlic-chili paste and stir-fry for 30 seconds, being very careful not to burn the garlic. Add the sweet onion mixture and stir-fry for an additional 2 minutes, or until the onion is slightly translucent but still carries a crunch. Season with the oyster sauce, fish sauce, black pepper, and sugar. If the dish looks too dry, add a few tablespoons of stock or water to moisten. Turn off the heat and transfer to a serving platter.

3. Finish with Thai basil and holy basil. Serve immediately with nahm plah prik.

Opposite page: Three-Flavor Pork Ribs (top, page 144) and Stir-Fried Venison (bottom).

Three-Flavor Pork Ribs

SERVES 4 • PREP TIME: 45 MINUTES • COOK TIME: 15 MINUTES

THREE-FLAVOR IS A VERY POPULAR Thai dish commonly served with fried fish. The three flavors refer to sweet, sour, and salty; this dish isn't supposed to be spicy, and is very fragrant with lots of ginger, garlic, and coriander root. Once a popular fish dish on Maenam's menu, we decided to run it as a special one evening featuring braised pork ribs, and we've kept it as a pork dish ever since.

Braised Pork Ribs:

1 rack pork back ribs

½ cup ginger or galangal trim (or mixed)

4 cups chicken stock

Pinch of salt

For the Braised Pork Ribs:

1. To clean the pork ribs, using a sharp knife, loosen the thin membrane on the bone side of the rib and rip it off whole with your hand. Slice the pork ribs between the bones to separate them.

2. Transfer the ribs to a 6-quart pot along with the ginger and/or galangal trim, and cover with stock. Bring to a boil over high heat. Add a pinch of salt, then simmer over low heat for 45 minutes. Do not overcook. Remove from heat and allow the ribs to cool slightly in the braising liquid, about 30 minutes.

Three-Flavor Sauce:

¾ cup garlic cloves

¾ cup roughly chopped coriander roots

¾ cup peeled and roughly chopped ginger

2 tsp coarse sea salt

1 tsp white pepper

1 cup mixed chili peppers, deseeded and roll-cut

1 cup palm sugar

¼ to ½ cup water (optional)

1 cup Tamarind Water (page 233)

½ cup fish sauce

For the Three-Flavor Sauce:

1. Using a mortar and pestle, pound the garlic, coriander roots, and ginger with the salt and white pepper to make a paste. Add the chili peppers and pound until they are bruised. Fry the paste in a wok over medium heat until the paste becomes golden and aromatic. Season with the palm sugar and stir to incorporate. Add ¼ cup of water to dissolve the sugar and simmer until the sauce thickens, reserving the other ¼ cup to loosen the sauce if needed.

2. Add the tamarind water and fish sauce. Simmer to reduce the sauce to the approximate consistency of a loose curry. It should taste sweet, sour, and salty. This will yield the amount of sauce you'll need for the stir-fry.

Stir-Fry:

1 cup canola oil

Fish sauce (optional)

½ cup fresh Thai basil leaves

½ cup sliced baby corn

¼ cup Fried Shallots (page 235)

¼ cup Fried Garlic (page 235)

2 large deep-fried dried guajillo chilies, to garnish

Handful of Fried Thai Basil (page 235), to garnish

For the Stir-Fry:

1. In a wok over high heat, preheat the oil to 350°F. Deep-fry the slightly cooled-off ribs for about 5 to 7 minutes. Ensure that the edges of the ribs become crispy and get a nice sear.

2. Once the ribs are golden brown and crispy, pour out the oil and add the three-flavor sauce. Toss together and cook over high heat until the ribs are well coated. Season with fish sauce if needed. Finish with Thai basil, baby corn, fried shallots, and fried garlic. Transfer to a serving platter and garnish with deep-fried chilies and fried Thai basil.

Recipe pictured on page 143.

Stir-Fried Beef Shin with Holy Basil

SERVES 2 TO 4 • PREP TIME: 2 HOURS • COOK TIME: 15 MINUTES

PAD GAPAO IS ONE OF MY FAVORITE THINGS TO EAT in Thailand. Cooked to order by street-side vendors, it's simple and quick to prepare, usually served with sliced or hand-chopped beef or chicken. Holy basil is essential to this dish; it has a beautiful citrusy aroma and a firmer texture that holds up to heat well. This recipe, slightly elevated from what you would find on the streets of Thailand, incorporates beef shin that's braised then fried to create a crispy exterior on a highly gelatinous cut of meat. A wok-fried egg on top is optional but highly recommended!

Braised Beef Shin:

½ pound cleaned beef shin, cut into 1-inch cubes

8 cups chicken stock

¼ cup fish sauce

3 star anise

1 Tbsp black peppercorns

Stir-Fry:

4 garlic cloves

2 red Thai bird's eye chilies

1 tsp coarse sea salt

½ tsp white pepper

2 cups canola or peanut oil

½ cup thinly sliced fresh hearts of palm

½ cup sliced white onions

½ cup sliced (lengthwise) or roll-cut red chili peppers

½ cup sliced (lengthwise) or roll-cut green chili peppers

2 Tbsp grachai

2 Makrut lime leaves

2 stalks fresh green peppercorns

1 cup fresh holy basil leaves

2 Tbsp fish sauce

2 Tbsp oyster sauce

2 tsp granulated sugar

2 tsp white pepper

Nahm Plah Prik (page 232)

For the Braised Beef Shin:

1. In a large pot or 5- to 6-quart Dutch oven over high heat, cover the diced beef shin with water and bring to a boil. Remove from heat and rinse off any blood and coagulated fat under running water.

2. Rinse out the pot, return the cleaned beef shin, and cover it with stock. Add fish sauce, star anise, and black peppercorns and simmer until fork-tender, about 45 minutes depending on the size of the beef cubes. Remove the beef shin to a bowl and let cool.

For the Stir-Fry:

1. Using a mortar and pestle, pound the garlic and red Thai bird's eye chilies to make a paste; add salt and white pepper to act as an abrasive.

2. Heat the oil in a wok over medium heat. Lightly pat the braised beef shin dry with paper towel before adding it to the wok; this removes excess moisture and prevents oil splatter. Sauté until crispy, stirring constantly with a wok spoon for about 5 minutes. Because the high collagen content of the beef shin gives it a tendency to stick to the wok, scrape the wok and be careful not to let the meat burn.

3. Once the beef shin is crispy, strain off excess oil from the wok and add the garlic-chili paste, hearts of palm, onions, red and green chili peppers, grachai, Makrut lime leaves, and green peppercorns. Remove any crispy shreds that are stuck on the wok spoon, and continue to stir-fry until the paste becomes aromatic. Add the holy basil to the wok and sauté for 15 seconds. Season with fish sauce, oyster sauce, sugar, and white pepper. The beef should taste salty and hot with little hints of white pepper; the sugar is to balance the flavor, not to overpower it, and should not be detected. Transfer to a platter and serve with nahm plah prik.

Dry Curry Stir-Fry of Crispy Pork Belly

SERVES 4 • PREP TIME: 2 HOURS • COOK TIME: 10 MINUTES

DRY-STYLE CURRY STIR-FRY, also known as *pad prik king*, is a rich red curry stir-fry that's crispy and aromatic. There are many variants of this dish in Thailand, including fried fish and chicken; pork belly is another common version and is one of my favorites. I love to render the simmered pork belly slowly and brown it in the deeply aromatic curried oil; this also renders the pork fat into the dish, adding to the meal's richness. Be very careful to ensure that the pork belly is dried before frying, as it will splatter—a lot!

Braised Pork Belly:

½ pound pork belly

4 cups chicken stock

½ cup ginger and/or galangal trim

Pinch of coarse sea salt

Stir-Fry:

¼ cup canola oil

2 Tbsp pork fat (optional)

2 Tbsp Garlic-Chili Paste (page 142)

¼ cup Chu Chi Curry Paste (page 202)

1 Tbsp palm sugar

1 Tbsp Tamarind Water (page 233)

¼ cup chicken stock (optional)

1 Tbsp fish sauce

Handful of fresh Thai basil leaves, about 1 cup

1 Tbsp finely julienned Makrut lime leaves

1 Tbsp shredded grachai

2 red chili peppers, halved and deseeded

2 stalks fresh green peppercorns

Pork Crackling (page 42), to garnish (optional)

Fried Thai Basil (page 235), to garnish (optional)

For the Braised Pork Belly:

1. Place the pork belly in a 6-quart pot, pour in the stock to cover it, and add the ginger and/or galangal trim to scent the braising liquid. Bring to a boil over medium-high heat, then reduce the heat to low. Add a pinch of salt and simmer for 2 hours. Do not overcook. Remove from the heat and allow the pork belly to cool in the braising liquid, about 30 minutes.

2. When the pork has cooled down, remove it from the braising liquid and cut into slices that are ½- to 1-inch thick and about 2- to 2½-inches long. Dry the pork belly chunks completely with paper towel.

For the Stir-Fry:

1. In a wok over medium-high heat, place the canola oil and 2 tablespoons of pork fat, and fry the pork belly chunks in batches, about 6 to 8 minutes per batch. Be very careful of splatter. Do not overcrowd the wok because this will cause the oil temperature to drop dramatically. Also, the pork belly is very high in collagen at this stage and will stick together more as a result. Once all the pork belly is golden brown, return it to the wok. Add the garlic-chili paste and cook until the garlic turns golden brown, stir-frying constantly to prevent the garlic from burning.

2. Remove some of the excess oil from the wok, but make sure that there's still ½ cup of oil left. Add the chu chi curry paste and stir-fry until the curry dissolves and becomes aromatic. Stir in the palm sugar and tamarind water. Add the stock if the curry becomes too dry. Season with the fish sauce. Add the Thai basil, Makrut lime leaves, grachai, red chili peppers, and green peppercorns, and toss to incorporate. The dish should taste salty and spicy; the sugar and tamarind should not be detected.

3. Transfer to a serving dish and garnish with some pork crackling and fried Thai basil leaves.

Pork Cheek Braise

SERVES 4 TO 6 • PREP TIME: 30 MINUTES • COOK TIME: 1 HOUR, 45 MINUTES

THIS RICH THAI-CHINESE BRAISE was one of my grandmother's signature dishes, and I took pride in being her prep cook. She was meticulous in the kitchen and accepted no shortcuts. I remember her blanching the pork three times to extract the "porky" aromas. After each blanch, she watched me carefully scrub each piece with a clean toothbrush to free the meat of coagulated proteins and blood. Her slow braising process perfumed our entire house, and I could hardly wait to eat. I must admit, this recipe isn't as homey as my grandmother's, but the earthy flavours of white pepper and the fresh citrus aromas of orange peel transport me back to her kitchen when I make it.

Pork Cheeks:

5 pounds pork cheeks

Pinch of coarse sea salt

¼ cup crushed dried orange peels (see tip on page 54)

¼ cup crushed cassia bark

8 star anise

1 Tbsp white peppercorns

1 big bunch pandan leaves

5 quarts chicken stock or Master Stock (page 61)

1½ cups oyster sauce

1½ cups fish sauce

2 cups palm sugar

¼ cup water

¼ pound bok choy

1 Tbsp white pepper

1 Tbsp julienned orange zest

Serving:

⅛ pound bok choy, thinly sliced

2 Tbsp Fried Shallots (page 235)

2 Tbsp fresh coriander leaves

1 Tbsp Fried Garlic (page 235)

1 Tbsp Fried Garlic Oil (page 235)

1 Tbsp sliced green onions

1 red Thai bird's eye chili, sliced

For the Pork Cheeks:

1. Clean the pork cheeks to remove fat and silverskin. Place them in a 6-quart pot and pour in enough cold water to cover them. Add a pinch of salt and bring to a boil over medium-high heat. Remove from heat, drain completely, and rinse the pork cheeks under cold water until they're free of coagulated blood and proteins.

2. In a large 6-quart pot over medium heat, toast the dried orange peels, cassia bark, star anise, and white peppercorns for about 5 minutes, tossing periodically until they become aromatic. Stir in the pandan leaves, stock, and oyster and fish sauces. Bring to a boil. Turn down the heat and simmer for 15 minutes. Add the pork cheeks, cover, and simmer for 1 hour, until the meat is fork-tender. Turn the heat to medium-low and allow the pork cheeks to cool slightly in the stock before removing them from the pot. Strain the braising liquid through a strainer and set aside.

3. In a saucepan over medium heat, simmer the palm sugar and water together for about 10 minutes, until the mixture thickens slightly but is not caramelized. Monitor using a sugar thermometer to take it to a dark-caramel stage, about 350°F. Be extra careful not to burn the sugar, and check the color regularly on the back of a wooden spoon. Once the caramel reaches the dark stage, deglaze it with the strained braising liquid and reduce the sauce until it coats the back of a spoon.

4. Carefully place the pork back into the sauce. Add the bok choy to cook. Heat until the pork cheeks are soft and warmed through, about 5 minutes, and take care not to overcook the bok choy. Adjust to taste with more white pepper and fresh orange zest.

For Serving:

1. Transfer the pork cheeks to a large serving bowl with plenty of sauce and garnish with all of the serving ingredients. Serve immediately.

Coconut-Braised Soy Pork Cheeks

SERVES 4 TO 6 • PREP TIME: 1 HOUR, PLUS OVERNIGHT REFRIGERATION • COOK TIME: 3 HOURS

THIS DISH IS A GOOD EXAMPLE of a gray area in Thai cuisine. Some call it a *geng* or curry, while others serve it with very few herbs and call it a stir-fry or stew, or serve it as a soup with lots of lightened braising liquid. Common versions are also made with beef shin, beef short ribs, beef tongue, beef cheeks, or braising cuts of veal. I particularly enjoy serving this dish as a warm herb salad. The soy brine enriches the meat's flavor, while the natural sweetness of coconut milk and cream softly balances the soy. Together with lots of bright herbs and some fruit, you have a perfect salad for early spring or a gloomy wet fall.

Brine:

2 Tbsp granulated sugar

1 tsp white pepper

3 cups light soy sauce

3 cups tepid water

3 pounds pork cheeks

2 pandan leaves

2-3 pieces dried orange peel (see tip on page 54)

2-3 pods Thai cardamom

Braise:

3 cups Coconut Milk (page 205)

2-3 cups Coconut Cream (page 205)

2 Tbsp granulated sugar, plus extra to taste

¼ cup sliced galangal

6 Makrut lime leaves

3 stalks lemongrass, peeled

3 shallots

2-3 coriander roots or small handful of stems

2 Tbsp Fried Garlic (page 235), or to taste

For the Brine:

1. In a large bowl, dissolve the sugar and white pepper in the light soy sauce and water.

2. Add the pork cheeks, pandan leaves, orange peels, and Thai cardamom pods. Stir until the pork cheeks are evenly coated. Cover the bowl tightly with a lid or plastic wrap and refrigerate overnight.

For the Braise:

1. The next day, preheat the oven to 320°F. Wash the marinade off the pork cheeks under warm running water and drain well. In a 6- to 8-quart Dutch oven or large braising pot, cover the meat with the coconut milk and 2 cups of coconut cream, then add the sugar, galangal, Makrut lime leaves, lemongrass, shallots, and coriander. Cover with a lid and braise the meat in the oven until fork-tender, about 2 hours. Remove from the oven and allow the pork cheeks to cool in the braising liquid, about 30 minutes.

2. Once the pork cheeks have cooled, transfer them to a bowl, being careful not to break the meat apart. Strain the braising liquid through a sieve into a bowl, measure out 2 cups of braising liquid, and return it to the pot, storing the remaining braising liquid in the fridge.

3. Bring the braising liquid up to a boil over medium-high heat. Add more coconut cream if necessary to adjust the salt content; a rough estimate would be two parts braising liquid to one part cream. Season the sauce with sugar and fried garlic. It shouldn't be too thick and should taste salty and rich with little hints of sweet—subtle notes of garlic, pork, and soy should be apparent, but not dominant.

Recipe continued . . .

Finishing:

½ cup fresh coriander leaves

½ cup fresh mint leaves

¼ cup peeled and finely sliced lemongrass

2 Tbsp julienned Makrut lime leaves

1 cup fresh longans, peeled and deseeded

¼ cup Fried Shallots (page 235)

4-6 lime wedges, to garnish

5-6 toasted dried Thai bird's eye chilies, toasted, to garnish (optional)

For Finishing:

1. In a bowl, toss the coriander and mint together with the lemongrass and Makrut lime leaves. Add the longan and fried shallots at the last possible minute to prevent the latter from getting soggy.

2. Cut each pork cheek in half and allocate four to six halved cheeks per plate. Pour just enough sauce around the pork cheeks to cover the meat. Top with a loose pile of salad and garnish each serving with a lime wedge and toasted chilies.

Lobster Clay Pot

SERVES 4 • PREP TIME: 20 MINUTES • COOK TIME: 20 MINUTES

I MUST ADMIT THAT I WASN'T TOO CRAZY about this dish when I first had it in Thailand. The thought of farmed prawns with vermicelli wasn't appealing at all. On a more recent trip, however, we stopped for lunch by a riverside town near Ayutthaya to enjoy some wild river prawns. The quality of the prawns really made the dish and completely changed my mind. When I returned to Canada, I was playing around with wild spot prawns and lobster, and found that lobster's body meat really holds up nicely in this dish. To achieve rich crustacean aromas, you must bake this dish with the vermicelli; this process would cause prawns to overcook and become mushy. Lobster, on the other hand, has a much firmer texture that bakes well and provides a wonderful fragrance.

1 cup double chicken stock
(2 cups chicken stock reduced by half)

1 live lobster, about 1½-2 pounds

¼ cup coriander roots or stems

¼ cup garlic cloves

2 Tbsp roughly chopped ginger

½ pound pork jowl

¼ cup canola oil

2 Tbsp oyster sauce

1 Tbsp fish sauce

1 tsp dark soy sauce

1 tsp white pepper

2 cups presoaked vermicelli noodles (according to manufacturer's instructions)

¼ cup fresh coriander leaves (divided)

¼ cup sliced green onions (divided)

1 Tbsp Fried Garlic (page 235)

1. If using an oven, preheat to 400°F.

2. In a 4-quart pot, add the double chicken stock and simmer over medium heat to reduce by half.

3. Kill the lobster (page 19), remove the body meat, and cut the tail after you've dispatched the lobster by stabbing it through the head. Turn the lobster on its back to slice through its soft underside. Split the head in half, crack the claws and knuckles for ease of eating, and cut the tail into medallions instead of butterflying them. A 1½- to 2-pound lobster will give you four meaty 2-inch tail medallions—avoid slicing them any thinner than 2 inches or they'll overcook easily.

4. Using a mortar and pestle, pound the coriander, garlic, and ginger into a fine paste.

5. Using a sharp boning or paring knife, clean the pork jowl, ensuring it's free of glands and/or any extra stringy fat. Slice the pork jowl against the grain into thin bite-size pieces.

6. Preheat a clay pot on the stove over medium heat, then add the oil. When the oil is hot, cook the pork jowl for about 5 to 7 minutes, until the fat renders and the meat becomes crispy. Add the paste and toss until it becomes fragrant and light golden. Add the lobster pieces to sear and color them.

Recipe continued . . .

7. Deglaze the clay pot with the stock. Add the oyster sauce, fish sauce, dark soy sauce, and white pepper. Check that the stock is strongly seasoned before you add the vermicelli. Toss the vermicelli with the lobster to evenly mix through, place the head and claws on top for presentation, and sprinkle half of the coriander leaves and half of the green onions over the dish. Turn the heat up to high and ensure that the stock reaches a boil before covering with the lid. Bake in the oven for 8 minutes. If cooking on the stove, turn the heat to medium and cook with the lid on for 10 minutes.
8. Remove the clay pot from the oven, carefully removing the lid and making sure the stock is well absorbed. Gently toss the vermicelli one last time, taking care not to dislodge the head and claws too much, and finish on the stove for 1 minute over high heat to dry the base and make the vermicelli crispy. Finish with the remaining coriander leaves and green onions, and the fried garlic.

Southern-Style Stir-Fried Lamb

SERVES 4 • PREP TIME: 30 MINUTES • COOK TIME: 10 MINUTES

I TASTED THIS STANDOUT DISH on one of my first visits to the southern province of Krabi. Though lamb or mutton dishes aren't so common in Thai cooking, there are some excellent exceptions in the south, thanks to Muslim influences. I tried eight or nine variations at the restaurants in Krabi specializing in their regional cuisine and, upon returning home, created this recipe that captures the best aspects of each one. To me, this lamb stir-fry is quintessential southern Thai because of its intense spice level, sharpness from Makrut lime, pungency from shrimp paste, and fragrance from turmeric. Adjust the Thai bird's eye chilies accordingly, keeping in mind that the incredibly spicy heat really makes this dish. Though the lamb can be either sliced or minced, I personally prefer it sliced and then quickly wok-fried in hot oil to achieve a nice sear.

¼ cup canola or peanut oil

½ pound lamb loin or leg, sliced or minced

½ cup Kua Kling Curry Paste (page 203)

Fish sauce, to taste

Large pinch of finely julienned young galangal, plus extra to garnish

Large pinch of finely julienned Makrut lime leaves, plus extra to garnish

Large pinch of peeled and finely julienned fresh white turmeric (optional)

2-3 1-inch pieces of green peppercorn stalks

Pinch of finely julienned red Thai bird's eye chili, to garnish

Nahm Plah Prik (page 232)

1. Heat a wok over high heat until drops of water evaporate on contact. Add the oil to the hot wok and heat until shimmering. Add the lamb and sauté for 2 minutes to sear, breaking the lamb slices or mince apart while frying. Add the kua kling paste and continue stir-frying, being careful not to burn the paste. Once the paste becomes fragrant enough to produce a sneeze, season to taste with fish sauce. If the lamb is too dry, add a little water, but remember that the dish is not meant to be wet. Stir-fry for about a minute more, tossing in the galangal, Makrut lime leaves, white turmeric if available, and green peppercorn stalks.

2. Finish by garnishing with a little more galangal, Makrut lime leaves, and Thai bird's eye chili. The dish should be pungent, spicy, and salty. Serve immediately with nahm plah prik.

Southern-Style Dry Cumin Lamb Ribs

SERVES 4 • PREP TIME: 1 HOUR, 30 MINUTES • COOK TIME: 30 MINUTES

THESE RIBS ARE A CROSS BETWEEN a Muslim-style dish I had in the southern part of Thailand and the popular northern Chinese cumin lamb. Given that the Chinese version is also Muslim-inspired, I figure the two versions are probably spinoffs of the same original dish somewhere back in time.

Braised Lamb:

2 slabs baby lamb ribs

3 Tbsp coarse sea salt

1 onion

1 knob ginger

Cumin Spice Mix:

4 tsp cumin seeds

4 tsp coriander seeds

4 tsp green fennel seeds

4 bay leaves

3 tsp black peppercorns

3 tsp white peppercorns

1 tsp Thai cardamom pods

Frying:

4 quarts canola oil

2 sweet onions

1 red Anaheim pepper

1 yellow Anaheim pepper

2-3 Tbsp fish sauce, to taste

2 cups fresh coriander leaves (divided)

2 Tbsp sliced green onions, plus 1 Tbsp to garnish

2 Tbsp fried Thai baby garlic (see tip on page 235), to garnish

Few sprigs of fresh coriander, to garnish (optional)

For the Braised Lamb:

1. Using a sharp knife, cut between the lamb ribs and segment them into 14 or so individual bones, then rub them with salt. Roughly chop the onion and ginger. In a heavy 6-quart pot, add the lamb, onions, and ginger, and fill the pot with enough cold water to cover the ribs.

2. Bring the water to a boil over high heat, then reduce the heat to medium-low and simmer for about 45 minutes, until the meat is almost falling off the bone. Turn off the heat and let the ribs cool in the braising liquid for about 30 minutes.

For the Cumin Spice Mix:

1. Meanwhile, in a wok, toast all the spice mix ingredients over medium heat for 5 minutes, until fragrant, tossing to prevent them from burning. Using a mortar and pestle, pound the toasted spices into a spice-rub consistency. You want to preserve some of the original texture of the spices while breaking down the whole seeds. Almost all of the cumin spice mix will be used in this recipe; keep any extra in an airtight container in your pantry for up to 2 weeks.

For Frying:

1. In a deep fryer or large heavy pot over medium-high heat, preheat the canola oil to 350°F. Remove the lamb ribs from the braising liquid and pat them dry slightly with paper towel before placing them in the pot. Fry them in three batches until brown and slightly crispy, about 5 minutes each. Remove from the oil and transfer to a platter lined with paper towel to absorb excess oil. Reserve 3 tablespoons of the frying oil.

Recipe continued . . .

2. Cut the onions into wedges and the red and yellow peppers into ¼- to ½-inch strips. Preheat a wok over medium-high heat. Once hot, add the reserved lamb-frying oil and stir-fry the onions and peppers. When the onions are soft and translucent, season with fish sauce and add the lamb ribs. Toss with 1 cup of the coriander and the green onions, then season with 2 to 3 tablespoons of the spice mix. Check the seasoning and add more fish sauce to taste if required. The dish should taste salty and smoky with nutty flavors from the spice mix. Garnish with fried Thai baby garlic along with the coriander sprigs, green onions, and a sprinkle of the spice mix.

Stir-Fried Chanterelles and Baby Corn

SERVES 4 • PREP TIME: 10 MINUTES • COOK TIME: 5 MINUTES

THIS IS A QUICK DISH that focuses on the beauty of impeccably fresh ingredients. Fresh chanterelles and corn have long been a great match in many cuisines, and I've paired them together in this Thai flavor-profile dish. Avoid dried chanterelle mushrooms, as they'll release too much water once you rehydrate them. Using fresh baby corn is also key, as canned doesn't have the same flavor and texture.

½ pound fresh chanterelle mushrooms

¼ pound fresh baby corn (see tip)

2 stalks fresh green peppercorns

3 Tbsp canola oil

2 Tbsp Garlic-Chili Paste (page 142)

4-6 Tbsp fish sauce

Small pinch of granulated sugar

Small pinch of white pepper

½ cup fresh Thai basil leaves

1 Tbsp julienned ginger

1 Tbsp julienned grachai

1. Clean the mushrooms with a dry brush to remove any dirt stuck between their gills. If the cap is really dirty, use a slightly dampened dish towel to wipe off the dirt. Do not wash under water. Keep the mushrooms whole if they're small, and tear the larger ones in half. Cut the baby corn in half lengthwise down the middle.

2. Preheat a wok to medium heat, add the oil, then add the mushrooms, green peppercorns, corn, and garlic-chili paste and stir-fry together for 2 to 3 minutes. Season with fish sauce, sugar, and white pepper. Finish by folding in the Thai basil, ginger, and grachai. The dish should have a mild taste with a hint of richness from the Thai basil, but not too much as it will overpower the delicate mushrooms.

æ Fresh baby corn is now readily available in most specialty Asian stores and some specialty grocers. If canned is your only option, try to find brands that are minimally preserved by reading the ingredient list, and rinse them under cold running water for at least 30 minutes to release the brine flavor.

Recipe pictured on page 134.

Stir-Fried Green Eggplant with Pork Jowl

SERVES 4 • PREP TIME: 15 MINUTES • COOK TIME: 10 MINUTES

THAI LONG GREEN EGGPLANT is one of my favorite vegetables. Its sturdy texture is far better suited for high-heat cooking versus its more delicate Japanese cousin, allowing the eggplant to absorb the flavors of this simple dish that are built on the pork jowl rendering in the wok. The aromas of the lard and soybean paste are the perfect accent!

2 cups canola oil

1 pound pork jowl

½ cup cornstarch

1 cup water

2 garlic cloves

1 red Thai bird's eye chili

2 coriander roots, roughly chopped

1 Thai long green eggplant

½ cup soybean paste

1 Tbsp fish sauce

1 tsp granulated sugar (optional)

½ cup fresh Thai basil leaves

2 Tbsp Fried Garlic (page 235)

1. In a wok over high heat, preheat the oil to 350°F.

2. Clean the pork jowl with a sharp boning or paring knife, ensuring it's free of glands and/or any extra stringy fat.

3. In a medium-size bowl, whisk the cornstarch and water together until the slurry is the consistency of thick cream. Dredge the pork jowl in the slurry until it's completely coated, and drain off the excess slurry.

4. Gently lower the pork into the hot wok and cook for 7 minutes. Turn the pork jowl and cook for an additional 4 to 5 minutes, until fully cooked and the exterior is golden brown and crispy. Remove from the oil and transfer to a plate lined with paper towel to absorb the excess oil. Let the pork jowl cool slightly. Reserve the oil in the wok for frying the eggplant.

5. Meanwhile, using a mortar and pestle, pound the garlic, chili, and coriander roots together into a smooth paste. Set aside.

6. Once the pork jowl is cooled, slice it into ½-inch pieces against the grain. Cut the eggplant into 2-inch sections and split each into four pieces to get 2-inch-long sticks.

7. In the same wok, heat the oil over high heat until it's smoking hot. Add the eggplant and fry for about 3 minutes, until lightly browned. Turn off the heat and transfer the eggplant to a bowl with a slotted spoon or spider.

8. Drain the canola oil, keeping about 2 tablespoons in the wok. Bring the oil temperature back up over high heat. Return the pork jowl to the wok and cook for 5 to 7 minutes, until golden and crispy, monitoring to ensure the pork renders nicely without burning. Add the paste and toss until the pork jowl is fully coated. Cook until the paste is golden in color and fragrant. Add the pre-fried eggplant, taking great care not to burn the paste. Season with soybean paste and fish sauce, and sugar if needed. Add a tablespoon of water to help steam the eggplant. Don't overcook it; the eggplant should be firm to the touch but soft to bite.

9. To finish the dish, fold in the Thai basil leaves and fried garlic. Serve immediately.

Stir-Fried Black-Pepper Spot Prawns

SERVES 4 • PREP TIME: 5 MINUTES • COOK TIME: 10 MINUTES

SPOT PRAWNS ARE ONE OF MY FAVORITE DELICACIES from our local waters. Normally, I don't enjoy them cooked, but stir-frying them with a light cornstarch slurry protects them from overcooking. This recipe also works well with sidestripe prawns because they're small and delicious when eaten whole without peeling. Sustainably farmed white prawns are okay as well; if you're like me and enjoy eating the shells, make sure the prawns are small enough so the shells are thin and palatable.

4 quarts canola oil

2 cups cornstarch

1 cup water

2 Tbsp black pepper

2 Tbsp plus 1 tsp coarse sea salt (divided)

1 pound live BC spot prawns, or prawns of your choice

3 cloves garlic

2 red Thai bird's eye chilies

2 coriander roots, roughly chopped

3 Tbsp vegetable oil

2 Tbsp fish sauce

Pinch of white and black pepper

¼ cup fresh coriander leaves

¼ cup finely sliced green onions

1. In a deep fryer or a 6- to 8-quart Dutch oven over medium-high heat, preheat the canola oil to 350°F.

2. In a large mixing bowl, whisk the cornstarch and water together to form a slurry. Add the pepper and 2 tablespoons of salt, and keep whisking together until the slurry is the consistency of thick cream.

3. Dredge the prawns in the slurry until evenly coated, then carefully lower them into the hot oil and deep-fry for 2 to 3 minutes, until golden brown and crispy. It's important not to overcook the prawns, as they become mushy. Carefully remove them from the oil and transfer to a rack with paper towel beneath it to absorb excess oil.

4. Using a mortar and pestle, pound the garlic, chilies, and coriander roots together until they form a fine paste, using the salt as an abrasive. Preheat a wok over high heat, add the vegetable oil, and fry the paste until it becomes golden and aromatic. Add the crispy prawns along with the fish sauce and white and black pepper. Fold in the coriander and green onions, remove from heat, and toss all ingredients together thoroughly. Serve immediately.

Stir-Fried Clams with Ginger and Thai Basil

SERVES 4 TO 6 • PREP TIME: 10 MINUTES, PLUS SOAKING • COOK TIME: 5 MINUTES

2 pounds clams

¼ cup coarse sea salt, plus a pinch

2 stalks lemongrass, peeled

3 cloves garlic

2 coriander roots, roughly chopped

2 red Thai bird's eye chilies

¼ cup canola or peanut oil

¼ cup Makrut lime leaves

¼ cup chicken stock

Pinch of white pepper, or to taste

2 Tbsp fish sauce, or to taste

1 cup fresh Thai basil leaves

½ cup fresh coriander leaves

3 Tbsp julienned ginger

½ cup Seafood Nahm Jim (page 132)

1. Clean the clams by soaking them in a large bowl with sea salt under cold running water for at least 45 minutes; using running versus still water ensures that the clams have enough oxygen to stay alive. This also enables the clams to purge any sand and grit. Remove the clams from the bowl by hand, starting from the top down. Do not pour the clams into another bowl or simply pour out the water, as this retains all the sand that has settled to the bottom of the bowl.

2. Wash the lemongrass stalks and remove the upper green stems. Slice the lighter-colored ends into 2- to 3-inch pieces. Using a mortar and pestle, bruise the lemongrass pieces and set aside. Add the garlic, coriander roots, and chilies to the mortar along with a pinch of salt, and pound into a coarse paste.

3. Preheat the oil in a wok over high heat, then add the paste and fry for 1 minute. Once the paste is aromatic, add the clams, bruised lemongrass, and Makrut lime leaves. Stir-fry for 30 seconds, then add the stock, white pepper, and fish sauce. Cook for about 5 minutes, until the clams open. If any clams remain closed after 5 to 6 minutes of cooking, discard them. Taste to check the seasoning and adjust with fish sauce and white pepper if desired.

4. To finish the dish, remove from heat and stir in the Thai basil, coriander leaves, and ginger. Serve with seafood nahm jim (and, if you're so inclined, a cold beer).

Grilled Sea Bass with Salt Crust

SERVES 2 TO 4 • PREP TIME: 30 MINUTES • COOK TIME: 15 MINUTES

A VERY COMMON SIGHT in Thailand's markets is whole fish grilled over charcoal with a salt crust. The charcoal's aroma perfumes the delicate fish while the salt crust preserves its moisture. I really like using sea bass or sea bream and the trick is to stuff the cavity with lemongrass and any aromatics/herbs you might have lying around to help cook the fish evenly. Once cooked, the salt crust peels right off with the skin, exposing the wonderfully moist and silky flesh. This pairs perfectly with Seafood Nahm Jim (page 132), the standard Thai accompaniment for this dish.

1 whole 2-pound Mediterranean sea bass or sea bream (see tip)

3-4 stalks lemongrass, peeled

2 sprigs fresh dill

2 sprigs fresh Thai basil

1 cup egg whites, plus 1 Tbsp as needed

½ cup coarse sea salt or kosher salt

Handful of fresh coriander leaves, to garnish (optional)

1 cup Seafood Nahm Jim (page 132)

1. Prepare a charcoal grill to medium heat 25 to 40 minutes prior to grilling (both a gas grill or grill pan on the stove at medium-high heat also work but are not preferred). Spread out the charcoal to achieve an even medium heat for the fish.

2. Under running water, wash the inside of the fish's body cavity to remove any blood, and ensure that all remnants of the gills have been removed. Dry the fish thoroughly with paper towel; the salt crust will stick better when the fish skin is completely dry.

3. Using only the tops of the lemongrass, cut the stalks into 6- to 8-inch lengths. Bunch them together with the dill and Thai basil, and stuff the herbs down through the fish's mouth, pushing all the way back until the stomach cavity is filled.

4. In a medium mixing bowl, lightly whisk the egg whites until the strands are loosely broken apart. Don't overwhisk them, as this will cause the salt crust to expand too much during grilling. Lightly whisk in the salt until you achieve a wet slurry texture. If the mixture resembles wet sand instead, add another tablespoon of egg white and continue to incorporate until a paintable consistency is achieved.

5. Using a pastry brush, brush a thin layer of salt crust evenly over the top and bottom of the fish, no more than ⅛-inch thick. Place the fish on the grill immediately after coating. Grill the fish for about 7 minutes on each side, until the stomach cavity is cooked through and shows no signs of pink. Transfer to a platter and serve immediately with seafood nahm jim.

6. To serve, use a knife to carefully cut open the fish from the top along the dorsal fins, peel back the salt crust with the skin attached, and expose the meat. Top with fresh coriander if desired and serve with seafood nahm jim. Enjoy!

ðɛ When buying the fish, ask your fishmonger to gut and scale it for you.

Stir-Fried Sidestripe Prawns with Fennel Salad

SERVES 4 • PREP TIME: 30 MINUTES • COOK TIME: 20 MINUTES

SIDESTRIPE PRAWNS ARE FOUND on the Pacific Northwest coast from Oregon all the way up to Alaska, and their smallish size is perfect for this delicious and simple dish, which I love. Sidestripes are typically sold frozen in sea water without their heads. If you can't source these tasty gems, I suggest using ethically farmed white prawns from the United States. As long as the prawns are the size of your pinky, you can fry them with the shell on and eat it too—no peeling needed!

1 pound frozen sidestripe prawns

8-12 cups canola or peanut oil

1 cup cornstarch

2 cups water

1 Tbsp plus 2 tsp coarse sea salt (divided)

1½ tsp plus pinch of black pepper (divided)

1 small- to medium-size bulb organic fennel

2 Tbsp extra virgin olive oil

1 Tbsp lemon juice

½ cup Eight-Spice Sauce (page 141)

¼ cup fried Thai baby garlic or garlic cloves (page 235)

1. Thaw the frozen prawns by running cold water over them.

2. In a deep fryer or a 6- to 8-quart Dutch oven over medium-high heat, preheat the oil to 350°F.

3. In a large mixing bowl, use a whisk or your hands to mix together the cornstarch, water, 1 tablespoon salt, and 1 teaspoon pepper for the slurry. The slurry should be the consistency of thick cream so that it coats the prawn shells evenly.

4. Prepare a bowl of ice water. Slice the fennel bulb in half, keeping the fronds for garnish. Using a Japanese mandoline, slice the fennel paper-thin and place in the water.

5. Rewhisk the cornstarch slurry to recombine the settlements, and coat the prawns with the slurry. Fry the prawns in batches for 2 to 3 minutes per batch, until they are light and crispy. Remove the prawns from the oil and transfer to a plate lined with paper towel to absorb excess oil.

6. In a medium-size mixing bowl, toss the sliced fennel with the olive oil, lemon juice, 1 teaspoon salt, and ½ teaspoon pepper.

7. Preheat a wok over medium-high heat and stir-fry the fried prawns together with the eight-spice sauce, remaining 1 teaspoon salt, pinch of pepper, and fried garlic. Transfer to a bowl and serve with the dressed fennel and fennel fronds on top.

Curries

Opposite page: Massaman Curry of Braised Lamb Shank (page 177).

Introduction

STARTING OFF WITH A GOOD CURRY PASTE is the first secret to building a killer curry. Lots of people resort to using store-bought canned mixes or pastes, which are often too hot to eat on their own because the chilies aren't deseeded. But if you carve out a bit of extra time to make your own, it's easier to control the flavoring and you achieve a tastier result. All you need are a few key ingredients: lemongrass, galangal, shallots, coriander roots, and chilies. Choose large red chilies and remove the seeds—this allows you to use the chilies for color and aroma rather than spice. And the techniques to making each of the pastes (page 204), as you'll see, are very similar.

Secret number two for excellent curry is making Cracked Coconut Cream (page 206). When you add it to your curry paste, the separated coconut milk solids soften the paste without any added moisture, allowing it to fry more evenly. Making cracked coconut cream is a simple process of evaporating the water from canned or fresh coconut cream until the fat separates from the milk solids. It's worth it.

What not to do: fry the curry paste using canola oil only. The oil sears the outside of the paste like a puck, and you'll need way too much oil to soften it up. Most curries benefit greatly from being caramelized before frying, with only a couple of exceptions, like the Geng Gati Curry of Lobster and Smoked Sablefish (page 199), which is gently simmered in the coconut cream as its aromatics are much more delicate. In contrast, a curry like Panaeng Curry of Braised Beef Rib (page 179), that's meant to be rich, really benefits from frying and developing the flavor of the curry paste with cracked coconut cream.

As mentioned, always trust your senses when cooking. Undercooked curries are bitter and flavorless, so be sure to observe the curry paste's many stages of color and smell. As you cook it, the color will darken and the smell will develop in the pan. As evaporation continues, you should be able to smell the transition of raw ingredients such as garlic and shallots, drier ingredients like lemongrass and galangal, followed by any of the dry spices that may be present in the recipe as they get closer to the desired aromas through the cooking process. These are good signs that you're frying the curry paste properly.

Massaman Curry of Braised Lamb Shank

SERVES 4 • PREP TIME: 1 HOUR, 30 MINUTES • COOK TIME: 1 HOUR

MASSAMAN CURRY IS ONE OF THE WORLD'S most recognizable Thai curries, widely loved for its richness, nutty flavors, and fragrant dry spices such as cassia bark, cumin, and nutmeg. It's often served with beef in Thailand, and I've also had southern versions with goat. However, I prefer to use braised lamb shank because of its more delicate flavor. Lamb shank takes much longer to cook than smaller chunks of meat, so it's braised in a lighter stock perfumed with aromatics, as opposed to a thicker curry that would break down over the extended simmering process. I braise the lamb separately from the curry, then fry it after braising to help the meat hold up and absorb more flavor while it's cooking with the curry. And I always add the braising liquid back into the curry to enhance its richness—definitely a game changer!

4 lamb shanks, about 1 pound each

8 cups chicken stock or Master Stock (page 61)

2-3 pandan leaves

2 cups Massaman Curry Paste (page 202), plus handful of its spices for braising (see tip)

4 quarts canola oil

1 cup Cracked Coconut Cream (page 206)

¼ cup palm sugar

1 cup Coconut Milk (page 205)

1 cup Coconut Cream (page 205)

½ cup fish sauce

3 Tbsp Tamarind Water (page 233)

¼ cup diced potato, cut into 1-inch cubes

¼ cup pearl onions, blanched

¼ cup diced pineapple chunks

Handful of roasted peanuts, skinned, to garnish

Fried Shallots (page 235), to garnish

1. In a large 6- to 8-quart Dutch oven or heavy stockpot, cover the lamb shanks with water and bring to a boil over high heat. Remove the meat and rinse off any coagulated fat under warm running water.

2. Place the lamb shanks back into a clean 6- to 8-quart Dutch oven or heavy pot and cover with stock. Add the pandan leaves and a handful of the same spices used in the Massaman Curry Paste (page 202) to echo the flavors of the curry. Turn the heat to low and braise on the stove at a gentle simmer for 2 hours, until the meat is fork-tender. Once cooked, remove from the heat and allow the lamb shanks to cool in the braising liquid for 30 minutes. Remove the lamb shanks from the stock and place them on a baking sheet lined with paper towel to dry before frying. Reserve the braising liquid.

3. In a deep fryer or a 6- to 8-quart Dutch oven over high heat, preheat the canola oil to 350°F. Fry the lamb shanks two at a time for about 4 to 5 minutes per batch, until they develop a golden-brown crust. The crust will absorb the curry while preventing the lamb shanks from falling apart. Remove the lamb shanks from the hot oil and transfer them to a rack with paper towel beneath it to absorb excess oil. Dry the lamb shanks thoroughly with paper towel to prevent splattering when you add them to the curry.

4. In a large frying pan over medium heat, fry the massaman curry paste and cracked coconut cream until aromatic and blended. Stir in the palm sugar along with 1 cup of braising liquid, coconut milk, and coconut cream to slightly thin out the curry. Turn the heat down to medium-low and cook for 15 minutes. Season to taste with fish sauce and tamarind water. The finished curry should taste salty, sweet, and rich.

Recipe continued . . .

5. Add the potatoes and pearl onions to the pan and cook until the potatoes are soft. Add the fried lamb shanks to the curry and stir to coat evenly with the curry. Simmer for 5 minutes, basting constantly with the curry so that the meat doesn't dry out. Finish with the pineapple chunks before transferring to a serving dish. Garnish with the roasted peanuts and fried shallots.

æ When braising in simple stock, it's nice to add basic aromatics like lemongrass trim and a couple of pieces of galangal to the braising liquid, ingredients that are either already in the recipe or have similar flavor characteristics. After trimming lemongrass for the curry paste, don't throw it away. The dry ends still have a bit of flavor, so braise with them. When you're measuring galangal for the recipe, you may have a couple of pieces left over; just throw them into the pot. And Asians believe that ginger has a strong capacity to offset gaminess, so that's a great ingredient to add even though it's not in the curry paste. Don't add a bunch of dried spices like cumin—stick to fresh aromatics instead.

Recipe pictured on page 174.

Panaeng Curry of Braised Beef Rib

SERVES 4 • PREP TIME: 2 HOURS • COOK TIME: 2 HOURS

PANAENG CURRY IS POPULAR because of its richness and delicious aromas from the peanuts in the curry paste. The texture of the curry is supposed to be quite luxurious. In practice, it's usually a personal preference; some people like their panaeng curry to be quite thick, while others prefer it more runny. I like to keep it thicker to give it more body. You can adjust the thickness as desired using chicken stock before and after the simmering process. I always add more stock than needed at the outset and let it simmer out.

Curry:

2 cups Panaeng Curry Paste (page 206)

1 cup Cracked Coconut Cream (page 206)

½ cup palm sugar

¼ cup fish sauce, or to taste

2 Tbsp Tamarind Water (page 233)

½ cup Coconut Cream (page 205)

1 cup Coconut Milk (page 205)

½-1 cup chicken stock or Master Stock (as needed)

For the Curry:

1. In a Dutch oven or braising pot over medium-high heat, fry the panaeng paste with the cracked coconut cream for 10 to 15 minutes. Season with palm sugar, fish sauce, and tamarind water; the curry should taste sweet and salty.

2. Thin out the curry with the coconut cream and coconut milk, then add ½ cup of the stock. Simmer for about 10 to 15 minutes, until the oil separates from the curry. If the curry has become too thick after simmering, add more stock as needed.

Ribs:

2 pounds bone-in beef short ribs

2 Tbsp fish sauce

6 shallots, unpeeled

3-4 red and/or chili peppers, roll-cut and deseeded

2 Tbsp finely julienned Makrut lime leaves

½ cup fresh Thai basil leaves

Coconut Cream (page 205), to garnish

Fried Shallots (page 235), to garnish

Fried Garlic (page 235), to garnish

Fried Thai Basil (page 235), to garnish

For the Ribs:

1. Prepare a charcoal grill to glowing-red high heat 25 to 40 minutes prior to grilling (both a gas grill or grill pan on the stove at medium-high heat also work but are not preferred).

2. When the grill is close to the desired temperature, preheat the oven to 350°F.

3. In a bowl, marinate the short ribs in the fish sauce for 5 minutes.

4. Grill the short ribs; if using a grill pan on the stove, turn the heat down to medium. Grill on all sides until charred evenly, about 3 to 5 minutes per side depending on the size of the ribs.

5. Transfer the ribs to a Dutch oven and cover them with the curry. Place in the oven and braise for about 2 hours, or until the ribs are fork-tender. Remove from the oven and allow the ribs to cool in the curry.

Recipe continued . . .

6. Meanwhile, grill (or roast) the shallots on all sides for about 15 to 20 minutes, until the tops ooze with juice and the skins are charred on the outside. If their centers are still firm to the touch, place the warm shallots in a bowl and cover them with plastic wrap to let them steam through. Peel the shallots once they're soft throughout. If you wait until the roasted shallots cool off, the charred skin tends to stick to the flesh and it'll be more difficult and messier to peel them.

7. Return the Dutch oven to the stove over medium heat. Add the shallots to the curry along with the chilies and Makrut lime leaves. Cook for another 5 to 10 minutes, until you start seeing the coconut fat separating from the curry, and finish with Thai basil. Transfer to a serving dish, drizzle in the coconut cream, and garnish with fried shallots, fried garlic, and fried Thai basil. This curry should taste sweet, salty, smoky, and rich.

æ From time to time, I like cooking the beef short ribs sous-vide for this recipe as pictured here. You'll need a vacuum sealer, water bath, and immersion circulator for home use. When packing the short ribs into the plastic bag, I like to cover the bones with some extra plastic wrap so the sharp bones don't puncture the bag during cooking. In the bag, season the beef with 2 to 3 tablespoons fish sauce and a pinch of white pepper. Seal the bag at 100% vacuum, and cook the ribs at 140°F for 48 hours. After the ribs are done, you can sear them on a charcoal grill or grill pan and finish in the curry. The end result is fork-tender meat that is much juicier and has a steak-like texture.

Southern-Style Curry Custard with Sea Urchin

SERVES 4 • PREP TIME: 30 MINUTES • COOK TIME: 15 MINUTES

HOR MOK IS A CURRY-BASED steamed custard. I especially like this recipe because I wanted something to serve with the delicate texture of sea urchin. This is a play on scallop hor mok with the *geng gati* curry paste; however, for this dish, I like to strain the curry and get rid of the extra fibers. As a result, it becomes lighter and fluffier in texture, thus differentiating the two dishes. Lovely and subtle, it works very well with the delicate sea urchin or any other lightly flavored shellfish.

2 cups Geng Gati Curry Paste (page 203)

2 eggs

8 sidestripe prawns or small ethically farmed shrimp, peeled

¼ cup cubed black cod

½ cup fresh sea urchin roe, to garnish

¼ cup Dungeness crabmeat, to garnish

2 Tbsp freshly grated young coconut meat, to garnish

2 Tbsp Coconut Cream (page 205), to garnish

1 Tbsp finely julienned Makrut lime leaves, to garnish

Handful of fresh coriander leaves, to garnish

1 Tbsp deseeded and julienned red chili pepper (optional)

1. Pass the geng gati curry paste through a fine sieve into a mixing bowl, and lightly whisk in the eggs. Be careful not to incorporate too much air when whisking, or the custard will expand during cooking and collapse once removed from the steamer due to steam build-up. You're whisking to stir the mixture rather than beating the eggs to aerate them and increase volume. Pour the mixture into a medium-size soup bowl, then add the peeled prawns and the cod.

2. Cook in a steamer (see tip on page 197) for 12 minutes, or until the center is just firm to the touch.

3. Remove the custard from the steamer and garnish with the sea urchin roe, crabmeat, young coconut meat, coconut cream, and Makrut lime leaves. Finish with coriander leaves and red chili peppers. Serve immediately.

Dry Curry of Seared Albacore Tuna

SERVES 4 • PREP TIME: 20 MINUTES • COOK TIME: 20 MINUTES

CHU CHI PLAH IS A VERY POPULAR stir-fry with central Thai street vendors, who usually serve it with catfish. Though this is not a creamy dish, the dry, oily curry's richness gives a hearty boost to the catfish's delicate flavor. I enjoy serving this dish with lightly grilled fish—albacore tuna in this case.

3 Tbsp Coconut Cream (page 205)

7 Tbsp fish sauce (divided)

Pinch of white pepper

½ pound albacore tuna

½ cup Chu Chi Curry Paste (page 202)

¼ cup Cracked Coconut Cream (page 206)

¼ cup palm sugar

1 tsp tamarind paste

Large handful of Makrut lime leaves, finely julienned

Handful of fresh coriander leaves, to garnish

Small pinch of julienned chili pepper, to garnish

1. In a medium-size bowl, mix the coconut cream with 3 tablespoons of the fish sauce and a pinch of white pepper. Add the tuna and turn it over until it's evenly coated. Marinate the tuna for 15 minutes.

2. In a large frying pan over medium heat, stir together the chu chi curry paste and cracked coconut cream until well combined. Fry until the curry becomes dark, rich, and fragrant. Stir in the palm sugar. As the sugar melts, the curry will darken to a dark burgundy color. Once the sugar has melted, add the remaining fish sauce and tamarind paste. The curry should be quite sweet at the initial taste, and salty on the finish. Turn off the heat and let the curry sit at room temperature.

3. About an hour before you're ready to cook, prepare a charcoal grill to high heat (a grill pan on the stove over high heat also works but is not preferred). Cook the tuna for 1 minute per side, until the exterior is well seared while the inside remains rare. Transfer the tuna to a plate and let it rest for 5 minutes. Bring the curry back up to temperature on the stove over medium heat before serving.

4. Using a sharp knife, slice the tuna into ¼-inch-thick pieces. Spoon the curry onto a serving dish and fan the tuna slices over the curry. Sprinkle liberally with Makrut lime leaves and garnish with coriander and julienned chili. The freshness of the Makrut lime leaves should come through and balance the rich curry.

æ If you prefer fried fish, choose boneless white fish such as halibut or lingcod. Slice it into chunks, coat it in a cornstarch slurry, and fry until crispy. Then toss the fish into a hot wok with the finished curry, and the result will be equally delicious.

Green Curry of Halibut

SERVES 4 TO 6 • PREP TIME: 30 MINUTES • COOK TIME: 15 MINUTES

GREEN CURRY IS PERHAPS one of my favorite curries. I love its fragrance of Makrut lime and fresh turmeric, as I'm not fond of curries that are overly sweet and/or creamy. This particular recipe is special to me because it was on Maenam's opening menu in 2009. It was a tricky time during the recession—we were carrying over lots of debt from our previous restaurant, Gastropod—so my friend Jenice, who provides us seafood to this day, offered to sell halibut cheeks at her low supplier cost to help us turn our restaurant around. It's such a beautiful piece of fish to work with, and I actually prefer halibut cheeks over the meat itself. As clichéd as it might sound, halibut cheeks taste like chicken, but with a much firmer, meatier texture and flavor.

½ pound halibut, preferably cheeks

1 cup Green Curry Paste (page 202)

½ cup Cracked Coconut Cream (page 206)

1 cup Coconut Milk (page 205), or to taste

2 cups chicken stock or Master Stock (page 61), or to taste

¼ cup fish sauce, plus extra to taste

1 tsp palm sugar

½ cup sliced fresh hearts of palm or bamboo

¼ cup sliced apple eggplants and/ or whole pea eggplants

½ cup cut fresh baby corn

6-8 Makrut lime leaves

1 tsp white pepper

½ cup fresh Thai basil leaves

½ cup fresh holy basil leaves

1 Tbsp shredded grachai

1 Tbsp finely julienned Makrut lime leaves

1. Preheat a Dutch oven or braising pot over medium heat. Meanwhile, cut the halibut meat into 2-inch chunks and set aside. Fry the green curry paste with the cracked coconut cream until fragrant, about 5 to 6 minutes. Add the coconut milk and stock; you may need more stock depending on how spicy the curry paste is. Season with the fish sauce and palm sugar.

2. Add the fish, hearts of palm, eggplants, baby corn, and Makrut lime leaves. Continue simmering over medium heat until the fish is cooked and becomes opaque and firm to the touch, about 3 to 4 minutes. Season with the white pepper and more fish sauce if needed. Lastly, stir in the Thai basil, holy basil, grachai, and Makrut lime leaves and check the seasoning. It should taste quite hot and salty, but not be too thick.

æ Although we season curry before adding the liquid, it's crucial not to overseason initially, and to taste-test it again when the curry consistency is closer to the desired serving consistency. Because of water evaporation, you may need to adjust accordingly.

Red Curry of Braised Duck

SERVES 4 • PREP TIME: 1 HOUR • COOK TIME: 1 HOUR, 30 MINUTES

Duck:

2 duck legs

3 Makrut lime leaves

2 shallots

1 stalk lemongrass, peeled

2 Tbsp galangal trim

8 cups Coconut Milk (page 205)

1 cup Coconut Cream (page 205)

Curry:

1½ cups Red Curry Paste (page 203)

1 cup Cracked Coconut Cream
(page 206)

¼ cup palm sugar

¼ cup Tamarind Water (page 233)

¼ cup fish sauce

6 cherry tomatoes, halved

6-10 lychees, peeled and pitted

1 cup loosely packed fresh
Thai basil leaves

2 stalks fresh green peppercorns

⅛ cup finely julienned Makrut
lime leaves

Zest of 1 Makrut lime

For the Duck:

1. Place the duck legs and aromatics in a heavy 4-quart pot and cover completely with the coconut cream and coconut milk. Bring to a boil over medium-high heat, then turn down the heat to a low simmer. Braise until tender, about 1 hour to 1 hour and 20 minutes, then remove the duck legs to a bowl and reserve 2 cups of the braising liquid for the curry. Refrigerate or freeze the remaining liquid for future use; it will keep for 1 week in the fridge and 2 months in the freezer.

For the Curry:

1. Preheat a wok over medium heat. Fry the red curry paste in the cracked coconut cream until the mixture becomes aromatic. Season with palm sugar, tamarind water, and fish sauce. Add the reserved 2 cups braising liquid. Stir in the cherry tomatoes along with the braised duck legs and cook for 5 minutes. The curry should be neither too thick nor too thin, and should taste slightly hot, sour, and sweet.

2. Stir in the lychees, basil, fresh green peppercorns, and Makrut lime leaves. Transfer to a serving platter and grate a bit of Makrut lime zest over the dish to finish.

Geng Gari Roast Chicken

SERVES 4 TO 6 • PREP TIME: 2 HOURS • COOK TIME: 1 HOUR

GENG GARI IS ONE OF THE OLDEST STYLES of Thai curries. *Gari* denotes an Indian-influenced dish and is a derivative of the Indian word "curry." I love making the dish with poultry—pheasant, duck, chicken, and even turkey. Roasting the bird beforehand really enhances its savory character, and this is a fantastic dish for using up leftover holiday turkey! In this recipe, we're using the chicken from the Northern-Style Grilled Hen (page 50). You can either grill the chicken or follow the same recipe and roast it in the oven for this application.

1 large sweet onion, unpeeled

1 Russet potato, unpeeled

3 cups duck fat

½ recipe Northern-Style Grilled Hen (page 50)

2 cups Geng Gari Curry Paste (page 203)

2 cups Cracked Coconut Cream (page 206)

3 Tbsp palm sugar, or to taste

½ cup fish sauce, or to taste

1 cup Coconut Cream (page 205)

1 cup Coconut Milk (page 205)

1 cup chicken stock or Master Stock (page 61)

¼ cup Fried Shallots (page 235)

2 tsp Tamarind Water (page 233), or to taste

10 fresh longans, peeled and deseeded, to garnish

1 Tbsp fried Thai baby garlic (see tip on page 235), to garnish

1 Tbsp Fried Garlic Oil (page 235), to garnish

1. Preheat the oven to 350°F and adjust the racks to fit two roasting pans.

2. Place the sweet onion in a roasting pan, and roast in the oven until the top oozes with juice and the onion is soft to the touch, about 1 hour and 30 minutes.

3. Meanwhile, cut the potato into thick pieces, place them in the other roasting pan along with the duck fat, and confit them in the oven for 45 minutes. You should be able to pierce them easily with a fork but they shouldn't be falling apart; bear in mind that the potatoes still have additional cooking time in the curry. Remove from the oven and set aside.

4. When the onion is ready, remove it from the oven and let cool. Once it's cool to the touch, peel off the skin and cut it into wedges.

5. Slow roast one chicken from the Northern-Style Grilled Hen recipe (page 50) in the oven for about 1 hour, until tender; the breasts should be firm to the touch and the juices should run clear when you pierce the skin between the drumstick and the thigh. Remove it from the oven to cool before deboning it, saving the bones for chicken stock. If you prefer to serve bone-in chicken, cut it into quarters and then small wedges.

6. In a frying pan over medium heat, fry the geng gari curry paste with the cracked coconut cream for about 10 to 15 minutes. When the curry paste is properly fried, you'll be able to smell aromas of the dry spices in the paste, such as coriander seeds. Mix in the palm sugar and fish sauce until thoroughly incorporated. While stirring constantly, slowly add the coconut cream to thin out the curry. Continuing to stir, add the coconut milk and stock. Add the chicken and simmer in the curry for 5 to 10 minutes, until you can see the coconut oil glisten as it begins to separate from the curry.

Recipe continued . . .

7. Add the roasted potatoes and onions, along with the fried shallots. Taste the curry and season to your liking with more palm sugar, fish sauce, and tamarind water; it should be salty first and not too sweet. The tamarind is there merely to balance the curry and shouldn't be detectable at all. Transfer to a serving dish and garnish with longans, fried Thai baby garlic, and fried garlic oil.

æ Confiting the potatoes in duck fat adds another layer of richness and prevents them from breaking down in the curry.

Geng Gola of Grilled Duck

SERVES 4 • PREP TIME: 1 HOUR, PLUS OVERNIGHT REFRIGERATION AND RESTING • COOK TIME: 45 MINUTES

Marinade:

6 cloves garlic

2 shallots

3 Tbsp grated ginger

2 tsp coarse sea salt

1 coriander root, roughly chopped

1 tsp white pepper

½ cup Coconut Cream (page 205)

1 duck crown (legs and backbone removed)

For the Marinade:

1. Using a mortar and pestle, pound the garlic, shallots, ginger, salt, coriander, and white pepper into a fine paste, then fold in the cream.

2. Rub both the outside of the duck and the inside of the body cavity with the marinade, place in a bowl, cover with plastic wrap, and let sit in the fridge overnight.

Curry:

2 cups Geng Gola Curry Paste (page 203)

2 cups Cracked Coconut Cream (page 206)

½ cup fish sauce

¼ cup palm sugar

1 Tbsp Tamarind Water (page 233)

For the Curry:

1. In a large frying pan over medium heat, stir together the geng gola curry paste and the cracked coconut cream until thoroughly incorporated. Fry for about 10 to 15 minutes, until fragrant. Season with fish sauce, palm sugar, and tamarind water. This is a dry-style curry that does not need to be thinned out; it should taste salty, sweet, and rich.

2. Rub some of the cooked curry onto the duck, both bone side and skin side, and let it rest for 45 minutes on the countertop to come to room temperature. Meanwhile, prepare a charcoal grill to medium heat 25 to 40 minutes prior to grilling (both a gas grill or grill pan on the stove at medium-high heat also work but are not preferred).

3. Place the duck on the grill, bone side down, and grill for 5 minutes before moving it to the coolest part of the grill. Flip the duck over and cook it slowly, skin-side down, for about 30 minutes to render the fat, being careful to prevent the fat drippings from catching fire and burning. Baste the duck halfway through, then finish it off on the bone side for about 2 to 3 minutes over the warmer part of the grill. The duck skin should be crispy and not burned, and the inside of the duck crown should appear cooked; if probed with a meat thermometer, it should read between 130°F to 135°F. Let the meat rest for 10 minutes before carving.

Recipe continued . . .

Serving:

1-2 eggs

½ cup sliced long beans, cut into
2-inch pieces

¼ cup pickled ginger

¼ cup fresh coriander leaves,
to garnish

For Serving:

1. In a pot of boiling water, cook the eggs until soft-boiled, for 7 minutes,
then transfer them to a bowl and cool immediately under cold running
water. Blanch the long beans in the same pot of boiling water for 1 minute,
until soft, then place them immediately into an ice-water bath.

2. Arrange the beans on a plate together with a spoonful of the dry curry.
Carve the duck breast off the bone and cut it into thin slices (see tip).
Fan out the duck breast slices slightly and spoon more curry over them.
Peel the soft-boiled eggs, then break them in half with your hands and
plate them with pickled ginger on the side. Garnish with the coriander.

ə To slice a duck breast, remove it from the crown and slice it skin side
   down. Whenever you're slicing through something crispy, always place
   it skin side down on the cutting board to slice cleanly through the meat
   rather than going through the crispy skin.

Steamed Red Curry of Scallops

SERVES 4 TO 6 • PREP TIME: 30 MINUTES • COOK TIME: 15 MINUTES

HOR MOK IS A DELICATE STEAMED CURRY, almost like a custard or *chawanmushi*. It works really well with any seafood, but we prefer to use live scallops from Vancouver Island when they're available. For this recipe, homemade curry paste is extra crucial; store-bought versions are often loaded with salt, shrimp paste, and preservatives, creating a heavy-handed taste that overpowers the scallops' delicate flavor.

6 large U10 scallops, live with shell

¾ cup Red Curry Paste (page 203)

¾ cup thick Coconut Cream (page 205), at room temperature, plus more to garnish

3 Tbsp chicken stock

3 eggs

1-2 tsp granulated sugar, to taste (optional)

1 tsp fish sauce, or to taste (optional)

1 Tbsp finely julienned Makrut lime leaves, plus extra to garnish

30 fresh Thai basil leaves, plus extra to garnish

Deseeded and julienned red Thai bird's eye chilies, to garnish

1. Using a paring knife or small offset spatula to clean the scallops, slide it in sideways, pry open the two shells, and scrape along the top of the shell until the muscle releases. Repeat for the bottom of the shell. It's important to use a thin flexible knife so that you can scrape as close to the shell as possible without losing too much flesh. Remove the contents and rinse in salted water. Remove the skirt and innards, leaving only the scallop and the roe. Slice the scallop meat into two or three slices and keep the roe intact.

2. In a medium-size bowl, place the red curry paste. Add the coconut cream in a slow and steady stream while stirring continuously in one direction to ensure even mixing until fully incorporated. Having the cream at room temperature is key; if the cream is too cold, it will clump up and cause the mousse to split. Stir in the stock, followed by the eggs. Mix until thoroughly combined. To properly check the seasoning, place 2 table-spoons of the mix into a small ramekin as a sample, steam in a steamer for 5 minutes, until set. Taste and season with sugar and fish sauce if needed. Gently fold in the Makrut lime leaves and Thai basil.

3. Pour just enough of the mixture into each scallop shell to cover the scallop slices. Steam the curry in a steamer for 8 to 10 minutes, until it is set like a custard. Garnish with more Thai basil leaves, Thai bird's eye chilies, Makrut limes leaves, and thick coconut cream.

æ If you don't have a steamer, pour about 2 cups of water into a wide 6-quart pot. Place a heat-resistant bowl in the center of the pot, and put a plate atop it that leaves about ½ to 1 inch of space between the edge of the plate and the inside of the pot. Place the items for steaming atop the plate and cover the pot.

Geng Gati Curry of Lobster and Smoked Sablefish

SERVES 4 TO 6 • PREP TIME: 1 HOUR • COOK TIME: 30 MINUTES

THIS IS A BEAUTIFUL CURRY from the southern part of Thailand. It's one of the few coconut-based curries where you don't want to fry the curry paste; instead you simmer the curry paste with coconut cream. The result is an incredible aromatic curry with pungent spice notes and hearty turmeric flavors. In Thailand, this curry is typically served with crabmeat and is usually extremely spicy. Coconut cream is essential to this dish for balance, but I prefer this version, which is less spicy but equally aromatic. I also like using smoked sablefish, as the smoke stands up well to the robust flavors. You can also use smoked haddock or cod.

1 cup Coconut Milk (page 205)

1 cup Coconut Cream (page 205)

2 stalks lemongrass, peeled

5 slices galangal

5 Makrut lime leaves

½ cup Geng Gati Curry Paste (page 203)

¼ cup fish sauce, or to taste

¼ cup palm sugar, or to taste

1 live lobster, about 1 pound

3 ounces smoked sablefish

6 Makrut lime leaves, julienned

3 betel leaves, cut into ⅛-inch strips

¼ cup young coconut meat, grated or cut into ⅛-inch strips

Coconut Cream (page 205), to garnish

1. In a 2-quart pot over medium heat, bring the coconut milk and coconut cream to a simmer. Using a mortar and pestle, bruise the lemongrass, galangal, and Makrut lime leaves, then add them to the mixture. Continue simmering for 10 minutes, until the cream is lightly perfumed with the aromatics. Stir in the geng gati curry paste and simmer for an additional 15 minutes. It should taste fragrant and sweet. Turn off the heat until ready to incorporate the lobster and sablefish.

2. Season the curry to taste with fish sauce and palm sugar, keeping in mind that the shrimp paste in the curry paste is already salty. This curry should be salty, creamy, and spicy. It shouldn't be sweet, but the sugar is there for balance.

3. Kill the lobster (see pictorial, page 19). In a large stockpot with enough water to cover, blanch the lobster and extract the meat (page 17, step 3). Cut the smoked sablefish into 1½-inch chunks. Turn the heat back to medium to warm the curry. Add the lobster meat and sablefish chunks to the pot and simmer for about 5 minutes. Add the Makrut lime and betel leaves; stir to incorporate, and finish with the young coconut. Transfer to a serving platter, garnish with the coconut cream, and serve.

Red Gati of Grilled Tuna and Crab

SERVES 4 TO 6 • PREP TIME: 1 HOUR • COOK TIME: 30 MINUTES

THIS CURRY IS A HAPPY ACCIDENT. While one of the Maenam cooks was preparing a recipe for the Geng Gati Curry Paste (page 203), he used large guajillo chilies instead of small dried Thai bird's eye chilies. As soon as the curry paste was finished, we immediately knew something was off because of the color. But instead of throwing it away, we tried it out as a special with grilled tuna and crab. Go figure—the dish was an overwhelming success with great feedback from the guests. Though it shares practically the same ingredients as the geng gati, it has much darker complexity and richness from the guajillo chilies. Such a great example of how fun cooking is!

1 cup Coconut Milk (page 205)

1 cup Coconut Cream (page 205)

2 stalks lemongrass, peeled

5 slices galangal

5 Makrut lime leaves

½ cup Red Gati Curry Paste (page 203)

¼ cup fish sauce, or to taste

¼ cup palm sugar, or to taste

3 betel leaves, torn up

3 ounces Dungeness crabmeat (divided)

4 ounces albacore tuna

1 Tbsp cured salmon roe, to garnish (optional)

1. Prepare a charcoal grill to high heat 25 to 40 minutes prior to grilling (a grill pan on the stove at high heat also works but is not preferred). Spread out the charcoal to achieve an even heat.

2. In a 2-quart pot over medium heat, bring the coconut milk and coconut cream to a simmer. Using a mortar and pestle, bruise the lemongrass, galangal, and Makrut lime leaves, then add them to the pot. Simmer for 10 minutes, until the cream is lightly perfumed with the aromatics. Stir in the red gati curry paste and simmer for an additional 15 minutes. The curry should taste fragrant and rich. Unlike with the geng gati, you want to showcase this richness, so simmer it for about 10 more minutes to reduce and thicken the curry.

3. Season to taste with fish sauce and palm sugar; the curry should be rich, aromatic, and salty with a touch of sweetness. Finish the curry by adding the betel leaves and half of the crabmeat. Simmer for 3 minutes. Turn off the heat until ready to serve.

4. Grill the tuna to medium-rare doneness, about 1 minute per side, until the exterior is well seared while the inside remains rare. Transfer the tuna to a plate and allow it to rest for 5 minutes before slicing.

5. Using a sharp knife, slice the tuna into ¼-inch-thick pieces. Spoon the curry onto a serving dish and fan the tuna slices over the curry. Garnish with the remaining crabmeat and salmon roe, if desired.

æ Instead of oiling the tuna before grilling it, marinate it quickly in coconut cream and fish sauce. The fat content of the cream will behave like oil and prevent the fish from sticking to the grill while giving it a nice smoky flavor as it cooks.

Curry Pastes

MAKES ENOUGH FOR 2 TO 3 CURRIES

HOMEMADE CURRY PASTE IS single-handedly the most important component of making a good curry. Most store-bought varieties contain too many preservatives and are often way too spicy. Each of these curry paste recipes yields enough for two or three recipes. Take your time to source the necessary ingredients; pounding them out by hand using a mortar and pestle is extremely satisfying, and is a great source of stress relief!

Also, it's important not to be overambitious and try to do an entire batch of curry paste all at once—if your mortar is full, it will take much longer to break down the ingredients in it. A mortar is at its most efficient when it's a third to half full, so break the recipe into manageable portions, pound it out in batches, and stir all the batches (see page 204) together in a large bowl to finish.

Panaeng Curry Paste

1 nutmeg seed

½ cup roasted peanuts, skinned

3 large dried guajillo chilies, deseeded

½ cup peeled and sliced lemongrass

½ cup sliced galangal

2 Tbsp coriander root, roughly chopped

⅔ cup garlic cloves

1 cup roughly chopped small shallots

Chu Chi Curry Paste

5 large dried guajillo chilies, deseeded

¼ cup peeled and sliced lemongrass

½ cup dried prawns

¼ cup sliced galangal

¼ cup sliced grachai

2 Tbsp roughly chopped coriander root

½ cup garlic cloves

½ cup peeled small shallots

Massaman Curry Paste

1 tsp whole cassia bark (small thumbnail portion)

1 tsp whole cumin seeds

3 pods Thai cardamom

3 cloves

1 blade mace

¼ nutmeg seed

½ cup roasted peanuts, skinned

1-2 dried guajillo chilies, deseeded

⅓ cup peeled and sliced lemongrass

⅓ cup sliced galangal

¼ cup coriander root

⅓ cup garlic cloves

¼ cup small shallots

Green Curry Paste

2 tsp white peppercorns

1 tsp coriander seeds

½ tsp cumin seeds

30 small green Thai bird's eye chilies

1 cup peeled and sliced lemongrass

⅓ cup sliced galangal

3 Tbsp coriander root, roughly chopped

2 Tbsp peeled and sliced fresh turmeric

1 cup garlic cloves

1 cup small shallots

Zest of 2 Makrut limes

Khao Soi Curry Paste

3 Tbsp coriander seeds

8 large dried guajillo chilies, deseeded

1 cup peeled and sliced ginger

½ cup coriander root

½ peeled fresh turmeric

½ cup garlic cloves

1 cup small shallots

Geng Gati Curry Paste

12 dried red Thai bird's eye chilies

12 fresh red Thai bird's eye chilies

3 cups peeled and sliced lemongrass

1 cup sliced galangal

⅔ cup sliced grachai

¼ cup peeled and sliced fresh turmeric

½ cup garlic cloves

3 Tbsp shrimp paste

Red Gati Curry Paste

12 large dried guajillo chilies, deseeded

12 fresh red Thai bird's eye chilies

3 cups peeled and sliced lemongrass

1 cup sliced galangal

⅔ cup sliced grachai

¼ cup peeled and sliced fresh turmeric

½ cup garlic cloves

3 Tbsp shrimp paste

Geng Gola Curry Paste

¼ cup roasted peanuts, skinned

6 large dried guajillo chilies, deseeded

½ cup toasted grated coconut (see tip on page 126)

1 cup sliced peeled ginger

3 Tbsp coriander root, roughly chopped

1 cup garlic cloves

1 cup peeled small shallots

Kua Kling Curry Paste

⅓ cup small green Thai bird's eye chilies

½ cup peeled and sliced lemongrass

1 cup peeled and sliced fresh turmeric

½ cup sliced galangal

½ cup garlic cloves

½ cup peeled small shallots

3 Tbsp shrimp paste

Zest of 2 Makrut limes

Geng Gari Curry Paste

¼ cup coriander seeds

5 tsp cumin seeds

1 Tbsp green fennel seeds

1 tsp white peppercorns

1 blade mace

2 large dried guajillo chilies, deseeded

½ cup peeled and sliced lemongrass

½ cup sliced galangal

¼ cup roughly chopped coriander root

⅓ cup garlic cloves

1 cup peeled small shallots

Red Curry Paste

1 Tbsp white peppercorns

2 tsp coriander seeds

6 cloves

½ nutmeg seed

8 large dried guajillo chilies, deseeded

1 cup peeled and sliced lemongrass

¼ cup sliced galangal

5 roasted shallots, peeled

⅓ cup garlic cloves

1 cup peeled small shallots

1 Tbsp shrimp paste

Zest of 1 Makrut lime

Recipe continued . . .

When you make any Thai curry paste, always use a stone mortar and pestle. The following method will work with each one of these recipes.

1. Always presoak your dried chilies before adding them to the mortar and pestle; they'll need a minimum of 2 hours' soaking time, so plan ahead.

2. If applicable, toast the whole spices in a pan over medium heat until they become aromatic. Toss them slightly so they don't burn; your kitchen will smell like a spice market within 10 minutes.

3. Slice your aromatics against the fibers so they'll break down more easily. Using a large mortar and pestle, pound the driest and hardest ingredients first. In most cases, this means pounding the dry spices into a fine powder before adding the nuts and then the chilies. Pound everything into a fine paste.

4. Pound the medium-dry ingredients next, such as galangal and turmeric.

5. Next, pound the wettest ingredients, such as shallots and garlic, using your wrist to strike the pestle down on the front side of the bowl, then grinding it on the backside of the bowl. You may also need to use your opposite hand to cover the mortar to prevent splashing.

6. Once you've achieved a fine paste, if your curry paste calls for it, add the shrimp paste to the mortar and pound until it's thoroughly incorporated.

7. If your curry paste calls for Makrut lime zest, use a Microplane grater to grate it directly into the mortar and pestle, and incorporate thoroughly.

8. Curry pastes will keep in the fridge for 2 weeks and in the freezer for 2 months if wrapped properly.

Coconut Cream and Coconut Milk

MAKES ABOUT 8 CUPS TOTAL • ASSEMBLE TIME: 1 HOUR PLUS REST TIME

MAKING FRESH COCONUT CREAM AND MILK is easy. Although it takes a bit of practice and time, you get both out of one recipe! The amount of cream versus milk produced in this recipe depends on the fat content of each coconut.

12 brown coconuts
6 quarts water

1. Crack the coconuts open with a hammer. Using a flat-head screwdriver, carefully separate the flesh from the hard brown shell.

2. In a large pot over medium-high heat, bring the water to a simmer. Using a blender, blend the coconut meat with the hot water in even batches at high speed until the coconut meat becomes a fine pulp.

3. Line a strainer with cheesecloth and place it over a large bowl. Pour the contents of the blender into the lined strainer, and squeeze the cheesecloth to extract all the liquid. Refrigerate for 3 to 4 hours. The thick coconut cream will rise to the top, while the thinner liquid at the bottom can be used as coconut milk.

4. Fresh coconut cream and milk are very volatile and go rancid quickly. If you're not using either right away, bring it to a boil in a pot over medium-high heat, then remove it from the stove and let it cool down before either refrigerating for up to 2 days, or freezing in smaller batches for up to 2 months.

Cracked Coconut Cream

MAKES 2 CUPS • ASSEMBLE TIME: 30 TO 45 MINUTES

CRACKED COCONUT CREAM IS ESSENTIAL for cooking curry paste, and it's easy to make.

4 cups Coconut Cream (page 205)

1. In a tall, heavy pot over medium heat, bring the coconut cream to a simmer, monitoring closely so that it doesn't bubble over. Simmer for about 20 to 30 minutes, depending on the fat content of your coconut, stirring occasionally so it doesn't stick to the bottom of the pan. Keep simmering until it "cracks" and you're able to see the cream splitting and releasing clear coconut oil.

2. The end product should look like coconut-milk curds that are a light grayish color, sitting in clear coconut oil, in a ratio of about three to one milk solids to clear fat. Cracked coconut cream is quite stable and can be kept in the fridge for up to 1 week.

æ If you're using canned coconut cream, that's okay too, but buy one that uses little to no emulsifiers, and don't shake the can—just let it rest for a little while before opening it. Spoon the thick cream off the top and place it in a saucepan. Reduce the coconut cream carefully over medium-low heat until it separates into clear coconut fat and grayish coconut-milk solids.

Desserts

Opposite page: Pandan Panna Cotta with Dok Jok Wafer (page 211).

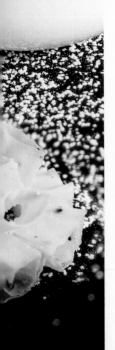

Introduction

TYPICALLY SPEAKING, I HAVE A HARD TIME eating heavy desserts in
Thailand after a big feast. Traditional Thai meals include so many different
flavors and dishes, and are quite eventful for the palate—we always end
up eating lots of rice and drinking lots of beer, leaving little to no room for
dessert. Rich Thai desserts do exist, but they're usually eaten in the afternoon
as a snack rather than at the end of a meal. Instead, I prefer a light, clean
finish and chose to include more refreshing desserts for this very reason;
Lychee Sorbet with Crushed Ice (page 217) and Coconut Shave Ice (page 213)
are two perfect examples: palate-cleansing, refreshing, and balanced.

Most of the desserts in this chapter aren't traditionally Thai at all. Just like at
the restaurant, they include seasonal produce in combination with fruits
typically found in Thailand. And since it's very common to have Thai desserts
that are both savory and sweet, I do love incorporating unconventional
ingredients into my desserts to achieve those flavors. The Heirloom Tomato
Salad with Grape Sorbet (page 222), is one example, featuring heirloom
tomatoes, Coronation grapes, and Italian prune plums at peak ripeness.
It offers a wonderful balance of sweet and sour, while the tomatoes bring
a beautiful savory counterpoint, adding umami to a dessert that normally
wouldn't have it.

Pandan Panna Cotta with Dok Jok Wafer

SERVES 4 TO 6 • PREP TIME: 20 MINUTES, PLUS REFRIGERATION • COOK TIME: 25 MINUTES

ALTHOUGH PANNA COTTA ISN'T what you'd think of as a Thai dessert, it's an ideal base for carrying the delicate fragrance of pandan leaves. We use coconut to really make the flavors sing; as an added bonus, it's dairy-free! Be sure to use good-quality coconut milk for this recipe. If you're buying coconut milk, set it on the counter and let it separate; measure out the cream and milk individually to control the creaminess of this dish. If you're making your own coconut cream (page 205), you can use all coconut cream in this recipe instead of half coconut cream and half coconut milk, as it will likely be less fatty.

Thin and crispy *dok jok* is one of my favorite Thai snacks/desserts. Both the panna cotta and the dok jok are beautiful desserts on their own, but I really enjoy them together, thanks to the great textural contrast. The dok joks stay crunchy for a few days, so make extras because one batch won't last very long! You will need a dok jok mold for this recipe (see tip).

Panna Cotta:

6 pandan leaves, sliced into ¼-inch chunks

2 cups Coconut Milk (page 205)

2 cups Coconut Cream (page 205)

2 cups granulated sugar

5 sheets gelatin (about 2 packages gelatin, ¼-ounce each)

For the Panna Cotta:

1. In a 2-quart pot over medium heat, simmer the pandan leaves with the coconut milk and coconut cream for 15 minutes, or until you can smell the floral and vanilla aromas. Stir in the sugar until thoroughly dissolved.

2. Transfer directly to a blender and blend on high until the pandan leaves are well incorporated and the mixture turns a vibrant green. Pour the mixture through a fine sieve to get rid of any excess fibers.

3. In a medium-size bowl, hydrate the gelatin sheets in cold water; it will take about 3 to 5 minutes for them to bloom and fully soften. To ensure even hydration, it's wise to drop the sheets into the water one at a time. When the gelatin sheets are soft to the touch, remove them from the water and squeeze out the excess liquid. Pour the water out of the bowl, then return the bloomed gelatin sheets to the bowl. Gradually pour small amounts of the pandan mixture into the bowl while slowly stirring with a whisk to dissolve the gelatin. Once all the gelatin dissolves, pour in the rest of the pandan mixture and stir evenly. Do not aggressively whisk the mixture, because you don't want to incorporate air bubbles into the panna cotta. Distribute the mixture evenly between four to six ramekins, depending on size, and refrigerate them for 6 hours, until they're set.

Recipe continued . . .

Dok Jok:

8 cups canola oil

1½ cups rice flour

½ cup tapioca flour

½ tsp coarse sea salt

½ cup granulated sugar

½ cup Coconut Cream (page 205)

1 egg

½ cup Limeized Water (see note on page 24)

1 Tbsp black sesame seeds

1 Tbsp white sesame seeds

Serving:

½ cup icing sugar (optional)

For the Dok Jok:

1. In a heavy 4-quart pot over medium-high heat, preheat the oil to 350°F.

2. In a medium-size bowl, mix the rice flour, tapioca flour, salt, and sugar. Stir in the coconut cream to form a dough. In a separate bowl, whisk the egg and then incorporate into the dough mixture. Slowly mix in the limeized water until you have a thin batter. Add the black and white sesame seeds to the bowl, stirring occasionally so they don't sink to the bottom.

3. Once the oil has reached the correct temperature, carefully place the dok jok mold into the pot for 5 minutes, ensuring the mold is the same temperature as the oil. In the meantime, line a tray with paper towel, and have one glass bottle close at hand for opening the dok jok.

4. When the mold is hot, remove it from the oil and dab it on the paper towel to shake off excess oil before submerging the mold into the batter, ensuring the top of the mold is still visible. If you submerge it in the batter completely, you won't be able to slide the wafer off the mold. Once the batter sears onto the mold, about 5 seconds, place the coated mold back into the oil while holding the mold in place so it floats in the middle of the pot. Shake the mold up and down to slide the wafer off into the oil, and continue to make the next one. Fry only two or three wafers at a time, and always ensure the temperature of your mold is hot enough. Using a spider, gently flip the wafer after 2 minutes. When the wafer is light golden, remove it from the hot oil and place it on the paper towel-lined tray to blot any excess oil. Let the wafer rest for 20 seconds. While it is still hot, place the wafer on the mouth of the glass bottle. Using both hands, shape the wafer until it looks like a beautiful lotus flower—this may take some practice. Work quickly, because the wafer becomes crispy and near impossible to shape as it cools.

For Serving:

1. To serve, remove the panna cotta from the fridge. Place a dok jok atop each ramekin and dust it with icing sugar.

æ Dok Jok molds are readily available online, and you can also track them down in Thai specialty stores.

Recipe pictured on page 208.

Coconut Shave Ice

SERVES 6 • PREP TIME: 45 MINUTES, PLUS FREEZING • COOK TIME: 5 MINUTES

SHAVE ICE IS A POPULAR DESSERT in just about every culture. Typically in Asia and specifically in Thailand, plain ice is shaved and topped with lots of condensed milk and candied fruits. I wanted to make a lighter version, so I used fresh young coconut water to naturally sweeten the shaved ice instead of adding too much condensed milk. This recipe also calls for more fresh fruits instead of candied fruits, resulting in a more refreshing and cleaner-tasting dessert. Although you can use any of your favorite fruits, I prefer to stick with a Thai flavor profile and use tropical fruits from Southeast Asia.

Coconut Ice:

2 young coconuts

1 cup simple syrup (see tip on page 223)

For the Coconut Ice:

1. Crack open the young coconuts and extract the coconut water (about 4 cups) and the meat.

2. Dice the young coconut meat and set aside in a bowl. In a separate bowl, mix the coconut water with the simple syrup.

3. Prepare an ice-cream and sorbet maker according to the manufacturer's instructions and churn the sweetened coconut water for 6 minutes, then freeze it for 2 hours before using. To serve, use an ice pick and break apart the large ice chunks to get smaller snow-like pieces of coconut ice.

Pandan Jelly and Foam:

4 cups chopped pandan leaves, cut across the grain into ½-inch pieces

4 cups simple syrup (see tip on page 223)

8 sheets gelatin (about 3 packages gelatin, ¼ ounce each)

1 drop jasmine extract (optional)

For the Pandan Jelly and Foam:

1. Blanch the leaves in boiling water for 1 minute, then transfer to an ice bath. Once the pandan leaves have cooled, squeeze out the extra water and place in a blender with the simple syrup, then blend until fine. Set aside for 10 minutes before straining to let the color mature.

2. In the meantime, hydrate the gelatin sheets in a bowl of cold water; it will take about 3 to 5 minutes for them to bloom and fully soften.

3. Strain the pandan syrup and add the jasmine extract. Place the bloomed gelatin sheets into a large stainless-steel bowl and melt the gelatin on the stove over low direct heat. Whisk the pandan mixture into the melted gelatin. Place 2 cups of the pandan-gelatin mixture into a bowl and refrigerate it so that it sets as jelly, and reserve the other 2 cups for the foam in the next step. Once the jelly is set, dice it into ¼-inch chunks for serving.

Recipe continued . . .

4. To make the foam, start with two large bowls one atop the other: the bowl on the bottom half filled with ice water, and the bowl on top empty. Pour the reserved 2 cups of the pandan-gelatin mixture, about ¼ cup at a time, into the empty bowl and continue whisking it on ice until it becomes foamy. Place each batch of the foam into a plastic container and repeat with the next ¼ cup of the pandan-gelatin mixture until all of it has been foamed. Don't whisk too much of the pandan-gelatin mixture at a time, as the gelatin may set before you achieve a foam. Keep the foam in the freezer until you're ready to plate.

Fruits:

20 fresh lychees, peeled and deseeded

20 fresh longans, peeled and deseeded

2 cups watermelon cubes

2 fresh passion fruit, pulp scooped out

½ cup diced ripe mangos

½ cup diced sour green mangos

½ cup sliced jackfruit

¼ cup condensed milk, to garnish (optional)

For the Fruits:

1. In a large bowl, place the diced coconut meat and all the fruit and toss gently until fully combined.

2. Assemble the dessert by layering the coconut ice in six individual dessert bowls with the fruit mixture. The idea is to get a little of everything with each bite of the dessert. Once you've built the dessert, garnish with the pandan jelly and foam, drizzle a little condensed milk on top, and serve.

Lychee Sorbet with Crushed Ice

SERVES 4 • PREP TIME: 20 MINUTES, PLUS CHURNING AND FREEZING • ASSEMBLE TIME: 5 MINUTES

THIS IS A SUPER-EASY DESSERT, extremely refreshing and perfect for the summer!

2 (20-ounce) cans lychees, puréed

4½ cups simple syrup (see tip on page 223) (divided)

3 Tbsp glucose or corn syrup

2 Tbsp freshly squeezed lime juice

2 pounds fresh lychees, peeled and deseeded

2 Makrut limes

4 cups ice

1. To make the sorbet, using a blender on high speed, blend the lychee purée, ½ cup of simple syrup, glucose, and lime juice until smooth. Prepare an ice-cream and sorbet maker according to the manufacturer's instructions and churn the sorbet. Keep in the freezer until needed, up to 2 weeks.

2. Slice the fresh lychees into quarters. Pour the remaining simple syrup into a large mixing bowl. Using a Microplane grater, grate the zest of Makrut limes into the simple syrup. Cut the Makrut limes in half and squeeze the juice through a small strainer into the simple syrup.

3. Wrap the ice in a clean dish towel and crush it with a rolling pin until it breaks down into coarse chunks of ¼ to ½ inch. Add the fresh lychees to the syrup bowl, spoon a good amount of crushed ice into the syrup, and mix together. Plate into four dessert bowls and scoop or quenelle the sorbet on top to finish.

Rice Doughnuts

MAKES 20 TO 30 DOUGHNUTS • PREP TIME: 10 MINUTES, PLUS OVERNIGHT REFRIGERATION • COOK TIME: 10 MINUTES

THIS RECIPE IS A PERFECT WAY to use up leftover rice. We only serve jasmine rice at the restaurant, but you can use fluffier longer-grain rice when you're making these doughnuts at home—glutinous rice would make the doughnuts too tough. The key to this recipe is to make the dough while the rice is still warm. Leftover rice from the fridge is too hard and doesn't blend well, giving you lumpy rice in your doughnuts.

2 tsp dry yeast (about 1 packet)

1 cup warm water

1½ cups granulated sugar (divided)

3 cups warm cooked rice

2½ cups all-purpose flour

1 tsp coarse sea salt

½ tsp nutmeg

6 eggs

8 cups canola oil, for frying

1. In a small bowl, whisk the yeast into the warm water to activate it. In a large bowl, combine ½ cup of sugar with the rest of the ingredients (other than the oil), add the activated yeast, and blend with a hand blender until smooth. Cover with plastic wrap and let it rise overnight in the fridge.

2. In a deep fryer or a 6- to 8-quart Dutch oven, preheat the oil to 350°F. Pour the remaining sugar onto a plate or tray. Remove the dough from the fridge and punch it down. Using an ice-cream scoop, separate the dough into golf ball-size portions and drop them into the hot oil one at a time. They will float to the top shortly after you drop them into the oil; use a spider to flip them over so that they cook evenly. Depending on the size of your deep fryer or pot, you can fry up to six to eight dough balls simultaneously; just ensure that they don't clump or stick to each other. When the doughnuts are golden brown, remove them from the oil and roll them in sugar to coat them evenly. Serve immediately.

Opposite page: Rice Doughnuts (left) and Yam Doughnuts (right, page 220).

Yam Doughnuts

MAKES 40 TO 60 SMALL DOUGHNUTS • PREP TIME: 1 HOUR, 30 MINUTES • COOK TIME: 15 MINUTES

YAM DOUGHNUTS ARE A BEAUTIFUL LITTLE SNACK that I eat every time I visit my wife Kate's hometown in Lamnarai. An elderly couple sells them from their street stall just outside a noodle shop. They ring the bell when a new batch is ready, and people in the noodle shop rush to grab the fresh ones. I worked on so many different ratios of flours to match the texture—in the end, it was just tapioca flour that gives these doughnuts their distinctive toothsome texture. Together with the roasted yam, the taste is delightful!

Palm Sugar Caramel:

½ cup palm sugar

¼ cup water

¼ cup Coconut Cream (page 205)

2 tsp coarse sea salt

Doughnuts:

2 large yams

8 cups canola oil

2 cups tapioca flour

1 cup granulated sugar

3 Tbsp baking powder

¼ cup Limeized Water
(see note on page 24)

Icing sugar, for dusting (optional)

For the Palm Sugar Caramel:

1. In a 2-quart saucepan over medium heat, combine the palm sugar and water. Bring to a simmer to melt the palm sugar. Monitoring the temperature with a sugar thermometer, bring the sugar mixture to a dark-caramel stage (350°F). Remove from heat and stir in the coconut cream and salt. Let cool to room temperature before using.

For the Doughnuts:

1. Preheat the oven to 350°F. Roast the yams whole until they're soft, about 60 to 90 minutes. Let them cool slightly but not completely, as the skin will shrink and cling to the flesh. Once cool to the touch, remove the skins and mash the yams with a fork. If the mashed yams are overly wet, place them in a colander and let them sit for 30 minutes to drain off the excess liquid.

2. In a deep fryer or 6- to 8-quart Dutch oven, preheat the oil to 350°F.

3. Meanwhile, place the yams in a medium-size bowl and mix in the balance of dough ingredients until it's the consistency of soft Play-Doh. If the mixture is too dry, add a touch more limeized water to moisten. Roll the dough into 1-inch-thick logs and cut into even sections, then roll into round balls about 1 to 2 inches in diameter. Smaller doughnuts will be crispier, while larger doughnuts will still have a thin crispy crust but will be chewier because of the tapioca.

4. Drop the balls of dough into the hot oil one at a time. Depending on the size of your deep fryer or pot, six to eight dough balls is ideal. They will float to the surface shortly after you drop them into the oil; use a spider to flip them over so that they cook evenly. When the doughnuts turn golden brown and form a crispy shell, carefully remove them from the oil and transfer to a rack with paper towel beneath it to absorb excess oil.

5. Drizzle with palm sugar caramel and dust with icing sugar. Serve immediately.

Recipe pictured on page 218.

Heirloom Tomato Salad with Grape Sorbet

SERVES 6 TO 8 • PREP TIME: 20 MINUTES, PLUS FREEZING • ASSEMBLE TIME: 5 MINUTES

TOWARD THE END OF EVERY SUMMER, I look forward to emails from Milan of Stoney Paradise Farm, also known as the Tomato Man, telling me that his crops are ready. He grows the best heirloom tomatoes and picks them the morning of delivery so they're all vine-ripened and sweet like candy. There's a week or two when his tomatoes and grapes cross paths, just as tomato season winds down and grape season begins. I love his Sungold tomatoes so much that my food costs go up dramatically when they're in season because I eat so many of them. Milan also grows delicious heirloom grapes, Coronation being one of my favorite varieties. This dish represents everything I love in a dessert—fresh, light, and simple.

Coronation Grape Sorbet:

2 pounds Coronation grapes, picked (can substitute Concord grapes)

6 Tbsp simple syrup (see tip)

¼ cup glucose or corn syrup

1 Tbsp lemon juice

For the Coronation Grape Sorbet:

1. If you don't have an ice-cream and sorbet maker, place a baking sheet in the freezer for 3 hours.

2. Place all the sorbet ingredients in a blender and blend on high for 3 minutes. Depending on the size of your blender, you may need to do this in two equal batches. Strain the contents through a fine strainer. Pour the grape mixture into an ice-cream and sorbet maker, and prepare according to the manufacturer's instructions. Remove from the machine and place in the freezer.

3. If not using an ice-cream and sorbet maker, pour the grape mixture over the frozen baking sheet, spread evenly, and return it to the freezer. Every 30 minutes, remove the tray from the freezer and scrape the mixture with a fork to break up the ice crystals. Repeat this at least 8 to 10 times before transferring the grape mixture to a container and storing it in the freezer overnight. If your sorbet is too hard the next day, cut it into chunks and pulse it roughly in a blender for 1 minute, then refreeze it again for 3 hours.

Tomato and Plum Salad:

1 pound ripe Sungold tomatoes

1 pound Italian prune plums

¼ cup simple syrup

1 Tbsp honey

1 Tbsp lemon juice

Pinch of coarse sea salt

2 Tbsp finely sliced fresh Thai basil or tarragon

For the Tomato and Plum Salad:

1. Slice the tomatoes into halves or quarters depending on their size. Using a paring knife, cut the plums in half and remove the pits, then dice the plums into similar-size chunks as the tomatoes. Place the tomatoes and plums in a medium-size mixing bowl.

2. In a small mixing bowl, mix the simple syrup together with the honey, lemon juice, and salt. Drizzle the honey syrup over the tomatoes and plums, gently toss until evenly coated, and fold in the Thai basil.

3. Plate the tomato and plum salad into six to eight bowls. Remove the sorbet from the freezer and place a quenelle or scoop of it atop the salads.

æ • Tomatoes are so much more flavorful when harvested while in season. Go to your local farmers' market and pick up a few types of heirloom tomatoes for this recipe, such as Green Zebras, Carolina Golds, and Sungolds—standard hothouse tomatoes and even Roma tomatoes are flavorless. The idea is to mix and match varieties of heirloom tomatoes for flavor and texture; some have great crunch to them, while some of the tiny ones have a lovely pop; some are nice and sour, while others are incredibly sweet.

• Simple syrup is just an equal-parts mixture of water and sugar.

• If you don't have glucose for this recipe, use corn syrup. Honey is also a good substitute; however, in this case it will introduce a new flavor into the sorbet. Glucose gives the sorbet a nice smooth texture. If you prefer your sorbet to be softer, add another 2 tablespoons of glucose.

Custard Apple in Smoked Coconut Cream

SERVES 4 • PREP TIME: 30 MINUTES • COOK TIME: 5 MINUTES

THIS SIMPLE DESSERT CAN BE SERVED either warm or chilled, and it tastes best with fresh coconut cream (page 205). It can be substituted with other sweet and luscious Thai fruits—fresh jackfruit is another one that I especially enjoy in this recipe.

2 cups Coconut Cream (page 205)

1 pandan leaf

¼ cup granulated sugar

1-2 tsp coarse sea salt

1 jasmine candle (see tip)

1-2 ripe custard apples

1 tsp toasted sesame seeds

¼ cup freshly grated young coconut meat

Gold flakes, to garnish (optional)

Dok Jok (page 212), for serving (optional)

1. In a heavy 4-quart pot over medium heat, place the coconut cream, pandan leaf, sugar, and salt and bring to a simmer, then turn the heat down to low and continue simmering gently until the sugar melts and the mixture has picked up some flavor from the pandan leaf, about 20 minutes. Pour the hot coconut cream into a large metal bowl. Place the jasmine candle in a small ramekin, light both ends, and let it float atop the coconut cream. Let the candle burn for 30 seconds to 1 minute, then blow it out and quickly cover the bowl and candle with plastic wrap so that the coconut cream absorbs the jasmine-scented smoke. Keep covered for about 30 minutes.

2. Using a paring knife, mark an "X" on the top of the custard apples. Carefully peel back the thick skin to reveal the soft white flesh. Gently cut the fruit into four wedges, and carefully scrape off the large black seeds.

3. Taste the cream; it should taste gently smoky, floral, and sweet with a hint of salt to balance. Spoon the cream equally into four bowls, and place a segment of custard apple into each, then sprinkle with the sesame seeds, young grated coconut, and gold flakes. Place a dok jok atop each if desired. Serve immediately.

æ Jasmine candles, called *tian op* in Thai, are U-shaped candles with wicks on both ends. Typically used in making Thai desserts, the candles are lit for only a couple of seconds before the flame is blown out; the candle smoke is used to infuse ingredients with a wonderful jasmine fragrance. You can track them down either online or at specialty Thai shops.

Fermented Rice Sorbet

SERVES 4 TO 6 • PREP TIME: 30 MINUTES, PLUS FREEZING • COOK TIME: 10 MINUTES, PLUS BAKING

FERMENTED RICE IS A POPULAR CHINESE DESSERT in the wintertime, often served in hot soup with an egg swirl and dumplings. When raw, it has a flavor similar to sake and pairs really well with yuzu. While experimenting with it at the restaurant, we made it into a sorbet using the rice starch as a stabilizer. It quickly became one of my favorite desserts, a modernized version of that from my childhood memories.

Sorbet:

2 cups fermented rice and liquid

2 Tbsp glucose

2 Tbsp yuzu juice

½ cup simple syrup (see tip on page 223)

For the Sorbet:

1. Place the fermented rice and liquid, glucose, yuzu juice, and simple syrup in a blender and blend on high for a minimum of 2 minutes, until smooth and there is no graininess in the sorbet mix.

2. Prepare an ice-cream and sorbet maker according to the manufacturer's instructions, and pour the sorbet mix into the machine. Once it reaches the consistency of soft-serve ice cream, remove from the ice-cream maker and chill for at least 3 hours in the freezer before serving. The sorbet will keep in the freezer for up to 2 weeks.

Salad:

1 cantaloupe melon

1 honeydew melon

1 ear of corn, blanched and cooled

3 Tbsp simple syrup (see tip on page 223)

1 tsp yuzu juice

For the Salad:

1. Slice the cantaloupe and honeydew melons in half to remove the seeds, and use a melon baller to scoop out the flesh into a large bowl. Slice the cooked corn off the cob and add to the bowl with the melon balls.

2. Stir in the simple syrup and yuzu juice until the melon balls and corn are well coated. Chill in the fridge and remove 5 minutes before serving, allowing the salad to come to room temperature for fuller flavor.

Meringue:

1 cup granulated sugar

½ cup water

4 egg whites

For the Meringue:

1. Preheat the oven to 175°F.

2. In a small saucepan, place the sugar and water, and bring them to a boil over high heat until the syrup reaches the softball stage, or 240°F on a sugar thermometer.

3. In a high-sided copper or stainless-steel mixing bowl, beat the egg whites with a hand mixer or stand mixer until they form soft peaks.

4. With the mixer set to slow speed, slowly and carefully pour the hot sugar syrup into the egg whites, and mix until incorporated. If the mixer speed is set too high, you risk the chance of being burned by sugar splatter. Turn the mixer back to high speed and whip until the meringue mixture is glossy and maintains stiff peaks.

5. Line a large baking tray with a thick silicone mat, and evenly spread the meringue mixture to a thickness of ⅛ to ¼ inch. Place the meringue in the oven on the center rack and bake for a minimum of 6 hours, until crispy and hard throughout; depending on ambient humidity, it could take up to 12 hours. The low oven temperature ensures that the meringue bakes evenly without discoloring.

6. Remove the meringue from the oven and place the baking tray on a rack to cool completely before serving.

7. Assemble the dessert by spooning the melon-and-corn salad mixture equally into the bottom of four to six dessert bowls. Break the meringue into random chip sizes. Spoon a quenelle of sorbet atop each portion of salad and sprinkle meringue chips over the sorbet to finish.

Condiments

Sweet Vinegar

MAKES 2 CUPS

1 cup granulated sugar

1 cup white vinegar

¼ cup thinly sliced serrano chilies

¼ cup thinly sliced shallots

1. In a medium pot over medium heat, combine the sugar and vinegar, and stir until all the sugar has dissolved. Set aside and let cool.

2. In a lidded glass container, combine the serrano chilies and shallots, and pour the cooled vinegar solution over them. Store in the fridge for up to 3 months.

Chili Oil

MAKES 2 CUPS

2 cups canola oil

1 cup dried guajillo chilies, deseeded

½ cup Fried Shallots (page 235)

½ cup Fried Garlic (page 235)

2 Tbsp Toasted Chili Powder (page 234)

½ tsp kosher salt

1. In a medium-size pot over medium-high heat, preheat the canola oil to 300°F. Fry the guajillo chilies one or two at a time until fragrant and the chilies darken slightly to a dark burgundy color, but not black, about 20 seconds. Remove the fried chilies from the oil and transfer to a baking tray lined with paper towel to absorb excess oil. Cool the hot oil until it reaches a temperature of 250°F.

2. In a metal container, combine the fried shallots, fried garlic, toasted chili powder, and salt, and pour in the cooled oil. Set aside at room temperature and let cool. Once cool enough to handle, pour the mixture into a blender together with the fried guajillo chilies and blend on medium-high until a coarse mixture is achieved. Transfer to a lidded container and store in the pantry for up to 1 month; beyond a month, it begins to lose its flavor and aroma.

Chili Vinegar

MAKES 2 CUPS

1½ cups diced orange chili peppers

4 red Thai bird's eye chilies

1 Tbsp galangal

1 garlic clove

1 tsp granulated sugar

1½ cups white vinegar

1. In a blender, blend all the ingredients together on high. Skim off any excess foam.

2. Pour into a lidded container and store in the fridge for up to 1 month.

Fermented Soybean Sauce

MAKES 2 CUPS

¾ cup fermented soybean paste

¾ cup pickled chilies with liquid

¼ cup pickled garlic

¼ cup roughly chopped coriander roots

¼ cup chopped ginger

2 red Thai bird's eye chilies

2 garlic cloves

2 Tbsp dark soy sauce

1. In a blender, blend all the ingredients together on high until smooth.

2. Transfer to a lidded container and store in the fridge for up to 1 month.

Ginger-Scallion Sauce

MAKES 2 CUPS

3 cups chopped green onions

2 cups chopped peeled ginger

1 cup vegetable oil

2½ Tbsp coarse sea salt

1. In a food processor, blend the green onions and ginger together on medium-high into a rough paste.

2. In a medium-size pot over medium heat, preheat the vegetable oil to 300°F; it should be just shy of smoking. Add the ginger and green onion paste to the oil and fry for 1 minute.

3. To finish, season with sea salt. Let cool completely before transferring to a lidded container. Store in the fridge for up to 1 week and use before the vibrant green color fades.

Cucumber Relish

MAKES 2 CUPS

½ cup rice vinegar

¼ cup water

¼ cup granulated sugar

Large pinch of coarse sea salt

1 cucumber, peeled, deseeded, and diced

1 red Thai bird's eye chili, sliced

1 shallot, sliced

1. In a medium-size bowl, combine the vinegar, water, sugar, and salt and stir to dissolve.

2. In a glass container, combine the cucumber, chili, and shallots. Pour the vinegar solution over the mixture and stir to combine. I encourage you to use this right away for peak freshness and crunch; however, you can cover with a lid and store in the fridge for up to 2 days.

Peanut Sauce

MAKES 2 CUPS

2 Tbsp canola oil

¼ cup Red Curry Paste (page 203)

½ cup skinned and ground roasted peanuts

2 cups Coconut Cream (page 205)

¼ cup granulated sugar

¼ cup Tamarind Water (page 233)

1 Tbsp kosher salt

1. In a medium-size frying pan over medium heat, preheat the canola oil to 300°F. Fry the red curry paste and ground peanuts until fragrant.

2. Stir in the coconut cream, sugar, tamarind water, and salt and simmer for 10 minutes. Remove from heat and let cool before transferring to a lidded container. Store in the fridge for up to 1 week.

ə Because this sauce should be served hot, reheat in a small pot over medium heat before serving. As you're reheating it, more oil will be released; therefore, you may wish to add a couple of tablespoons of coconut milk to re-emulsify it.

Nahm Jim Jiao

MAKES 1½ CUPS

½ cup Tamarind Water (page 233)

¼ cup Toasted Rice Powder (page 117)

¼ cup Fried Shallots (page 235)

¼ cup sliced pak chi farang

¼ cup finely sliced shallots

¼ cup freshly squeezed lime juice, plus extra to taste

¼ cup fish sauce, plus extra to taste

3 Tbsp granulated sugar, plus extra to taste

Large pinch of Toasted Chili Powder (page 234), plus extra to taste

1. In a medium-size bowl, stir all the ingredients together until well combined. Check seasoning and adjust until equally sweet, salty, sour, and spicy.

2. Transfer to a lidded container and store in the fridge for up to 3 days.

ə This is a great accompaniment for grilled and fried meats, such as grilled steak or the Fried Chicken Wings (page 30).

Nahm Plah Prik

MAKES ½ CUP

3 Tbsp fish sauce

3 Tbsp lime juice

1 shallot, finely sliced

4-6 red Thai bird's eye chilies

Small handful of coriander leaves, to garnish (optional)

1. In a small bowl, stir the fish sauce and lime juice together. Add shallots and chilies and stir to incorporate thoroughly. Garnish with coriander leaves. This typical condiment for Thai stir-fry dishes should taste equally salty, sour, and spicy.

2. You can transfer to a lidded container and store in the fridge for up to 3 days, but it tastes best when made fresh before serving.

Sweet Chili Sauce

MAKES 2½ CUPS

½ cup roughly chopped coriander roots or stems

½ cup garlic cloves

Pinch of kosher salt

1 cup deseeded and chopped chili peppers

4 cups white vinegar

3 cups granulated sugar

Large pinch of kosher salt

4 cups water

1. Using a mortar and pestle, pound the coriander roots, garlic, and salt into a coarse paste. Grind the chilies in a meat grinder, or pulse them in a food processor until the chili pepper bits are evenly sized to about ⅛ inch. Combine with the paste.

2. In a large pot over medium-high heat, stir together the chili paste, vinegar, sugar, salt, and water. Bring to a simmer. When the sauce reaches a temperature of 220°F, continue simmering for 5 more minutes. Remove from heat and let cool.

3. Transfer to a lidded container and store in the fridge for up to 2 months.

Tamarind Water

MAKES 4 CUPS

1 (14-ounce) bag tamarind pulp

6 cups water

1. Cut a brick of tamarind pulp into small pieces and soak overnight in water.

2. The next day, use your hands to massage the water into the tamarind and loosen it up. Once the water is well saturated with tamarind, pass it through a strainer and keep only the tamarind water. Store it in the fridge for up to 1 week. Tamarind water goes rancid quickly so don't make too much at once.

æ Prepressed tamarind water is available in some Asian specialty markets. Because it has to be shelf-stable, it must be pasteurized; as a result, it tastes mustier than freshly pressed tamarind water.

Caramelized Tamarind Sauce

MAKES 1 CUP

½ cup palm sugar
¼ cup water
½ cup Tamarind Water (page 233)
¼ cup fish sauce
Zest and juice of 1 lime

1. In a small saucepan over high heat, melt the palm sugar in water. Cook for 4 to 5 minutes, stirring occasionally, until the sugar syrup reduces to a dark caramel. Check the color of the caramel with a light-colored spoon—be careful not to burn yourself.

2. Once the syrup reaches dark-caramel stage, stir in the tamarind water, fish sauce, lime zest, and lime juice until fully incorporated. The sauce should taste equally salty, sweet, and sour with a refreshing lime finish.

3. Transfer to a lidded container and store in the fridge for up to 1 week.

Toasted Chili Powder

MAKES ½ CUP

1 cup dried Thai bird's eye chilies

1. In a wok over medium heat, dry-toast the chilies, constantly tossing the wok to prevent the chilies from burning. Keep tossing the chilies until they turn dark red/borderline black. (At this point, you'll start to have issues holding back coughs—that's when you know they're properly toasted.)

2. You can either keep the chilies whole to use in soups or salads, or pound them using a mortar and pestle to make your own chili powder. Be extra careful not to accidentally inhale the chili powder while you're grinding it. Keep it in a lidded container in the pantry for up to 2 weeks.

Fried Shallots

MAKES ½ CUP

4 cups canola oil
1 cup thinly sliced shallots,
about ¹⁄₁₆ inch

Fried Garlic

MAKES ½ CUP

4 cups canola oil
1 cup thinly sliced garlic cloves,
sliced lengthwise to about ¹⁄₁₆ inch

1. In a medium-size pot, preheat the oil to about 330°F. Fry the shallots or garlic for about 5 minutes, stirring them occasionally. Toward the end of the cooking time, turn them over a few times with your spider and remove them from the oil when they're light golden brown.

2. For the fried shallots, use two forks to spread them out evenly to cool on a wire rack lined with paper towel. This ensures that the shallots cool off and crisp up more quickly.

3. For the fried garlic, keep in mind that it will retain heat when you remove it and darken quite a bit as it cools.

4. Reserve the fragrant garlic oil for finishing and stir-frying.

5. Store fried aromatics in a lidded container in the pantry for up to 2 weeks.

ℑ You can buy deep-fried shallots and garlic in stores, but they're most often old, stale, and coated with starch-like flour for crispness, which adds unwanted texture.

You can also use Thai baby garlic; just use a mortar and pestle to pound them with a pinch of salt until the garlic breaks down into bits that are about ¹⁄₁₆ inch to ⅛ inch. Fry the garlic pulp using the same method. Note that you'll need to pass the oil through a fine strainer to fish out the garlic completely. The Thai baby garlic will carry over a lot of heat and continue cooking, so speed is of the essence in separating it from the oil. After straining, spread the garlic out onto a pan lined with paper towel to dry. Keep the skin on Thai baby garlic when you're frying it, as the skins and tiny cloves have beautiful texture and aroma.

Fried Thai Basil

MAKES 1 CUP

4 cups canola oil
1 cup fresh Thai basil leaves
(preferably larger leaves that
look nicer)

1. In a medium-size pot, preheat the oil to 330°F. Using a spider, gently place the Thai basil leaves into the oil. Be very careful: there's a lot of moisture in the leaves, and the oil will splatter. Fry the basil leaves for about 10 seconds per side, until they start to hold their own shape. Remove them from the oil with your spider, and dry on paper towel-lined trays.

2. Once cool, the leaves should be firm and crispy. Store in a lidded container in the pantry for up to 1 week.

Cocktails

Opposite page: Saim Sunburn (page 242) and Thai Ginger (page 239).

Introduction

THROUGHOUT THE YEARS, many bartenders have graced the Maenam bar with their talents. My request of them has always been the same: please make flavor-forward cocktails that are ingredient driven, rather than booze driven. Here are some classic recipes we've used over the past decade—they all pair really well with spicy food!

Recipes make 1 cocktail.

Thai Ginger
by Tanya Roussy

Cassia Rye Mix:

1 cup rye

1 piece cassia bark

½-inch piece galangal, grated

½ cup passion fruit purée

Thai Ginger Cocktail:

2½ ounces Cassia Rye Mix
(see here)

1 ounce freshly squeezed lime
juice

¾ ounce vanilla syrup (see tip)

1 (16-ounce) bottle ginger beer

1-2 drops Angostura bitters

1. To make the cassia rye mix, infuse the rye with the cassia bark for 24 hours. Strain, then mix in the galangal and passion fruit purée before straining again. Store in the fridge for up to 3 weeks.

2. To make the cocktail, pour 2½ ounces cassia rye mix into a cocktail shaker with ice. Add the lime juice and vanilla syrup. Shake well and serve in a highball glass over ice. Top with ginger beer and a couple of drops of Angostura bitters.

æ To make the vanilla simple syrup, split 1 vanilla bean lengthwise and scrape the inside of it with the back of your knife. In a saucepan over medium heat, bring 2 cups of simple syrup (page 223) to a simmer. Add the vanilla bean pod, and vanilla bean scrapings and infuse for 5 minutes, continuing to simmer. Remove from heat, let cool, and keep refrigerated in a lidded container for up to 3 weeks.

Tang Kwa Luck
by Kristi Linneboe

Cucumber-Infused Gin:

1 cup gin

⅓ cup roughly chopped
cucumbers

Lemongrass Simple Syrup:

1 stalk lemongrass, peeled

1 cup simple syrup (see tip
on page 223)

Tang Kwa Luck Cocktail:

2 ounces Cucumber-Infused
Gin (see here)

2 tsp ginger juice

1 ounce freshly squeezed
lime juice

¾ ounce Lemongrass Simple
Syrup (see here)

Long pepper, grated, to garnish

1. To make the cucumber-infused gin, infuse the gin with the cucumber for at least 3 days.

2. To make the lemongrass simple syrup, using a mortar and pestle, bruise the lemongrass. In a saucepan over medium heat, bring the simple syrup to a simmer. Add lemongrass and infuse for 5 minutes, continuing to simmer. Remove from heat, let cool, and keep refrigerated in a lidded container for up to 3 weeks.

3. To make the cocktail, pour 2 ounces cucumber-infused gin into a cocktail shaker with ice. Add the ginger juice, lime juice, and ¾ ounce lemongrass simple syrup. Shake well and double-strain into a coupe glass. Garnish with the long pepper.

Bai Ho La Pra
by Kristi Linneboe

5-7 fresh Thai basil leaves, muddled

1¾ ounces tequila

¼ ounce green chartreuse

2 tsp ginger juice

1 ounce lemon juice

¾ ounce vanilla simple syrup
(see tip on page 239)

1 Thai basil leaf, to garnish

1. Add all of the ingredients (other than the final basil garnish) to a cocktail shaker with ice. Shake, then double-strain into a coupe glass.

2. Garnish with a single basil leaf.

Gin-nae
by James Welk

1½ ounces London dry gin

¾ ounce dry vermouth

¾ ounce Lemongrass Simple Syrup (page 239)

¼ ounce citric acid

3 fresh Thai basil leaves, bruised, to garnish

1. Fill a glass cocktail mixing pitcher with ice. Add all ingredients (other than the garnish) to the pitcher and stir thoroughly. Strain into a rocks glass and top with ice.

2. Garnish with the Thai basil leaves.

Rusty Bumper
by Tanya Roussy

Salted-Plum and Cumin-Infused Brandy:

1 cup brandy

½ tsp toasted cumin seeds

3 sour Chinese salted plums

1 strip fresh orange rind

Rusty Bumper Cocktail:

1½ ounces Salted-Plum and Cumin-Infused Brandy (see here)

1 ounce lemon juice

½ ounce Cointreau

½ ounce simple syrup (see tip on page 223)

1 strip fresh orange rind, to garnish

3-4 drops Peychaud's bitters, to garnish

1. To make the salted-plum and cumin-infused brandy, infuse the brandy with the cumin, Chinese salted plums, and orange rind for at least 10 days. Store in the fridge for up to 1 month.

2. To make the cocktail, pour 1½ ounces of the infused brandy and the remaining ingredients (other than garnishes) into a cocktail shaker with ice. Shake well, double-strain into a rocks glass, and top with ice. Garnish with a fresh orange rind and gently drop the bitters on top.

Scotch Tom Rick
by James Welk

Turmeric-Infused Scotch:

1 cup Scotch

2 tsp chopped fresh turmeric

Scotch Tom Rick Cocktail:

1¾ ounces Turmeric-Infused Scotch (see here)

1 ounce lemon juice

¾ ounce simple syrup (see tip on page 223)

¼ ounce Amaro Averna

2 big drops Angostura orange bitters

1. To make the turmeric-infused Scotch, blend the Scotch and turmeric in a blender at medium speed. Strain into a glass bottle or container and keep in the fridge for up to 2 weeks.

2. To make the cocktail, pour 1¾ ounces of the Scotch into a cocktail shaker with ice. Add the remaining ingredients. Shake well, and double-strain into a chilled coupe glass.

Ma Kham Whan
by James Welk

Coffee and Lime-Leaf-Infused Bourbon:

1 cup bourbon

1 tsp coffee beans

4 macerated Makrut lime leaves

Ma Kham Whan Cocktail:

2 ounces Coffee and Lime-Leaf-Infused Bourbon (see here)

2 tsp ginger juice

1½ ounces Tamarind Water (page 233)

¾ ounce Makrut lime leaf simple syrup (see tip)

2 drops Fee Brothers Old Fashioned Bitters

Curled rind of ½ lemon, to garnish

Bruised lime leaf, to garnish

1. To make the coffee and lime-leaf-infused bourbon, infuse the bourbon with the coffee beans and macerated lime leaves for 1 to 2 days. Strain into a glass bottle or container and keep in the fridge for up to 2 weeks.

2. To make the cocktail, pour 2 ounces of the infused bourbon into a cocktail shaker with ice. Add the remaining ingredients (other than the garnishes). Shake well, double-strain into a rocks glass, and top with ice. Garnish with the lemon rind and lime leaf.

ℬ To make Makrut lime leaf simple syrup, using a mortar and pestle, bruise 1 cup of Makrut lime leaves. In a saucepan over medium heat, bring 2 cups of simple syrup to a simmer. Add the bruised Makrut lime leaves and infuse for 5 minutes, continuing to simmer. Remove from heat, let cool, and keep refrigerated in a lidded container for up to 3 weeks.

Siam Sunburn
by Jon-David McIntyre

Bird's Eye Chili and Lime-Leaf-Infused Tequila:

1 cup tequila

½ red Thai bird's eye chili

3 Makrut lime leaves

Siam Sunburn Cocktail:

1¾ ounces Bird's Eye Chili- and Lime-Leaf-Infused Tequila (see here)

1 ounce lemon juice

1 ounce passion fruit purée

¾ ounce butterscotch liqueur

1 egg white

2 drops Bittered Sling Condesa Bitters

1. To make the infused tequila, infuse the tequila with the chili and Makrut lime leaves for 3 days. Store in the fridge for up to 3 weeks.

2. To make the cocktail, pour 1¾ ounces infused tequila and the rest of the cocktail ingredients (other than the bitters) into a cocktail shaker with ice. Shake vigorously for 30 to 45 seconds to aerate the egg whites. Strain into a coupe glass. Float the bitters on top.

On Wine at the Maenam Table

by Kurtis Kolt

As a guy well steeped in Vancouver's restaurant scene, where I have run restaurants and quite often worn the wine director hat, I've had the pleasure of witnessing the genesis and evolution of Chef Angus An. Angus and I became casual friends during his early Vancouver restaurant years. I was a fan of Gastropod, Angus's first restaurant. But admittedly, I was more excited by the prospect of Maenam, as it brought a style of dining to the city we hadn't seen before. And it wasn't until a year or two into Maenam's short history when we developed a more solid bond. In a particularly busy season while—between freelance gigs—I ventured into the world of writing and consulting, I stepped onto the floor for a few cameo serving shifts, which buoyed both my income and my penchant for being at the helm for people's food and wine experiences.

Chef An's elevated cuisine was beyond what most people considered Thai dining experiences to be. But what I noticed most as a wine guy was that, well, hardly anyone was drinking wine. Sure, there were a few Singha beers on tables here and there, but most guests were content with water—maybe sparkling mineral water if they were feeling fancy. While Maenam had built a tidy wine list with many worthy selections, guests more often than not flicked past those pages to ponder other options. That conundrum stayed with me when Angus approached me to consult on his wine program, something I ended up doing over the next few years.

There are wines that work well with certain dishes, and there are wines that people want when they dine out, regardless. It's plausible that when it comes to elevated Thai cuisine, this disparity is greater than with other culinary styles. One of the challenges is that there's an array of dishes on the table at the same time, with everyone tucking in and taking disproportionate amounts of each dish apiece. There are likely elements of sweet, sour, salty, bitter, and heat all going on at a well-balanced, but loud, volume. So, I'm not here to tell you to have the Chardonnay with the chicken, or the Cabernet with the beef. Thai food needs wines that are dynamic and will hit a range of flavors quite well.

They say there are no specific rules for food and wine pairing, and that we should enjoy whatever works best for us. Nevertheless, here are some guidelines to finding those pairings that should more than likely work for most.

White Wines

Flavor is key, and if there's one thing I recommend keeping in mind, it's to think of any flavor a wine may carry and consider if that actual component would work well as an ingredient in the dish(es) it's going with. Hey, there's a reason that we enjoy a crisp Chardonnay from Chablis (lemon! apple!) when we're eating fresh oysters, rather than a California Petite Sirah that's laden with elements of mocha and sweet blueberry compote.

Equally important is the heat a dish may have as a component—the spice element. On the white wine side of things, don't go too dry. I know, I know, we love our crisp Marlborough Sauvignon Blancs. Unfortunately, when eating most spicy dishes, we're likely to lose all of their lovely citrus and orchard fruit, and the heat a dish expresses will only get hotter.

This is why we often look to the various shades of Riesling, where orchard fruit and citrus notes can spike rich or spicy dishes perfectly, and hints of residual sugar on the finish can envelop heat with ease. Germany is a no-brainer for provenance; go toward a Kabinett or Spätlese level, or the more generous Riesling offerings from New World regions like Central Otago in New Zealand or the Clare Valley in Australia, or—if you can find them—gems by our local British Columbian producers from the Okanagan Valley.

For Thai food, certain pairings that appear to work on paper can often throw us into a tailspin in practice. In doing our due diligence on testing food and wine compatibility, Angus and I have found that Gewürztraminer—a floral and tropical variety we thought would be a home run—can often come across as metallic or overwhelmingly herbal. With specific dishes, sure, it can be successful, but as a dependable pairing across the board, we're likely to relegate it to a well-appointed aperitif.

Chardonnays juicy with orchard fruit do indeed work well, or if something more opulent is required, the honey-drenched peaches and apricots of Viognier can charm many a dish.

Red Wines

While it may not be the automatic instinct, we can also attest to the appropriateness of red wine with a surprising number of these dishes.

Do look at Pinot Noir. The round, plummy character and earthy, mushroomy attributes of the variety can sing loud. Just make sure there's a bit of oomph to any selection you make; subtle, ultra-pale, nuanced versions will be lost in the noise.

While they are popular, it seems many Cabernet Sauvignons of the world just don't work. Breaking them down, red bell peppers, chocolate, eucalyptus, and such—the notes we often attribute to the variety—are flavors we hardly associate with Thai food.

I'd venture the biggest surprise has been the success of Grenache or Grenache-Syrah blends, whether from France's Rhône Valley, Australia's Barossa Valley, or beyond. Let's face it: they can be big and boozy, and alcohol is known to accentuate heat

in spicy dishes. Tannins can also be an issue, and wines that carry those bitter, astringent compounds from grape skins, stems, or oak aging definitely bring that astringency to savory or those otherwise perfectly spicy plates we love. The perfumed berry fruit and baking spices that Grenache blends express often add yet another layer of complexity and deliciousness.

•••

Over the last few years, it's been encouraging to see an increasing number of bottles hitting the tables at Maenam; it's pretty much flipped to become the rule, rather than the exception.

At the very least, the brilliant array of Chef Angus An's flavors on the table are certainly worthy of a toast.

Seasonal Sample Menus

Thai food is all about sharing. Dishes are served family style, and typical Thai menus are very balanced with seasonal ingredients. When planning a meal, it's important to build a diverse collection of dishes that complement each other. For example, you would never order five curry dishes or five ultra-spicy dishes together without having any light, cleansing dishes to refresh your palate. A balanced meal generally consists of some snacks, soup, salad, relish, stir-fry, curry, and dessert. If you're incorporating a rich soup, you should follow up with a lighter salad. As mentioned, it's also important to remember that Thai food is always meant to go with rice. Rice is actually your main course, and you choose all the other dishes to encourage everyone to eat more rice.

Many of our new customers at Maenam find it challenging to build a family-style menu, so they often leave the decisions to us. I'm always inspired by the season when creating dishes, and I've put together four sample menus to kick-start your creativity. These menus differ in seasonality as well as difficulty of preparation.

During spring and summertime, I love cooking outdoors. I'm less inclined to do loads of prep work indoors on heavy stews and braises, and lean toward lighter, quicker meals. The spring and summer menus are easier to execute, fun to cook outside, and lighter but still balanced to the palate. In colder months, though, I'm happy to spend more time in the kitchen stewing and braising tougher cuts of meat, so I've selected richer, more robust dishes for the fall and winter menus. You may find these heartier spreads more difficult and time-consuming, but the end result is incredibly rewarding!

Spring

Difficulty: Medium-Easy

SERVES 4 TO 6 FAMILY STYLE

Prawn Cakes (page 37)
Hot Sour Soup of Spot Prawns (page 83)
Larp Tartare of Beef (page 115)
Salmon Relish (page 53)
Stir-Fried Black-Pepper Spot Prawns (page 166)
Geng Gari Roast Chicken (page 191)
Pandan Panna Cotta with Dok Jok Wafer (page 211)

THE SPRING MENU IS very seasonal, as the anticipation of fresh produce all winter often excites most cooks to create something light and fresh. One of the marks of spring for me is always the beginning of spot prawn season. It starts in early May, and it marks the height of warmer spring weather when the flowers are in full bloom. This particular menu is relatively easy to execute and is more seafood-focused, dedicated to spot prawns. If spot prawns aren't readily available where you are, use live wild prawns to create the same menu.

Summer

Difficulty: Easy

SERVES 4 TO 6 FAMILY STYLE

Scallop Ceviche (page 15)
Hot Sour Soup of Halibut and Thai Basil (page 100)
Grilled Beef Salad (page 117)
Southern-Style Stir-Fried Lamb (page 159)
Green Curry of Halibut (page 186)
Custard Apple in Smoked Coconut Cream (page 224)

THIS MENU WAS INSPIRED by the summer weather and the desire to go outside and fire up the grill. You'll probably notice there's no relish on this menu. I left it off intentionally, as I find that people's appetites tend to diminish during the hotter months. The salad featuring grilled Wagyu beef is one of the easiest to make—and one of the tastiest. It balances perfectly with the cleansing ceviche and the hot sour soup, while the lamb and green curry dishes both offer welcoming heat and complexity. Fresh halibut is also readily available in the summertime and perfect for the season, and is meaty without weighing you down. This should be the easiest menu to execute, and you get to do it while cooking on your grill and enjoying an ice-cold beer.

Fall

Difficulty: Medium

SERVES 4 TO 6 FAMILY STYLE

Steamed Mussels with Lemongrass and Thai Basil (page 49)
Hot Sour Soup of Braised Beef Shin (page 99)
Chicken with Blood-Orange Salad (page 131)
Grilled King-Crab Relish (page 56)
Black-Pepper Crab (page 137)
Red Curry of Braised Duck (page 189)
Coconut Shave Ice (page 213)

THIS IS A FUN MENU with lots of shellfish. It may take a little longer to prepare, but it isn't overly difficult. Fall weather is always unpredictable. But whether it's brisk and sunny, or dark and gloomy, beef shin soup is what I crave. Its hearty, robust flavors balanced by fresh herbs go hand in hand with this transitional season. I threw in the Coconut Shave Ice dessert as a reminder that summer isn't that far gone, and we are still clinging on.

Winter

Difficulty: Medium-Hard

SERVES 4 TO 6 FAMILY STYLE

Chiang Mai-Style Sausage (page 38)
Nam Prik Num (page 41)
Hot Sour Chicken Soup with Chanterelles (page 89)
Larp Duck Salad (page 111)
Coconut-Braised Soy Pork Cheeks (page 153)
Massaman Curry of Braised Lamb Shank (page 177)
Yam Doughnuts (page 220)

FOR THE WINTER MENU, I chose four dishes from Chiang Mai, the cooler, northern region of Thailand. The weather there is slightly cooler than the rest of the country, and Chiang Mai's food tends to be much heartier and more soulful. The smoked sausage, nam prik num, hot sour soup of chanterelles, and duck larp are all typical Chiang Mai dishes. You definitely won't regret the extra time it takes to prepare the sausages and nam prik— they're well worth the wait. To be efficient, I recommend braising the lamb legs and pork cheeks while preparing the rest of the dishes. My ideal winter afternoon is cooking with a glass of wine at the ready, and I built this menu with that in mind.

Ingredient Glossary

Banana leaf (1): Banana leaves can be found both fresh and frozen at Asian specialty stores. They're not meant for eating, but rather are used for wrapping curries or desserts and for lining plates.

Basil, holy (2): Holy basil is very popular in Thailand but is often difficult to find in North American markets because of its short shelf life. It has a furry stem and citrus-like aromas. With a tougher texture that holds up to heat well, holy basil is often used in curries and stir-fries. One of my favorite dishes with this ingredient is Stir-Fried Beef Shin with Holy Basil (page 146).

Basil, Thai (3): Thai basil is one of the more commonly used basil varieties in Thailand. Also called purple stem basil, it has a licorice-like flavor and a strong aroma—particularly delicious in soups and curries. Thai basil doesn't like to be too cold or wet, so wrap it in a paper towel and store in the vegetable crisper drawer of your fridge.

Bean, long (4): Also known as snake beans, long beans have a similar flavor to French beans but are less waxy. They're often used in papaya salad for their subtle sweetness and crunchy texture.

Betel leaf (5): Widely used for the popular snack Lobster Miang (page 17), betel leaves have a bittersweet flavor with lots of tannins. When shopping for them, choose dark green leaves as opposed to the lighter-colored ones often sold right next to them. The lighter green ones are mostly used for wrapping chewing betel nuts, while the darker ones are the type eaten as food.

Bird's eye chili, dried Thai (6): Dried Thai bird's eye chilies are used for their heat. When incorporating them into a dish like larp (page 111), we toast them in a wok until they are dark red and extremely pungent, slightly glowing from the natural oils being released. Be sure to toast them in a well-ventilated kitchen or be prepared to cough—a lot. When dealing with any chilies, either dried or fresh, definitely wash your hands before rubbing your eyes.

Bird's eye chili, green Thai (7): The Thai name for this pepper, *prik kee noo*, translates into "mouse poo chili," referring to its tiny size. Green bird's eye chilies are quite spicy, and they're pounded into curry pastes or simmered in soups.

Bird's eye chili, red Thai: Also known as dragon's eye chilies, these chilies aren't as hot as the small green ones, but are just as aromatic. Their stems also carry a lot of fragrance and are often pounded together with the chilies into curry pastes or used in soups.

Cardamom, Thai (8): Thai cardamom is similar to Chinese white cardamom, floral and subtle compared to the green cardamom that most people are familiar with. Cardamom grows in pods with seeds inside, and it's crucial to roast them over medium heat to release their flavors, then bruise them to break apart the pods.

Cassia bark (9): Cassia is very similar to cinnamon, but much more subtle and earthy. I prefer cassia in my savory dishes, as cinnamon always tastes too sweet for me. Cassia bark is readily available at Chinatown spice merchants.

10.

11.

12.

13.

14.

15.

Celery, Asian: The stems of Asian or Chinese celery are almost straw-like, usually growing in bunches with lots of leaves. It's stronger in flavor than Western celery, and both the leaves and stems are used in cooking. Asian celery is excellent in soup and adds refreshing depth to any dish.

Cha-om (10): Also known as stink fern, cha-om is a wild fern with a distinct sulfur-like aroma. The tender leaves are picked off the thorny stems and are often used in curries and omelets.

Chili, guajillo (11): These large dried chilies are readily available in Latin stores, and they're commonly used in our curry pastes. Deseeding and deep-frying them produces a beautiful coffee aroma, perfect for finishing dishes or infusing into stews. These chilies don't carry a lot of heat and are often used for aroma and color.

Chili jam (12): This condiment is made from fried chilies, fried garlic, fried shallots, and palm sugar. Despite its name, it isn't spicy at all; rather, it's sweet and aromatic, adding great richness to dressings and soups.

Chili pepper (13): Long chilies in North America are often referred to as hothouse peppers or bell peppers. They come in assorted colors—green, red, yellow, and orange—and they're great in stews, soups, and stocks.

Chili powder: We don't like using store-bought chili powder. Simply toast the chilies as described in the recipe on page 234; once they've cooled, break them down into a powder with a mortar and pestle. If using a blender, be very careful not to breathe in the fumes.

16.

17.

18.

19.

20.

Chinese chives (14): Chinese garlic chives are commonly found in Asian supermarkets. They have flat leaves and are usually double the length of typical chives. Chinese chives are most notably used in Pad Thai (page 74) and a wide array of other Thai-Chinese dishes.

Coconut milk (15): Try making your own coconut milk by following the recipe on page 205. If you're buying coconut milk, choose brands that contain few to no emulsifiers, such as Aroy-D; this allows the coconut milk to separate as you cook and form Cracked Coconut Cream (page 206).

Coriander (16): Commonly called cilantro, coriander leaves are often used for salad, while the roots are used in infusions and pastes and the seeds are dried and used as a spice in curries and stir-fries. If coriander roots are not readily available, I often substitute coriander stems; they contain more water and less flavor, so I generally double the amount that's called for with roots.

Coriander seeds (17): When the seeds of the coriander or cilantro plant are dried, they have a nutty, citrusy, floral aroma. Coriander seeds lend sweetness to any dish and are commonly found in stir-fries and curries.

Coriander, Thai (18): You can find Thai coriander in Southeast Asian specialty stores; look for leaves that are smaller yet more fragrant and floral than coriander. It's used in the same way as coriander.

Corn, baby (19): There's nothing better than fresh baby corn. I dislike canned baby corn that you typically find at grocery stores, as the taste isn't even remotely comparable. Look for it at specialty grocers or Asian green grocers—once you've tasted it fresh, you'll never buy canned again.

Cumin seeds (20): Like fennel seeds, cumin seeds originate from India. They're a common ingredient in curry dishes and are occasionally used in stir-fries. Cumin seeds carry a distinct nutty aroma and peppery

21. **22.** **23.**

24. **25.** **26.**

27. **28.** **29.**

flavor; toasting them before use enhances their nutty characteristics. Always buy whole cumin seeds, as powdered cumin is essentially flavorless in comparison, and be careful not to mistake them for caraway seeds.

Dill (21): Also known as *pak chi lao*, dill is an herb that's commonly found in the northeastern region of Thailand. It's particularly delicious in soups, curries, and salads.

Eggplant, apple (22): Commonly found in Southeast Asia, apple eggplants are about the size of

a golf ball, with a light-colored top and green bottom. Apple eggplants can be served raw in salads or cooked in stir-fries and curries.

Eggplant, pea (23): Pea-size Thai eggplants are bittersweet in flavor and retain a great textural pop even after being simmered for a long time in a curry. They're very commonly found in curries and relishes.

Eggplant, Thai long green (24): Thai long green eggplants are wonderful. They look like a longer green version of Japanese eggplant, but have a very different texture. While their Japanese cousin often becomes too soft when cooked, Thai long green eggplants are firm and hold their shape. Because they're sturdy and stand up to heat well, they're especially delicious in stir-fries.

Fennel seeds (25): Fennel seeds are indicative of an Indian influence on Thai food. Their sweet licorice flavor adds depth to dishes such as Geng Gari Roast Chicken (page 191). When buying them, look for bright green color and strong floral aroma. I always prefer to source bulk spices from spice merchants so that I can see, smell, and taste the spices before buying them.

Fish sauce (26): There are many different types of fish sauce on the market. A clean-tasting fish sauce with strong flavor works best for the recipes in this book. My preferred brands include Squid, Megachef, and Red Boat.

Gai lan (27): Also known as Chinese broccoli, gai lan is one of the most popular Chinese vegetables. Great when stir-fried on its own or with oyster sauce and crispy pork belly, it's often sliced up and added into stir-fries such as Pad Si Ew (page 71), giving a great crunchy contrast to the soft chewy noodles.

Galangal (28): Galangal is not to be confused with ginger, nor are the two interchangeable in recipes. There are many different types of galangal, and you can find them in Southeast Asian stores either fresh, frozen, or dried. Always buy it fresh if it's available; look for young shoots with tender skin and pink tips. Galangal has a very distinct citrus aroma, and it's key to making a great hot sour soup (page 87).

Garlic, Thai baby (29): Thai baby garlic cloves are very tiny and have an elegant garlic flavor without any unpleasant pungency. Because they're so small, we pound them before frying and often serve them with the skin on for extra texture.

Ginger (30): When it comes to ginger, I prefer young ginger over the older roots. Young ginger's lighter-colored skin is tender, and it often has pink tips—delightful when

30.

31.

julienned and added to salads. Older ginger roots are ideal for soups, stews, and stocks.

Grachai (31): Also known as finger root or wild ginger, grachai is available fresh, but is more commonly found either frozen or in jars. Grachai has an earthy, bitter flavor that's unique, and it's great in stir-fries and curries. It's also used in certain northeastern Thai soups.

Lemongrass (32): Most lemongrass sold in North America comes from Mexico. I find it less flavorful than Thai lemongrass, and I use it for curry pastes and infusions because it's hardier and more robust. For soup and salad, I like to

32.

33.

34.

35.

36.

37.

import the Thai variety, which is younger and much more fragrant. When using lemongrass, peel off the outer two or three layers and use the bottom half of the stalk, which has more flavor.

Mace (33): Mace is the sheath of the nutmeg seed inside the nutmeg fruit. It looks like a dehydrated flower and is a beautiful orange color. Mace has a similar flavor profile to nutmeg but is much brighter in character and lighter in flavor with a more floral aroma.

Mah kwan (34): A relative of Sichuan pepper or prickly ash,

mah kwan is quite floral with strong mandarin-peel aromas. It's commonly used in northern Thai cuisine and is a key ingredient in larp (page 111). Mah kwan can be difficult to track down, but Sichuan pepper can be used as a substitute.

Makrut lime (35): Also known as kaffir lime, its zest is extremely fragrant and is often used for green curries, dressings, nahm jims, and desserts. Each Makrut lime carries only a scant amount of juice, which is very aromatic but quite bitter.

Makrut lime leaf (36): Makrut or kaffir lime leaves share the beautiful

perfume of the fruit. They're a key ingredient in many soups and are often used in curries and stir-fries to impart fragrance and flavor. Tough and sturdy, they should be sliced as thinly as possible when put into a salad to avoid irritation. Be very careful of the thorns on the stems when buying, cleaning, and cooking them.

Mint (37): Mint is often used in Thai salads. Its cool, crisp flavor is a wonderful balance for intense Thai spices, and it's often added to spicier salads for that very reason; Grilled Beef Salad (page 117), Larp Duck Salad (page 111), and Larp

38.

39.

40.

41.

42.

43.

Tartare of Beef (page 115) are good examples.

Mint, Vietnamese (38): Also called Vietnamese coriander by some, this herb is commonly found in northern Thailand and is one of the main ingredients in larp (page 111). It has a woody stem and a distinct soapy, peppery flavor.

Nutmeg (39): Whole nutmeg is the seed of the nutmeg fruit. Its distinct nutty flavor is excellent in curries such as Panaeng Curry of Braised Beef Rib (page 179). Toast the nutmeg seeds whole, then grate them with a grater or crush

them with a mortar and pestle. They are tough and difficult to break down.

Orange peel (40): Dried orange peel is a common ingredient in Thai-Chinese dishes. It's readily available from Chinatown spice merchants; however, the type they sell is generally used for medicinal purposes and is often bland in flavor. I prefer to dehydrate my own mandarin peel; simply keep the peel after eating mandarin oranges, and dry it in a food dehydrator or piloted oven (see tip on page 54).

Oyster sauce (41): A common ingredient in Thai-Chinese dishes, this sauce is rich with savory oyster flavors and oozes umami. Its thick consistency is used to give sauces added body and texture. I use Lee Kum Kee's Panda oyster sauce.

Pak chi farang (42): *Farang* means foreigner, while *pak chi* means coriander. Sawtooth coriander is another common name for this delicious herb, derived from the saw-like edges of its leaves. Highly fragrant in both smell and taste, it adds a beautiful aroma to soups and salads. Source it at Southeast

44. **45.** **46.**

47. **48.** **49.**

Asian markets or at Latino markets under the name "culantro."

Palm sugar (43): Palm sugar is made from boiling down palm-tree sap. It's commonly found in a hard disk shape; mash the disk using a mortar and pestle before using. If available, buy it in jars, as the sugar is much softer and more pliable with fuller, rounder flavor.

Pandan (44): These long sword-like leaves can be found both fresh or frozen; dried pandan leaves are used for tea. Their floral, grassy flavor lends itself especially well to desserts, and they're often used in infusions for both sweet and savory dishes.

Papaya, green: Unripe papaya is most often used in salads but is also found in soups and curries. Green Papaya Salad (page 107), or som dtam Thai, is widely considered to be the most popular dish among Thais. Green papaya is neutral in flavor but full of crunch; when served as a salad, it picks up the flavor of the dressing well and offers a cooling effect to balance all the chilies.

Peppercorn, green (45): You can find green peppercorns fresh or pickled in jars. Personally, I'm not fond of the jarred ones, as the brine flavor is often rather unpleasant. Fresh ones are ideal for using in curries and stir-fries; bear in mind that they don't have a long shelf life and tend to turn black after a week in the fridge. Don't throw them away, though—dehydrate them, and you'll have the best black pepper you've ever tasted.

Radish, preserved (46): Preserved, or dried, radish is a common Chinese preserve made from sundried salted radishes. It has a distinct toothsome, crunchy

50.

51.

52.

texture. The drying process gives the radish ample amounts of umami, and it's an essential ingredient in Pad Thai (page 74).

Rice, jasmine (47): Rice is the most important part of a Thai meal. *Kao suay*, or "beautiful rice," is how Thai people refer to it. Be sure to experiment with different brands, as not all rice is created equal. When cooked properly, jasmine rice is unparalleled for its aroma and textural balance. Use a pandan leaf to perfume the rice once it's cooked.

Rice, Thai sticky (48): Thai sticky rice is common in northern Thailand and has a delicious aroma and texture. A longer-grained rice, it's not cooked in water like regular rice; instead, soak it in water overnight and steam it in cheesecloth.

Shallots (49): Thai shallots are very hard to find but definitely

worth hunting for, as the small Chinese shallots aren't nearly as nice. If you can't track down any Thai shallots, substitute Western shallots instead. Thai shallots are crunchy and subtly sweet. They're used in stir-fries, curries, salads—just about everything. Thais even sprinkle fried shallots on desserts.

Shrimp paste: Shrimp paste is a common ingredient in Southeast Asia, made with shrimp that's crushed with salt and then fermented. It carries a rich shellfish aroma with a salty, pungent flavor and is used in curry pastes, soups, relishes, and dressings.

Soybean paste (50): This nutty, salty paste is made from fermented soybeans and is commonly used in vegetable stir-fries and some relishes. I prefer a paste with whole beans to maximize its texture, while others prefer thicker paste with broken beans—almost like a

chunky-versus-smooth peanut butter debate. Healthy Boy is my preferred brand.

Soy sauce, dark (51): With a dark molasses flavor, dark soy sauce is often used as a coloring agent in Asian cooking. Take care to add only small amounts to light soy sauce so as not to overpower a dish with its flavor. Look for Healthy Boy brand.

Soy sauce, light (52): Thai cooking uses more fish sauce than soy sauce, but the latter is almost always included in Thai-Chinese dishes. I prefer light soy sauce for its more delicate flavor, and opt for Chinese soy sauce over Japanese varieties when preparing Thai dishes. Look for Healthy Boy brand.

Star anise (53): Star anise is a spice commonly used in Thai-Chinese dishes. It has a strong licorice-like perfume and is a key element in Chinese five spice.

53.

54.

55.

56.

57.

Water spinach (56): Also known as morning glory or *ong choy*, water spinach has long pointy leaves and straw-like stems. Two varieties are readily available: dark green (skinny straw) or light-green (thick straw) aquaponic. I personally prefer the dark green type for its firmer texture and fuller, sweeter flavor.

Buy it from Chinatown spice merchants to ensure freshness. Look for star anise that is dark in color and has a strong aroma; older ones are pale with a dull aroma.

Tamarind water (54): Tamarind water is widely used in Thai cooking as a souring seasoning. It is watered-down tamarind seeds and pulp, and it's quite easy to make (page 233).

Turmeric (55): Turmeric is available in both fresh and powder form. Don't substitute the powder for fresh turmeric, as they're vastly different in flavor. When handling turmeric, wear gloves and know that it will likely stain anything it touches. Its peppery, earthy aroma and flavor are distinct in many types of curry. Turmeric is currently in the culinary limelight because of its antioxidant characteristics, and can be sourced fresh at most supermarkets.

Winter melon (57): Winter melon isn't commonly sold whole due to its size; you can usually buy it in slices or wheels. When fully grown, it can weigh about 30 to 40 pounds and reach about 30 inches in length. It's most often used in soups because of its cool, refreshing flavor and a sponge-like texture that absorbs broth well. Remove the thick green skin and the seeds before cooking it.

Acknowledgments

A lot of people have pitched in to help make this cookbook a reality. But before I mention them, I'd like to express my heartfelt gratitude to the people who have guided me to become the person and the chef I am today. My late grandparents for their constant support and belief in me. My parents, my wife, Kate, and my son, Aidan. Without your love, help, and encouragement, my career simply wouldn't have been possible.

During my third year in Fine Arts at UBC, Professor Ken Lum expressed especially keen interest during my exit interview. He noticed my photography series on food and wanted to know if I was continuing on to get a Master of Fine Arts or if I was moving on to other pursuits. When I told him I had dreams of becoming a chef and wanted to move to New York to cook, his eyes lit up. In many ways, Ken was the very first supporter of my culinary pursuits, and he eventually became my first business partner in getting Gastropod and Maenam off the ground. I'd very much like to thank you, Ken, for believing in me.

At about the same point in my life, I idolized chef/restaurateur John Bishop and often attended his cooking classes. I'd pick his brain about cooking and the path I should take to realize my ambitions, and he very kindly had all the time in the world for my myriad questions. Thank you so much, John.

There are many great chefs in Vancouver, but none has had more influence on me than chef/restaurateur Pino Posteraro. Since the beginning of my culinary career, he has always looked out for me and has always been ready with assistance, advice, or simply a listening ear when I've needed it the most. He treats me like his own family—often welcoming Kate, Aidan, and me to spend Christmas at his home—and I couldn't be more grateful.

A huge thank you to my business partners: Jeff Wang, Matt Macdonald, Mark Shieh, Elizabeth Mah, and Mimi Cheung. Although each of you has come on board during different stages of this evolution, we've always collectively shared the same passion: food!

The Vancouver restaurant industry is a close-knit community, with chefs who support each other, along with wonderful suppliers and farmers who are always looking out for us. I'd like to give an extra-special shout-out to Robert Belcham, Joël Watanabe, Hamid Salimian, and Jenice Yu. It's incredible when colleagues become dear friends, and you've all been a treasured part of my journey over the past 12 years.

Kurtis Kolt, thank you for your contribution to this book and to Maenam's wine program over the years. I'd also like to thank all the wineries, distilleries, and breweries along with the wine reps, spirits reps, and beer reps who so readily taste-test their newest products with us in the ongoing search for the perfect pairings to this beautiful cuisine.

Massive thanks to Joie Alvaro Kent and Darren Chuang for all your diligence, your eloquent words, your beautiful photographs, and your patience in putting up with me over the two years that it took us to create this book together. Thank you to the entire crew at Appetite by Random House: Robert McCullough, Lindsay Paterson, Katherine Stopa, Terri Nimmo, and the marketing, publicity, and sales teams for your unwavering support in helping me bring my cookbook to fruition.

I'd very much like to thank my two favorite chefs that I've ever worked with: Normand Laprise and David Thompson. Normand, thank you for teaching me the importance of simplicity. My years in your kitchen at Toqué are the fondest memories of my career. David, thank you for sharing with me your personal journey with Thai food. The lessons I learned and the people I met at Nahm have been a tremendous influence in shaping the chef and restaurateur I've become.

Huge gratitude to my close friends Young Tze Kuah and Peter Chan: I deeply treasure the constant friendship and support you give me. Thank you for always having my back. And I'll be forever grateful to the late Jim Clark, who helped me purchase Gastropod and guided me over many years through legal and real estate matters. You are dearly missed.

Thanks to Shannon Heth and Nicola Humphrey, my diligent PR people for the past 10 years. I appreciate everything you've done to spread the good word about Maenam.

Thank you to all my recipe testers: Elizabeth Li, Sarah Westwood, Jonathan Yuen, Lee Gibson, Tricia Raeburn, and Sarah Garrett, along with my staff members and culinary students at Vancouver Community College, Northwest Culinary Academy of Vancouver, and Pacific Institute of Culinary Arts. All your hours of cooking and curry-paste pounding have been invaluable in helping me fine-tune the recipes for this book.

I'd also like to thank Vollrath Co., Puddifoot, Staub, Churchill, Revol, and Atkinson's for their kind support in providing the finishing touches to our photographs.

Last but certainly not least, props to each one of my work family, all of the team members both past and present: Mike Tuangkitkun, Justin Cheung, Brandon Intharangsy, Jennifer Chiang, Michael Peters, Waraphan "Bank" Chanthong, Warakorn "Tempo" Suriyawong, Boonyawee "Bonnie" Khummuang, Emily Waters, Tara Thom, Tanya Roussy, Kristi Linneboe, Ben De Champlain, James Welk, Jon-David McIntyre, Tessula Whitford, Brooke Delves, and everyone else who has been a part of our tight-knit staff. Without all your hard work, Maenam wouldn't be the story that it is today.

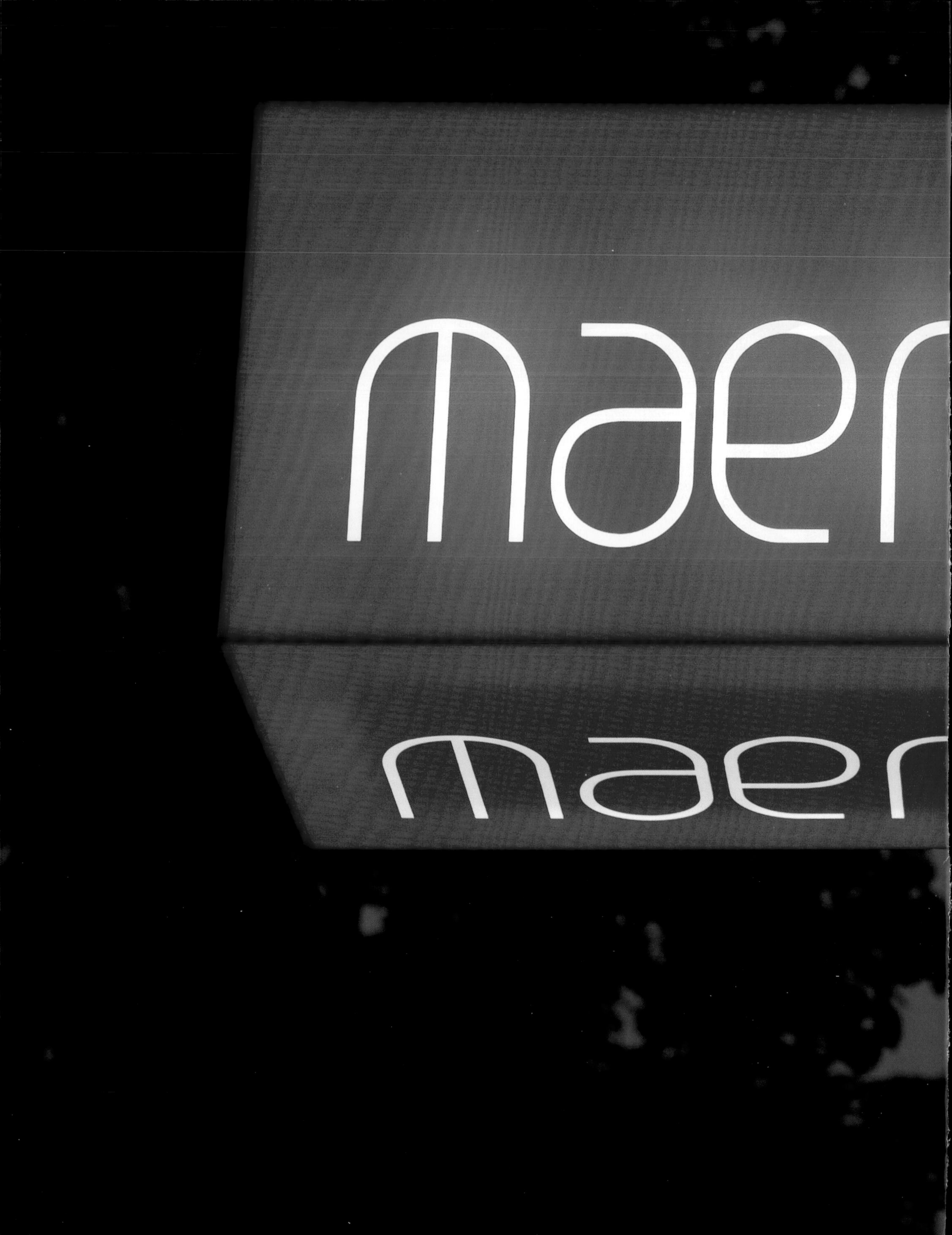
maer
maer

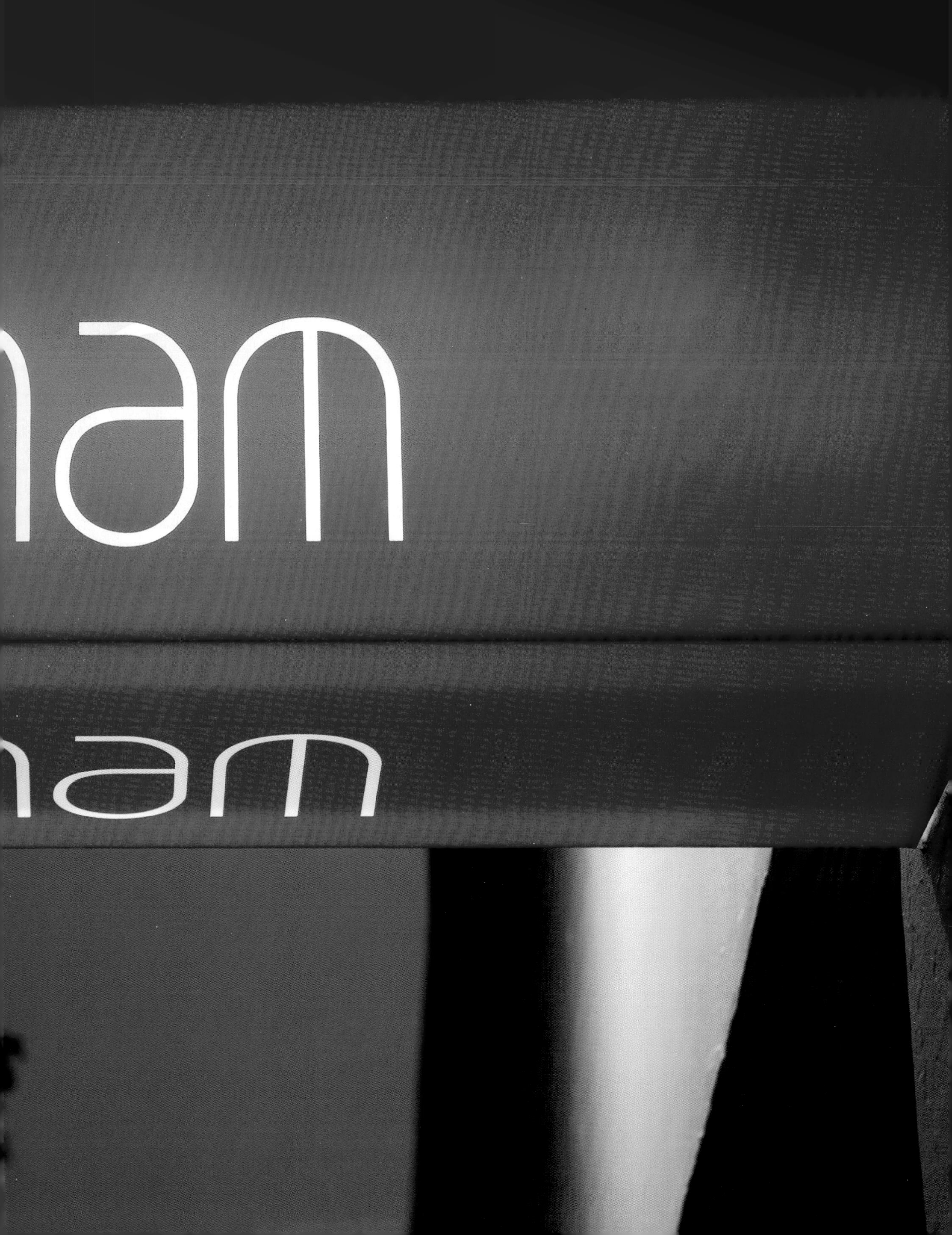
nam
nam

Index